Your Personal
Survival Guide
to the 21st Century
by Roy Sheppard

your personal
SURVIVAL
GUIDE to the 21st
century

Roy Sheppard

Published in 1998 by Centre Publishing, London, England

A catalogue record of this book is available from the British Library.

ISBN 1-901534-01-4
Cover design by Barrie Cutler.
Book design and typesetting by Antony Parselle
Edited by Ian Johnston
Rear cover photograph by Frankie Blagden

All trademarks and copyrights acknowledged.

Printed and bound in England by Biddles Ltd.

ATTENTION COLLEGES & UNIVERSITIES, CORPORATIONS AND VOLUNTARY & PROFESSIONAL ORGANISATIONS.

Quantity discounts are available on bulk purchases of this book for educational purposes, charity fund-raising and gift giving. Special books, booklets or book excerpts can also be created to fit your specific needs.
For more information please contact:
Centre Publishing, Suite 2, 170 Kennington Park Road, London, SE11 4BT, England
Tel: 00 (+44) 171 820 8511. Fax: 00 (+44) 171 793 7962.

To contact the author

Please write to the above address.
Unfortunately, Roy Sheppard is unable to enter into personal correspondence.
Roy Sheppard's email address is; roy.sheppard@virgin.net

Acknowledgements

So many thanks are in order. Without the help of a dedicated team of friends, colleagues and other professional specialists, this book could not have been written and produced. Thank you to everyone who has offered ideas, tips, snippets of additional information and recommendations to improve the text. I consider myself truly lucky to know such a group of intelligent, knowledgeable and skillful individuals.

I am indebted to you all: Frankie and Sally Sheppard, Ian Johnston, Chris Howe, Margaret Coles, Ian Pearson of BT Labs, John L. Petersen at The Arlington Institute, Tom Nash at The Institute of Directors, Sue Spenceley-Burch, Mike Burch, Kathryn Booth, Stuart Booth, Alison Cork, Stephen Herd, Lolita Fierro, Peter C Joyce, Dennis Sherman, Ellie Garvin, Pamela Gawler-Wright, Peter Dykhuis, Barrie Cutler of Cutler Whitehead for what I can only describe as an outstanding book cover design, David Cooper of Direct Marketing Solutions and Antony Parselle for his book design and typesetting work.

Dedication

To Frankie, my wife.

Thank you for all your support and pearls of wisdom.
There isn't a necklace large enough to hold them all
– and if there was, we couldn't afford it!

Table of Contents

Table of Contents

Table of Contents

Preface

This book is about you and your future. It deals with many of the most pressing issues which will affect you and millions of others in the decades to come. It offers ideas, solutions and strategies to stack the odds in your favour for a more successful and secure future. It's a 'what-you-can-do-about-it' kind of book.

Rather than merely devoting the book to pointing out the problems we will all face in the coming decades (which is about as useful as a bandaid on a gunshot wound), it is important that a variety of solutions are also offered. These have been gleaned from more sources than I could possibly remember. Years as a communications consultant and interviewer have ensured a constant stream of ideas flowing into and out of my head. Where ever possible I have included the source of particular trains of thought, advice and survival strategies. My apologies in advance to anyone who has not been credited.

You will find hundreds of questions dotted throughout the text. These are specifically designed to help you assess your own situation and formulate your own specific strategies to cope with the changes ahead.

Everything is changing. How we cope with, manage and adapt to change in the future is fundamental to our personal survival. This is why an entire chapter is devoted to the subject of change and how we deal with it - especially change within the workplace.

You will notice a heavy bias towards aspects of work and business in the text. How and where business is conducted, will increasingly affect everyone's lives. Even if you do not work in paid employment, you will almost certainly be affected by the radical changes taking place in business. A deeper understanding of these business trends is essential for everyone as we head towards the 21st century.

Global corporations are becoming more powerful than many national governments. Business is the only source of wealth creation for any country. It affects us all. There has always been trade, but never like what we are witnessing in business today. In future decades, businesses will continue to operate across geographical boundaries with scant interference from governments. Politicians know that if they do not agree to the growing demands of business, they will take their considerable money, resources and employment opportunities to the regions and countries where they will receive the best incentives. Too many regulations which penalise businesses (as has happened in Canada, The United States and Germany) result in the relocation of many businesses. Why pay for hefty statutory healthcare, unemployment benefits and pensions when you can operate from a country which has lower labour costs, no unions or costly social security to pay for? In particular, many more manufacturing companies are moving to areas of the world such as Asia where operating costs can be reduced greatly, leading to higher profits for these increasingly cost-conscious corporations. For some, their corporate survival demands it as competition intensifies everywhere.

The constant demands from shareholders to maximise short term profits means business decisions are made without regard for the longer term consequences to us as individuals. Paradoxically, many of the largest business investors are the trustees of corporate pension funds. All too often our pension funds are used to invest in companies which develop the very technology which is putting so many of us out of work.

There is obviously so much more to life than just work. Most of what improves our quality of life involves doing things more slowly, taking the time to savour the moment. But the pace of life is increasing and will continue to do so. We are living in a fast forward society. More and more people have had enough and are turning their backs on the stress-inducing and ulcer-producing rat race, handing in the keys to the luxury company car, selling up and moving to the countryside for a simpler, yet improved lifestyle. Those who 'downshift' in this way, are deciding to earn less and spend more time raising their families away from the noise, pollution and dangers which have become so much a part of city and town life. Developments in communications technology and the concepts of teleworking are making such fundamental lifestyle changes ever more feasible.

This book includes a vast array of topics. It encompasses sociology, economics, personal finance, business, management science, change integration, electronics, biotechnology, time management, gender studies, nutrition, behavioural psychology and psychotherapy. In many ways the text represents a 'pull together' of many different and, at times, conflicting views. In therapy, it is said that the nearer you get to the truth, the more paradoxes exist. Paradox itself plays a central role in tomorrow's world. For example, China is the world's largest communist country - but there are more Chinese millionaires than from any other country on this planet. Today, there are an estimated 100,000 dollar millionaires in Asia alone. The number in this region is growing all the time and will continue to do so into the 21st century.

No one can predict the future, but based on many of the changes which have already happened and are continuing to happen today, it is possible to 'forecast' the trends and changes which may not have yet 'trickled down' into your life. Yesterday's changes are affecting you today in many areas of your life; today's changes will affect you tomorrow.

Tomorrow's changes in society and business will affect us sooner than we think. Many for the better - some for worse.

Roy Sheppard
Central London, England. December 1997

Chapter 1
Your Future in Your Hands

Bad things happen to good people. Good things happen to bad people. And in today's changing world, they happen much quicker.

As M. Scott Peck asserted as the opening words of his book *The Road Less Travelled*, "*Life is difficult.*" Obviously, so much of life is outside our direct control. But, by more fully understanding what choices we all have in life, we can improve (possibly dramatically) the probability of a more successful, secure and happy future, whilst minimising the downside risks and threats to our long term safety and security.

John Wiseman, former survival instructor for the SAS, writes in *The SAS Survival Guide*, "*Think of Survival skills as a pyramid, built on the foundation of the will to survive. The next layer of the pyramid is knowledge. It breeds confidence and dispels fears. The third layer is training: mastering skills and maintaining them. To cap the pyramid, add your kit. Combine the instinct for survival with knowledge, training and kit and you will be ready for anything.*"

One of the most important aspects of survival is the survivor's ability to recognise potentially dangerous risks to their life. Many of the places we live in are routinely described as 'a jungle out there'. Some areas are obviously more dangerous than others. It is easy to recognise the impending threat of a rapidly approaching elephant - get out of the way or you'll get flattened ... but it is less easy to spot the poisonous spider lurking under the leaf of the tree on which it habitually lives.

A true survivor has a strategy and a range of tools and techniques at his or her disposal and knows how and when to use them. You'd have to be pretty foolish or naive if you live in tornado country to ignore weather forecasts when satellite pictures clearly show bad weather ahead. But in reality, people do choose to deny what they don't want to believe. There are many documented cases of individuals who 'just knew' that the tornado wouldn't affect them. Some of them end up getting killed. Stuck in a desert miles from an oasis, you wouldn't waste water by pouring it away on non-essentials. But millions of people are doing just that - splashing out and pouring away what little money they may have, oblivious to the potential financial threats which may affect them in the next 20 to 40 years. They may be OK - but it's folly to assume so.

For a future flood - do you have a lifeboat?

Individuals trained to cope with a survival situation learn to think clearly and calmly. This calmness comes from preparation and the quiet confidence which comes when they are equipped with the most appropriate information and knowledge needed to identify potential threats. By applying this knowledge they can insulate themselves against future problems. Noah knew there was a flood on the way; his source of information and knowledge was pretty good. Who needs satellite pictures and Michael Fish when God takes you aside and tells you it's about to get a bit wet? But what happened? Even though it started pouring down - and did so for day after day after day, all his neighbours had a good laugh at old Noah's expense. Until, that is, they were all up to their armpits in flood and Noah was loading the ark. "Let us in, Noah old chap" would have been a common request. It wasn't recorded in the Bible, but if a CNN news crew had been there, I'm sure we'd have seen an exclusive interview with Noah. His detailed, in-depth analysis of why God had decided to create the flood and His plans for preserving the earth's wildlife and eco system could have be condensed and encapsulated within a single sound-bite - "Sodom all".

As you will discover in later chapters there are major and very real environmental, technological, work and financial threats on the horizon for millions of Britons and hundreds of millions of other, largely unsuspecting individuals throughout the world. We can choose to dismiss such threats - even though the trends are clear to see - and we can laugh at those who take their survival seriously enough to do something about it.

In Jeremy Rifkin's controversial and, at times, deeply disturbing book *The End of Work*, he forecasts massive global unemployment in the first decades of the new millennium as more and more companies 're-engineer', restructure and automate their manufacturing, service and administrative processes. He claims that entire job categories will be eliminated in the decades to come.

Your job could be one of them. But we can choose to ignore such findings. What the hell do the experts know anyway? No one can predict the future. True. But what if they are correct about even a small proportion of what is being forecast?

The job or career you or your kids are currently working in or training for could already be in decline and may be unable to provide you with a livelihood for more than the next few years. Rifkin's exhaustive research and evidence makes it clear that this cannot be dismissed as 'negative thinking' or being unnecessarily alarmist. We ignore it at our peril.

If you are prepared to look into the future and develop a survival plan for the 21st century you will be much better placed to look after yourself and your families. We have choices; we can ignore them by telling ourselves that 'it won't happen to me', someone else will find a cure, or we can take full responsibility for our futures and do something about it.

The new millennium is both exciting and frightening; exciting for those who realise the extent of the changes which are taking place and who act on their knowledge - and frightening for those who eventually wake up in a world which no longer wants or needs their low level skills and outdated attitudes and beliefs. Most of these workers remain unaware of what is already happening in the global marketplace. They are 'too busy' to notice. They may have a bit of a giggle at that beer advert which says CU@the.pub.no.anoraks. A contemporary version of laughing at Noah perhaps?

How this book was born

Let me share with you how this book came about. In the late 1980's I came across an anonymous quote which has literally transformed my life - as a result, my earnings have rocketed.

"The future belongs only to those who have adequately prepared for it."

It still has a deep and profound effect on the way I live, work and think. Those 12 words totally changed the way I thought about my future. It could do so for you too. No business can ever hope to be successful or continue to prosper without adequately preparing for its future. This involves deciding on its strategic plans and identifying areas which pose a real or possible threat to its future wellbeing. However, on an individual level, detailed planning tends to be relegated for 'some other time' - although as soon as a wedding or holiday needs arranging, detailed long term planning is immediately brought to the top of our 'to do' lists.

Planning for our long term success is often merely thought of in financial terms - even so, it is still given a low priority by millions.

In the mid 1980's I became a victim of circumstance and a lack of personal planning - simply because I was so wrapped up in what I was doing. At that time, I was certainly not prepared for my future. This brief story could provide a valuable lesson for others who could so easily find themselves in similarly dire financial straits.

From 1984-1989 I was seen to be highly successful - on prime time TV most nights of the week in London, England, presenting the early evening news for the BBC. On the face of it, life was good. I was also recognised where ever I went, invited to parties and movie & theatre premieres.

But in reality, as a freelancer, life was difficult. I was overworked and seriously underpaid. A counterpart in New York City earned about $700,000 dollars a year - my fee for presenting the early evening news on BBC television was £75 (about $120) per programme. When I read the *Breakfast Time* news alongside Jeremy Paxman, Frank Bough and Jill Dando, my fee was £12.50 per news bulletin ...Oh, the glamour of television!

Then, after five years it simply stopped. The news programme was re-vamped and out went the faces associated with the 'old' programme. I was given less than ten days notice. It would have been less if I hadn't found out about my forthcoming demise from a colleague.

I had been leading a typically hand to mouth existence as a freelancer - within days, there was nothing. Simultaneously, the entire TV industry was thrown into turmoil for about three years as all the commercial TV companies prepared for the first franchise bids under Prime Minister Margaret Thatcher's plan to de-regulate the television industry. Few new programmes were made which meant fewer opportunities for out-of-work TV presenters - many of whom were national household names. Competition was certainly intense in those days - and the money was often poor (although I'm told it was not as bad as it is today - and it's getting worse).

For months I had no work. For the first time I started to think more and more about my own future and what I wanted to achieve, how I wanted to live, who I wanted to live with and what contribution I could make to the lives of the people around me - friends and family as well as colleagues and clients. By carefully analysing what was stopping me from achieving what I decided was important to me gave enormous peace of mind and confidence to stride towards the future.

Interestingly, in just three years after starting this process I successfully increased my earnings by three hundred percent compared with when I was fully employed, whilst working less hours and taking more time off to pursue personally interesting projects.

You too could benefit from a similar approach.

Copying 'The HP Way'

The concept of preparing for my own future had so much power that I even developed "the future" as a new hobby. This pastime covered all elements of the future, although it was not long before I found myself being drawn towards the future development of technology and how it was being used in business and got quite excited about such developments - avidly reading everything I could find on the subject in newspapers and magazines. This was further fuelled by the regular long and detailed conversations I had with many leading business people in Britain, Europe and the United States. One particular executive springs to mind; Joel Birnbaum is in charge of Hewlett-Packard's worldwide research and development arm. Joel is responsible for developing the products and technology which will create the future success of Hewlett-Packard in the next century. He has an annual budget of nearly two billion dollars. HP takes the preparation of their future very seriously indeed.

I have worked with Joel on two different occasions. The first involved a conference in Berlin, Germany, for 800 of Hewlett-Packard's sales and marketing staff. Joel's presentation was electrifying. A softly spoken man, the content of his talk must remain highly confidential (even though it has since been superseded) but it clearly described the technology that would be in use in just five years time. Cynics in the audience were reminded that five years previously, a collection of similarly outrageous technological products had been forecast. Every one of those predictions was commercially available at the time of the conference, strongly indicating that many of the products then in development would similarly be available in the future.

I was excited about the massive improvements in productivity and efficiency that this new technology would bring about. As someone who uses computer technology on a daily basis, I apply this automation to my everyday work. However, I feel slightly embarrassed to admit that, in the past, I did not consider the impact on those people who are unable to buy into the technological dream.

There is a huge number of low-skilled, low paid (or unemployed) people who are computer illiterate because they cannot afford or do not see the value of acquiring such skills. Society will pay a high price for marginalising them, just as the United States is continuing to pay the consequences for abusing the human rights of the black slaves they 'imported' as cheap labour nearly three hundred years ago.

Too busy to care

Other consequences of past behaviour will certainly come back to haunt us. Our belief that Nature can be forced into submission will ultimately prove disastrous. We all know that the damage inflicted by humans on our planet since the beginning of the industrial revolution (less than three hundred years ago) has been massive. But let's be honest - just for once. Society doesn't care enough about global warming, deforestation, industrial and nuclear pollution. We don't care enough that the earth's protective ozone layer is disappearing - in any case some scientists say it isn't disappearing, so let's choose to believe them instead of the majority of specialists who say it's a HUGE problem. So what, if a load more Australians and New Zealanders are getting skin cancer because of the growing ozone hole above them? So what, if everybody stopped manufacturing CFCs today, it will still take 17 years for today's CFC emissions to reach the upper atmosphere? In the book *Your Money or Your Life*, authors Joe Dominquez and Vicki Robin state "*As consumers, we are becoming like a cancer on the Earth, consuming our host.*"

Have a nice day!

The belief that everything will turn out fine is one of society's 'vital lies' as author Daniel Goleman describes them. By convincing ourselves in this way, we give ourselves permission to ignore the unsavoury facts. Anyone who thinks "As an individual I can't do anything about it", falls into the 'vital lie' trap. If we as individuals did care enough, we would do far more about these issues. We are lulled into believing that such important issues will be solved by others. Perhaps it's just as well - we're too busy anyway, too pre-occupied with who's having the latest affairs in our favourite TV soap, or picking our numbers in the National Lottery. Politicians won't or can't do it. Why? Simply, because they can't do it on their own. Tony Blair, the British Prime Minister, in his first party conference following the Labour election win, exhorted the nation to go with the government to join in the effort and work together towards a solution to many of society's problems.

Favouring falsehoods

But canny politicians still perpetuate 'vital lies' to ensure they do not lose votes or upset the largest employers. Politicians can't tell the truth, because the system which holds society together relies on these lies. Take the following examples of 'vital lies':

- Politicians can and will put the world right
- A government can and will look after you when you are sick, disabled, poor, unemployed or old
- More funding equals better education
- White, middle aged, middle class men know everything, all the time (I am one!)
- Criminals will be caught and 'justice' will prevail
- If we have more and bigger nuclear weapons than the 'bad guys' we will win
- The more money you earn, the happier you will become
- 'Consequences' will never be as bad as the doom mongers predict
- Science and technology will solve society's problems
- "Trust me, I'm a doctor"

- Put your money into bricks and mortar - it's as safe as houses.
- Eating low fat, reduced sugar foods will make you healthy
- Coca-Cola doesn't make you fat and fart

We may be brought up not to tell lies - our parents insist we tell the truth to them, but for years many of us see them telling lies and dealing dishonestly with family, friends, colleagues and employers. Just about everybody tells lies - some do it all the time. Good, 'honest' people routinely tell lies by refusing to express their real opinions and views to friends, neighbours and especially to colleagues. We become adept at telling half truths to protect ourselves or to preserve our reputations as 'nice' people. We are often afraid of the consequences of telling the truth. Fear is increasingly driving our behaviour. Most of all we tell lies to ourselves. It alleviates the anxiety and dulls the pain. Or so it seems.

It takes bravery or sheer stupidity to be the deliverer of bad news in business - so it's often safer to tell the 'preferred' version of the truth or to just keep quiet. Telling the truth to an insecure boss (and there are certainly enough of them) when the news is unpleasant, can be a serious CLM (Career Limiting Move). Men have become accustomed to playing the deception game in business. Women seem to have a problem playing this game - a sense of fair play and openness can become an impediment to progress in this male-dominated, dishonesty-driven world. Women are better at telling lies in other ways. Yet neither gender holds a monopoly on good or bad behaviours. We learn to protect ourselves by hiding from the truth. But does it protect us?

Truth - the final frontier

In my work as a communications consultant I am constantly seeking ways at their conferences to convey the truth to clients' staff, suppliers and management without offending those who pay my fees. There are sometimes much easier ways to earn a living. Countless preliminary client conversations have begun with earnest executives declaring that the conference must be positive at all times. *"It is bad for staff morale if they hear anything other than good news"*. Delve deep enough and you will often discover the real motives for such beliefs. If staff hear bad news, executives are afraid that they will be seen as mere human beings who haven't solved all the company's problems. One example comes to mind: the President of a U S company was invited to attend a European meeting for approximately four hundred of its staff. As a closed minded, arrogant man, he insisted on hearing exactly what was going to happen the following morning. He was not convinced that an open and honest approach would be appropriate. The agenda had been carefully worked out in the weeks leading up to the event, no one was keen to change it for his benefit, nor were they confident enough to challenge him. The European President and Marketing Director referred him to me. After a 90 minute heated discussion, the agenda remained intact. And the following day progressed as planned. The audience responded particularly well to the honesty and openness. He did not. Interestingly, as part of the event everyone took part in a business game. The team in which this man took over, came last. He later dismissed it all as a 'waste of everybody's time'. Senior management are afraid he will one day run the company (into the ground).

His bullying tactics within the company limit and restrain open and frank communication among the staff. In my experience, this obsession with being 'positive' at all times tends to come predominantly from American owned companies, where positive mental attitude (PMA) is seen as strength of character. Sometimes PMA is wholly inappropriate especially if it is used as a suppression mechanism. PMA business books have a great deal to answer for.

Living in a society and working within a business environment which does not encourage and reward honesty, makes it far more difficult for each individual to be honest with him/herself, to see situations as they really are, rather than through a rose-tinted version of reality which PMA so often demands. Your ability and confidence to be objective by refusing to accept these 'vital lies', will help you to think about and plan for a more secure future in the 21st century.

At the end of each year, New Year celebrations take place all over the world - from small family get together's to the hundreds of thousands who congregate in places like New York's Times Square or London's Trafalgar Square. It's a time when everyone appears to have a good time - often helped by large quantities of alcohol. But does everyone enjoy the new year celebrations? I'll be honest - I don't. May be you are the same? The end of one year and the beginning of another is more a time for quiet reflection rather than boisterous revelry. I enjoy a good party like most people, (I don't remember some really good ones!) but New Year's Eve isn't the best time for me. I tend to reflect on the past year and the year ahead by asking myself a series of questions.

The value of questions

As a radio and television interviewer, I learned many years ago that if you ask someone a vague question, you will invariably get a vague answer. Vague answers tend to make for rather dull interviews, so the secret of good interviewing is to ask specific questions. The quality of your future success is down to the quality of the questions you ask yourself - because they will affect the quality and accuracy of your answers. These in turn will influence your future behaviour and ultimately the quality of the results you get.

Many people ask glib, superficial questions or pose none at all. While others just experience a nagging sense of something not quite right about their life.

Quite deliberately, this book is littered with questions - some are straight forward, while many are not intended to be answered instantly. As the author of this book, my role is to provide you with provoking questions. You already have most of the answers inside you. By providing you with detailed information and knowledge about future trends and what impact they are likely to have on your life, your answers should become better informed.

Self-reliance is a pre-requisite for the future - this cannot be achieved by a universal prescription - only you can decide what is best for you.

It's easy to skim over some of the trickier questions. But if you decide to invest some time in thinking about each question and formulating your answer, you will gain a deeper and richer insight into your future potential. Remember, these questions and answers are purely for you - no one else need ever see them. Your answers may change over time - indeed, I hope they do. Preferably, write them down and you will gain far more from this book. Use a computer, if you can, to create a personal and confidential file, print out your answers and store them in a specially prepared binder. If no computer is available, buy a notebook specially for the purpose - it will also provide a handy place to write down other ideas and strategies you should pick up while reading.

A small tip - if you choose the notebook option - don't buy a cheap one. Invest a little money in it - your future life can be one of higher quality - let that be reflected in your choice of notebook. A cheap one just doesn't say the right things to your subconscious mind about the importance of your future.

Answer each question as fully as you can - some will take a while. Who said life should be easy? Don't take the line of least resistance by skipping over the more difficult ones. Some of the answers you give will not always be what you actually believe deep down - they'll be a knee-jerk reaction. But the more you think about the questions, the more you will uncover your true beliefs and feelings about your core values, aspirations, desires and ambitions. This process can involve a lot of soul searching and delving deeply into yourself. As you get into it, you may find you surprise yourself with the greater clarity you bring to key areas of your life. It's powerful stuff.

Most of the questions have been worded precisely so that they cannot be answered using a simple 'yes' or 'no'. There are no 'right' and 'wrong' answers. The aim is to help you see who you are and where you want your life to lead. Without this knowledge it is difficult or even impossible to work out a strategy to take you there. These answers are the first stage of mapping out the future you want.

Many years ago Frankie (my wife) and I chose to devote a major part of a holiday in the French countryside to asking each other these and many other questions. Sitting alongside the Burgundy canal in the sunshine, we took it in turn to ask each other a steady stream of previously prepared questions. These provoked many additional questions all of which we used to encourage a free flow of thoughts and ideas. The whole process was helped along by the occasional bottle of our favourite local white wine!

When we subsequently told friends and colleagues what we had done, a significant proportion of people said "Some holiday!" They seemed to think that it represented 'work'. They didn't understand that this process brought us far closer together - which meant that we had a more intimate and enjoyable holiday. We discovered things not only about each other which we had not understood or realised, but also about ourselves. It's true that some aspects of the process were quite difficult at times, but the rewards made it worthwhile. In Peter Senge's book *The Fifth Discipline Fieldbook* he and his co-authors advocate exactly the same approach.

Many of us are brought up being told what we want by parents and teachers. They try to influence our decisions by recommending actions which in their views are far safer and more sensible. Asking yourself deep questions is all about exploring who you are and the choices and possibilities open to you. It can only be achieved if your views and feelings are not skewed or diluted by others.

If you choose to conduct this exercise with someone else in the way I have just described, there are a number of ground rules which I recommend you follow. The first rule is that the person asking the questions must not try to redirect or misinterpret the desires and goals of the other person. Simply write or type as accurately as you can, exactly what the other person says. It is not your role to impose your views - however well meaning they may be. Alternatively, record the conversation (your self-consciousness about being 'on-tape' will disappear very quickly) then transcribe the recording later, adding any other thoughts as they occur to you.

Accept that this process takes time. Don't be in too much of a rush to finish the conversations - indeed set yourself a time limit of say, 45-60 minutes per day. This approach gives you time to think between sessions.

In late 1996, I was invited to join 400 senior partners in Barcelona for Price Waterhouse's European Corporate Finance and Corporate Recovery Division

Conference as their keynote speaker and 'Business Oprah Winfrey'. The conference was entitled "Creating the Future". My four talks over three days focused on how to "Create Your Own Future" within the framework of the company's strategy. I was there to challenge and provoke these high-ranking executives into questioning the ways they run their business and their own lives.

They, like most executives in business today, have so many on-going commitments and demands on their time, it can be difficult or even impossible to clear some space in their lives just to think about what they want out of life and their jobs. Thinking time is so often shunted down the 'to do' list in favour of what appear to be more pressing issues.

So, for one of the sessions everyone was given a few sheets of paper containing a list of questions. Their answers would remain private and confidential - they would not be collected or discussed with anyone. The purpose was to give these busy executives some thinking time with no interruptions. The assembled audience then sat in silence for twenty minutes as they worked their way through each question. They were designed to be difficult and thought provoking. Below are just some of the questions they were given - see how you get on:

- What are the consequences to you on a personal level, if you continue on exactly the same path, when you know that business from competitors will become tougher in the years to come?
- What talents and skills do you possess?
- What specific tasks do you enjoy?
- What are you good at that most people don't know about?
- What new skills would you like to have? And why?
- How would you describe your perfect life in detail? Where are you? What are you doing? Who are you with? How do you look? What are you wearing? How do you feel about yourself? What are you driving?
- As someone who is paid for the application of your knowledge, how much time each week do you invest in learning new and potentially more valuable knowledge?
- How much of the answer to the previous perfect life questions were a fantasy and how much were tangible and achievable goals?
- Who and what do you believe is stopping you from achieving this perfect life?
- What could you do today or this week to move you towards this vision of your future?
- How much money would you need to be happy in life? What is 'enough'?
- Exactly why did you choose such a sum?

- What new things have you learned in the last week?
- What excites you the most about your work?
- What do you want to achieve in your future career?
- It is your funeral. What would you want people to say about you? What would you want to be remembered for? What do you need to do now and in the years to come to guarantee such plaudits?

During an open forum discussion I chaired at the end of this event, a number of delegates referred to this exercise as being particularly useful to them. Answer these and the other questions you will find in later chapters. By more fully understanding what you are looking for in the future, your answers will help clarify your thoughts.

Without doubt, everyone is and will continue to be subjected to massive changes in the ways we live and work. We are seeing the start of it now. Highly sophisticated technology is already capable of performing 'intelligent' functions which have traditionally been performed by people. As computers become more powerful, and are able to process billions of calculations per second, people (who represent the most expensive and fallible component in many businesses) will be replaced by machines - increasingly by computer software.

In the next chapter we will look at many of the changes being predicted by the world's leading futurists and asking the question "What is the most likely impact these changes will have on the way you live and work?"

Chapter 2
Painting Pictures of the Future

Arthur C. Clarke, the writer and acclaimed futurist, has observed that there is a tendency amongst scientists and social commentators to over-predict the short term future, but to vastly under-estimate change in the longer term. Making predictions about the future is fraught with all manner of problems, although most are down to society's ever increasing complexity. The more complicated our lives become, the more difficult it is to assess the impact any change will have - however small or insignificant it may seem.

In this chapter we will look at many of the changes which experts agree will be a part of the next 20 to 30 years. This is not intended to present an optimistic or pessimistic view - merely to explain what is happening and why such predictions and projections are being made. Below you will find a collection of predictions by some of the world's leading futurists and management gurus. These are individuals who devote their lives analysing existing and future trends in society, business, finance, technology and demographics. They unravel complex, seemingly unrelated facts and behaviours to paint a picture of the future (refer to the extensive Bibliography at the end of this book for details of further material from these sources). Understanding the implications of their findings will present you with distinct advantages over those who believe they are too important or too busy to think much about the future.

Pick a 'wild' card

First, let's take the bleakest look into the future - don't read the next page or so if you are feeling depressed! In the book *Out of the Blue*, John L. Petersen of The Arlington Institute has produced a list of what he describes 'Wild Cards'; massive events and scenarios which could happen at almost any time. They are reprinted here with the author's permission.

The AIDS virus (or similarly deadly disease) mutates and becomes transmittable by air. There's another 'Chernobyl'. An asteroid hits the earth. A civil war erupts between former Soviet states and goes nuclear. Climatic instability takes a turn for the worse. A collapse of the sperm count. The collapse of the United Nations. A computer/chip/operating system maker blackmails a country (or the world). Computers/robots become capable of thinking like humans. Encryption is invalidated. A collapse of the world's fisheries. The end of the nation state. An energy revolution. Terrorism rises beyond the capability of government systems. An extraordinary US West coast natural disaster. Faster than light travel. Foetal sex selection becomes the norm. The first unambiguous contact with extraterrestrial life - the arrival of ET's. Fuel cells replace the internal combustion engine. Global electromagnetic communications are disrupted for the foreseeable future. A global food shortage. The growth of religious environmentalism. The Gulf or Jet Stream shifts location permanently. Computer hackers blackmail the US Federal Reserve. Major health and medical breakthroughs. Human cloning is perfected and a human mutation takes place.

The ice cap breaks up - oceans rise one hundred feet. Inner cities arm and revolt. An international financial collapse. A large-scale, lengthy disruption of national electricity supplies. Life expectancy approaches 100. The long term side effects of medications are discovered. The loss of intellectual property rights. A major break in the Alaskan pipeline leads to significant ecological damage. Major chaos in Africa. A major information systems disruption. A major technology or science research accident. A major US military unit mutinies and allies with the militia movement. Mass migrations. Nanotechnology takes off. New age attitudes blossom with the millennium. A nuclear terrorist attack on the United States or Europe. The rise of an American dictator. The rules of society change. Economic and/or environmental "war criminals" are prosecuted. A Second World nation demonstrates the development of nanotech weapons. The development of self-aware machine intelligence. A social breakdown in the US or Europe. A stock market crash. A sweeping medical breakthrough is perfected. Terrorists go biological. A Third World exodus. Time travel is invented. The US economy fails and there's a collapse of the dollar. Virtual reality and holography move information instead of people. Viruses become immune to all known treatments. A whole generation becomes effectively unable to read, write, think and work and there's a worldwide epidemic.

Not all of the above are necessarily harbingers of doom - so, when reading or hearing about these 'Doomsday scenarios', it is worth considering what positive role these potential disruptions and chaos could plays. In Charles Handy's *The Empty Raincoat* he writes *"Scientists call this sort of time the edge of chaos, the time of turbulence and creativity out of which a new order may jell...it [the universe] has also managed to produce from that disorder an incredible array of living creatures, plants and bacteria, as well as stars and planets. New life is forever springing from the decay and disorder of the old."*

Society

21st century life will become less predictable and more insecure. There will be more conflict generated by ethnic minorities, some of whom will try to impose their own religious and ideological beliefs on others; guns and bombs will continue to be used to attract attention to causes. Conflict will intensify within such institutions as government, business, and healthcare. Politicians and bureaucrats will continue to fight for control of a system which has become woefully inadequate at coping with the speed and complexity of tomorrow. Faceless bureaucrats will continue to exert their awesome power over whichever political party is in office, in order to maintain the status quo - and their jobs - for as long as they can. Integrated information technology will render many functions of government unnecessary. But which politicians are brave enough to dismantle these high cost yet obsolete departments?

Through the process of privatisation, government has divested itself of infrastructure services such as telecoms, railways, and gas & electricity supply. However, during the 1980's and 90's there was in fact an increase in centralisation and governmental control. As Simon Jenkins points out in his book *Accountable to None*, Margaret Thatcher's contempt for the public sector did not lead to a reduction of that sector's demands on the taxpayer. Where once nationalised industries made demands upon the exchequer, now their place is taken by a raft of quangos and regulators who are electorally unaccountable. The libertarian vision of a society with limited government seems unlikely as governments continue to impose more and more regulations which they justify as 'protection' for the consumer. In reality, this behaviour imposes unnecessary costs and limitations on businesses, making them less competitive. Nowhere is this demonstrated better than in the regulatory-ridden United States and Canada. It would seem that governments still believe or act as if their prime function is to regulate and legislate rather than to lead their nations into the 21st century. Whilst on one hand task force groups are set up by governments to remove red tape and bureaucracy, on the other hand, government continues to draft, pass, and enact new statutory regulations.

As more money is transferred electronically across international borders, the role of national governments will decline even further. Many of yesterday's mighty institutions are crumbling. The costs of Western government will continue to rise. Excessive taxes levied by any government will result in rapid physical and electronic migration to less onerous regimes. Business has the cash and the clout to dictate the terms.

Society will become split into the 'knows' and the 'know-nots' as well as the 'haves' and 'have-nots'. Tomorrow will not be like yesterday.

The Eastern promise

Despite efforts to ban satellite dishes by predominantly anti-Western governments and religions, Western values continue to spread. Many older, more traditional Eastern societies reject what they see as Western immorality as portrayed in films and on TV, where violence is glamourised and sex without emotion is seen as 'normal'. They may have a point; in the West, families continue to disintegrate, crime and violence is on the increase, the number of children borne out of stable relationships continues to rise, old people are treated with disrespect and Western populations suffer the ravages of cancer, heart disease, diabetes and sexually transmitted diseases. Many of these behavioural traits and afflictions are virtually unheard of in some Far Eastern countries, although the authorities there worry that their incidence is growing. The young want the consumer lifestyle, while the old guard, who have devoted their lives to preserving the traditions of their ancestors, will exert their considerable power to maintain the status quo. Expect a loud and bloody backlash in some countries. In others, expect increased racial and religious conflict as bigoted individuals with low IQ's sense they are losing out to harder working, better trained 'foreigners'. The real fights have yet to begin.

The US will continue to lose its dominant political, military, and economic position throughout the rest of the world. The Far East is already re-establishing itself as the global economic powerhouse. With 3 billion people in Asia - half of them under 25 - economies are exploding (and occasionally crashing!), gleaming cities are rising from former shanty towns at a breathtaking pace. As John Naisbett declares in *Megatrends Asia*, *"The West now needs the East a lot more than the East needs the West."*

Overseas Chinese are the most successful business people in the world. Their powerful family-style business networks own a significant proportion of the businesses throughout Asia and increasingly in North America. Their 'connections' into mainland China are also deep rooted and hugely influential. The perception of Asia as an area of dire poverty, coolies, and rice paddies has its foundations in truth, but within the last 40 years it has become the centre of world trade. How? Everyone is an entrepreneur. With no handouts, they have to be.

India's population is rapidly approaching 1 billion; over 150 million are well educated and middle class. Bangalore is a high-tech region, and is home to advanced computer software and aerospace industries.

Lee Kuan Yew, Singapore's authoritarian political leader, has proved, through his almost dictatorial policies, that there are effective alternatives to

Western democracy. Singapore is routinely described as a 'fine' city - you will be fined for any anti-social behaviour. It's illegal to chew gum, to drink alcohol in public, to beg in the streets, to spit, to 'forget' to flush a public toilet -the list is long. You are calmly reminded by otherwise chirpy cabin crew on your final approach into Singapore's Changi International Airport, that, if you take or sell illegal drugs, you risk execution. Canings and hangings are also a part of the harsh punishments handed out to criminals. The streets are generally spotless, with little or no graffiti to be seen. It's not just the taxi drivers in Singapore who quietly complain about these and other strictly enforced regulations governing their country. They call for Western democracy, taking for granted the fact that anyone in Singapore, unlike in cities like London or Washington DC, can walk the streets at just about any time of the day or night without fear. Crime obviously exists, especially amongst the young, but **nothing** like on the scale of democratic nations in the West. You have to see it at first hand to understand the modernisation of Asia, which is being defined as the most important development in the world today. Singapore in particular has created the infrastructure needed to be at the forefront of business, culture, and politics in the next century. Its telecom-munications system is the envy of the world. As someone who travels regularly on business, The Shangri La Hotel in Singapore ranks as my favourite hotel in the world. It's inspiring to realise that all of this has been achieved by a country which is only about the size of the Isle of Wight!

When I was last in Singapore, sitting at dinner in a Thai restaurant alongside the harbour quay, I was distracted and fascinated by the conver-sation on the next table; a group of middle class Singaporean men in their late twenties, were enthusiastically discussing business - in English. Wherever you go in Asia, English is the international business language. Millions of Asians are joining the middle classes and want to own the consumer goods their parents could never afford. And they are prepared to work damned hard for them. This is the norm in a modern society which encourages self-discipline, self-reliance, hard work, frugality, personal responsibility, honesty, innovation, education and looking after your family.

The West could learn a great deal from Asia, but Western arrogance usually gets in the way.

The control of society, business and religion throughout the world will no longer be the exclusive domain of white, middle class men. White women and Asian and Hispanic men & women will increasingly set our future agendas. Anyone with high quality technical skills would be wise to explore the employment opportunities in Asia.

The environment; burning holes in our fragile blanket

Nuclear and fossil power will decline as a source of energy, to be replaced by power generation from sustainable energy sources. The technology exists now to generate vast quantities of energy from the wind, the seas and the sun. Indeed, before the First World War there were 10,000 windmills operating in Britain alone. Since the Chernobyl nuclear disaster, how many governments regret building these 'artificial suns' which burn holes in the Earth's crust? It's a bit like encouraging everyone to smoke in bed! And, as any fan of *The Simpson's* will tell you, Montgomery Burns, the nuclear power station owner, is responsible for creating 3 eyed fish! It must be true because I saw them on TV!

There has always been enough power from the real sun, the wind and the waves in our oceans, if only we and government didn't accept the view of the fossil fuel and nuclear lobbies that sustainable energy is not 'commercially viable'. It's small wonder that they hold this view when you consider all the grants, tax incentives and regulations in favour of the large non-sustainable power providers. The longer they get away with what they tell us through public relations exercises and TV commercials, the more they can prolong the life of their terminally ill cash cow. Interestingly, they are beginning to re-position themselves as a 'renewable' source of energy.

Any visitor to the World Sustainable Energy Exhibition in Amsterdam in 1997, would have seen that today's technology is capable of generating vast amounts of 'clean' energy. Holland already produces 16% of its energy requirements via sustainable methods. More governments will follow. However, widespread bickering within the largely fragmented sustainable energy sector which cannot yet compete with the well established, highly organised, cash-rich fossil and nuclear energy producers, is inhibiting its progress.

Distributing electricity is highly inefficient and wasteful. It is estimated that there is a loss of up to 20% of the electrical power sent along the copper based power lines, whose pylons criss-cross the countryside. Technological developments in superconductivity will greatly reduce this power loss. Could this mean the need for less power stations? Perhaps.

China will become the major economic force on earth, followed by the rest of Asia. As Frank Ogden observes in *Navigating in Cyberspace*, "*It took the United States 200 years to produce one million millionaires. China did it in the last three.*" If China's economy continues to grow at its present rate, in about 20 years it will overtake the US as the world's largest economy. It will also overtake the US to become the world's largest polluter. It appears that its economy is more important than what it does to the planet (in this disrespect, China, as well as other developing countries, shares the same view as the US).

We may care about the environment, the problem is, we don't care **enough**. When it comes down to jobs, industrial output, food production and leisure, environmental issues invariably come last. Apparently the average American baby causes twice as much environmental damage as a Swedish baby during its life time. And the populations of developing countries want to emulate the consumptive lifestyles of America!

The population; exploding & exploiting

"The earth's resources cannot feed, clothe, house and educate a population that in the next 25 years will be almost 30% larger than the earth's present 5.6 billion people." Barry Howard Minkin

The British population is getting older. According to the OECD, the number of old people in Europe will double in 50 years. By 2050, up to half of the European population could be over 60. How many will have enough money to survive?

David K Foot, author of the Canadian bestseller *Boom Bust & Echo*, states: *"Demographics explain about 2/3rds of everything...the future doesn't just arrive suddenly one day. There are always early warning signs."*

Older people tend to become more conservative and cautious. There is a huge number of baby boomers competing for a declining number of senior management jobs. David K. Foot describes the baby boom as a rectangle of people growing older together, but business tends to resemble a triangle - which won't fit! Most get frustrated or depressed - especially if their company re-structures and flattens the triangle. The rectangle still won't fit. For many there's no way up the corporate ladder, so those with the most initiative form their own businesses. He claims it is easy to predict the impact of 'grey power' in about 20 years time, as the largest group of the population reaches retirement age. A growing population buys more consumer goods, an ageing one doesn't. Also, as people grow older, they commit fewer crimes. At least, at the moment they do, but who knows what future desperation will provoke; ramraiding grannies perhaps? Expect the number of poor people to increase - especially amongst the elderly in Britain. This will also occur in every other country. An estimated 1 billion people already live in real poverty.

People in their 40's tend to own properties in the countryside - with more entering that age group, expect a higher demand for rural properties. Those areas with the best hospitals will appeal more to older people who tend to use the health service more than the young. Low grade (by today's standards) mechanisation attracted millions to city factories at the birth of the Industrial Revolution. Many of those involved in the information revolution are now using technology to leave the cities. The next 50 years will see a migration of affluent 'knowledge' workers back to the countryside, where they will want to raise their families and enjoy an improved and more peaceful lifestyle, linked by telecommunications technology - phone, fax, satellite and computer modem - to their widely dispersed clients and colleagues. Will this lead to increased green-belt over-development?

Fear, confusion, and anxiety will become more widespread among a growing number of individuals, many of whom are worried about their jobs, families and future old age. The middle class will shrink in the West. According to Barry Howard Minkin about 6% of the US population lives a Third World existence of dire poverty. That's about 15 million people.

Britain has the highest pregnancy rate amongst teenagers in Western Europe with about 7,500 pregnancies a year. Approximately half of these are aborted. If the perception of government as a 'parent' continues, it will perpetuate the belief that young girls will be cared for if they get pregnant. This represents a good deal to individuals who believe they are not loved by their parent(s) or who are desperately keen to leave home. Get pregnant and have a baby which will love you unconditionally until it too suffers from years of subsistence living, and increased stress from its 'uncaring' parent. This pattern is well known to social workers. It does not provide young girls with the escape or status in society they crave. In 1971 there were 570,000 single parents raising a million children. By 1991, 1.3 million single parents were raising 2 million children. Bringing up a family (often alone) on a subsistence income creates tension and deprivation for the child(ren) which causes the pattern to repeat itself. But in the future, no government will be able to afford to pay to support this behaviour.

"In the year 2010 the percentage of population over 65 years old will be the highest ever in the United States, Japan, West Germany and the United Kingdom. In Latin America however, only 3% of the population will be over 65." Barry Howard Minkin

In the 30 years from 1950 to 1990, the global population more than doubled from 2.5 billion to over 5 billion. It has been forecast to grow from 6 billion today to nearly 9 billion within the next 30 years. In 1950 the population of Africa was half that of Europe, by 2025 it is predicted that Africa will have a population three times larger than Europe. Most of these people will be desperately poor. In underdeveloped countries, 70% of all water is used for agriculture. This could lead to massive water shortages - to the point where it has been predicted that the lack of water will lead some affected countries to war.

Biotechnologists are busily creating hundreds of new plant and animal life forms far more intriguing than existing cross breeds such as the mule (horse and donkey). Optimistic scientists such as Dennis Avery, author of the book *Saving the Planet with Pesticides and Plastics*, believes that such genetically modified plants will be able to feed these extra billions. Splicing, adding, and removing genes from animals to plants or vice versa, will create new breeds. Breeds which are salt-resistant and drought-tolerant and which can produce high yields without the need for large quantities of water or which are capable of growing abundantly without the need for expensive pesticides and which can thrive in areas of the world currently unable to support them. Already, since 1960, world food production has doubled and productivity from agricultural land has tripled. Growing sufficient food to feed an additional 3-4 billion hungry mouths without destroying the planet will be a further major challenge.

Expect an increase in vegetarianism and high quality pre-prepared vegetarian foods. With such massive growth in world population, there isn't enough grain available to rear enough animals to produce meat. Red meat producers and processors will suffer. Global fish yields are smaller due to over-fishing. This will become more acute.

Misery for millions

Because of well-meaning foreign aid, populations in third world countries are declining less rapidly than they used to. Human reproduction has always been high in these countries because largely uneducated parents knew many of their children would die or they can be added to the family workforce. Now that more children live, the result is massive over-population. In India - the world's second largest population - vast areas of land are devoid of trees, cut down to provide fuel for cooking. Future fuel shortages will result in misery for millions. In many countries, especially in Africa and Asia, up to 50% of the population is now under 15 years of age. These millions are entering the age range when men are statistically most likely to experiment with criminal and violent behaviour and women are reaching their prime child-bearing years. Widespread starvation and wars over food and water are likely consequences.

The Roman Catholic Church's anti-contraception, global recruitment campaign, especially in South America, will certainly not help the situation.

As society goes through such profound changes, those with the loudest voices will exert the most pressure to protect their self-interests. As the population ages, seniors will demand increased government spending in healthcare, housing and financial support. This power, influence and self-interest will create tension, dissent, resentment and anger amongst many young people, who will ultimately lose out.

The fights against crime

Terrorism, apparently unprovoked attacks and other random acts of violence against people, countries, and institutions will increase as the perpetrators desperately seek to express their dissatisfaction and frustration at their economic and political impotence. They will fail to see that those they hurt, maim and murder are equally powerless to make the changes or maintain the status quo they demand.

In the Dark Ages we built castles and forts to keep us safe. As society became more civilised there was less need for such strong houses. But today there is an increasing number of homes and businesses which operate behind high security walls and iron railings. Anyone visiting a business in an urban area is already faced with security guards and sophisticated surveillance equipment. Only recently we visited a friend who had moved into a new development in a deprived area of London. Getting into the compound in which she lived was like going into a prison. Inside, all the owners' cars were safe from vandalism and theft. More locks and railings had to be negotiated before we were greeted at a heavily locked front door.

Increased crime by the predominantly younger elements of society will continue. Most crime is committed by men aged between 16 and 30. With rising aspirations for material possessions, especially among young males everywhere, expect a corresponding rise in crime and violence in the approaching decades, as many turn to illegitimate means to satisfy their material wants. Demographically, the number of people entering this age group is rising, it is therefore reasonable to expect that more crimes will be committed. In Britain, there are more than 65,000 prisoners in jail and the figure is rising by about 200 inmates every week. The cost to society is at least £2 billion per year or £30,000 per inmate. You could live in a 4-star hotel for less than that. Building and maintaining prisons will be a growth industry for the private sector.

Security services will be a growth industry. Although surveillance cameras can be monitored from anywhere, even a different country. To alert the police only requires a 'phone call - it doesn't matter where you are.

According to a report in *Success* magazine (April 1996), 85% of inmates at San Quentin prison are illiterate. With more and more young illiterate people being imprisoned, there is perhaps an argument for introducing a policy whereby inmates will not be released until they can read and write to an acceptable standard. Such a policy could radically reduce future crime.

Older and better educated criminals will move away from 'high risk' activities in favour of the so called 'victimless' crimes of deception and fraud. Computer fraud and extortion will become more widespread. Sophisticated criminals, often with military intelligence expertise, will continue to blackmail large corporations with threats of a meltdown of their entire computer systems. The head of a corporation is told that their computer system will 'fall over' at a predetermined time. It does. The extortionist arranges for it to be put right within a short time and then calls again to say "Unless you pay $millions into our Swiss account, the next time it happens, we won't put it right." Governments, corporations and banks are all at risk. No one involved wants to talk about it - but electronic extortion already happens. It is a growth industry.

Drugs; sniffing, smoking and swigging

Humans crave stimulation. We all want to feel good - often at any cost. Illegal drug use amongst young people is at an all-time high (forgive the pun) and will certainly continue. If it is possible to eat, drink, smoke or inject stimulants, people will do so, either in an attempt to feel better about a sad life, or, if they feel good already, to seek a more intense high. Knowing that the behaviour is illegal also appeals to those who like the idea of being a rebel. In our 'instant gratification' society there is a widely held belief that there must be something wrong with you if you don't feel good all the time.

The growing 'normalisation' of illegal drugs in society has already led anti-drugs campaigners to move away from advocating a 'just say no' approach. They realise it's ineffective. In the US, disruptive kids of all ages are routinely given sedatives to 'calm them down' or supposedly make them more attentive. How long will it be before this becomes the norm in Britain too?

Until society, not simply government, can provide a more appealing alternative to illegal drug use, the 'problem' will continue and worsen.

Traditionally, young people are the highest illegal drugs users. And young men are the most likely to commit crime. The costs of drug-related crime committed by men are escalating to an alarming extent. Figures vary but it is estimated that up to 75% of all burglaries are commited to pay for a drug habit. Sort out the drug problem, and crimes involving burglary and violence would drop significantly. Prostitution amongst female illegal drug users would also drop as well as the spread of HIV amongst users who share needles. In May 1995, a government White Paper, *Tackling Drugs Together*, estimated the annual cost of just heroin-related crime at £864 million. That's approximately £338 million more than the government's annual expenditure to fight the problem. But alcohol-induced crime is far more costly to society. For example, up to 70% of murders are booze-related. But that does not seem to matter - alcohol abuse is socially acceptable and is highly lucrative for the government as a revenue source!

There are fewer men and women in their thirties and older who take illegal drugs. There are two reasons; they start their own families and exercise responsibility to their partners and children or putting it simply, they are dead. Instead of using illegal drugs, as people get older they become the largest users of alcohol and legally prescribed drugs, especially anti-depressants and sedatives to overcome stress. There are however, plenty of illegal drug-users in this age bracket - especially 'fashionable' and more expensive drugs like cocaine and the intellectual dope-smoking brigade. They presumably don't feature in government figures as much because a) they are more affluent and don't get involved in petty crime to support the habit, b) they are far more adept at not getting caught, or c) many of them are probably directly involved in producing the government figures or writing about them in the media!

Pharmaceutical companies are currently developing anti-ageing drugs aimed at the growing number of older people. The pharmaceuticals industry is gearing itself up with many other products for older people; drugs to offset the effects of the menopause, hormone replacement therapy, new anti-depressants and treatments for Alzheimer's and Parkinson's disease. So called 'smart' drugs to combat memory loss for such sufferers will also attract interest from young ambitious individuals if they believe their own mental performance can be improved by taking them.

Technology; the answer to every question?
Technology will continue to create as many problems as it solves.

The discovery of electricity, the invention of the telephone and aeroplanes have changed the world. It's difficult to imagine society without these inventions. The networking of computers will further transform the world - even though less than 1% of the world's population is currently 'wired'. Allowing millions of ordinary folk to communicate globally, almost instantaneously and at low cost, linked computers have already changed the world of business. There are major advantages to those who are, but monumental consequences for those who are not, a part of this new means of communication. Developing countries are building state-of-the-art optical fibre telecommunications networks, many of them leap-frogging the technology currently used in the telephone systems of developed countries. Even those living and working in the remotest parts of the world will have telephone access via Iridium, a series of low orbiting satellites currently under construction. Planning on a weekend walk in the Antarctic? Being permanently on-call, as more and more workers are, the office will be able to contact you instantly. What a lovely thought!

Nicholas Negroponte, in *Being Digital* also makes the interesting observation that one of the key recent changes in technology is that systems which used to use underground cables (e.g. telephones) now use radio & satellite transmission media (e.g. mobile telephones), and vice versa - most noticeably the rapid growth of cable TV distribution compared with airborne transmission. In the process, the capacities and capabilities of both systems have increased hugely.

Think of the average library - quiet, row after row of books - everything you could possibly want - except of course the actual book you are looking for! "I'm sorry, but it's out until a week on Thursday." says the cheerful librarian. Electronic libraries of the future will not have this problem. Hundreds of thousands of people can have the same book in its electronic form at exactly the same time if they want it. Such computer-based libraries will be 'retrievatories' rather than 'depositories' according to Nicholas Negroponte, Director of the Media Lab at MIT (Massachusetts Institute of Technology).

Within 30 years practically all knowledge will be stored and available electronically. This means anything you want or need to know will be available almost instantaneously from any where in the world - at a price, admittedly. Bomb disposal experts could find a CD-Rom by Military Ordinance Design quite useful. It contains descriptions and diagrams of every known explosive, bomb mechanism and fuse. Just the thing if you are facing a ticking device, with a design you have never seen before. Let's hope terrorists can't get it. Spend a moment thinking about the impact that the availability of all knowledge could have on your life - both positive and negative.

Does your work rely on knowledge? What if your customers could buy it more cheaply without any help from you? Or perhaps you would only be called upon to apply it? Constant information now gushes into our lives. How we sort and filter it will become a major issue for busy professionals. Nine out of 10 scientists who have ever lived are alive today. Each one is producing information and knowledge, much of it constantly distributed to colleagues around the globe. The growth of scientific knowledge is explosive and looks set to keep doubling every 12-18 months.

If you have trouble operating your feature-laden telephone, you are likely to face the next few decades drowning in technology. It may be difficult at first, but get to grips with it and make your life easier either by reading more manuals or paying for training courses. Technology designers may be trying extremely hard to make everything easier to use but there will be too much of it for most people to cope with. Information and technology overload will increase.

Expect more complexity not less.

While we are submerged in technology, over half the world's population has yet to make or receive a 'phone call. According to *The Economist*, an estimated 15 to 20 million new telephone lines will be installed every year for the next five years. China alone will install 97 million telephones lines within the next 10 years. One in 6 new telephone subscriptions worldwide is for a mobile 'phone. So far over 50 million mobiles have been sold and are most popular with young people - but not as a fashion accessory. Most lead a mobile lifestyle and don't know how long they will live in their current accommodation, so their number can travel too.

Expect the costs of long-distance telephone use to continue to drop as competition hots up amongst the growing number of telecom suppliers.

The mobility of telephony and the seemingly never ending increases in the power of computers have already created gigantic opportunities and considerable threats to many workers.

Using telephones to connect the world's computers together will create the single biggest change to life as we know it.

The effects of combining computers and telephony has only just begun. As technology continues to shrink in size and increase in power, it becomes possible to do more and more with the technology. Desktop publishing for the masses became possible with the introduction of powerful computers during the mid 1980's. Additional computer power is creating 'desktop studios'- broadcast quality audio and video recording and editing is already possible for would-be Steven Spielberg's everywhere. Computer software which instantly translates spoken and written material from one language to another will allow for rapid and accurate dictation. In Bosnia, American troops tested *Falcon* (Forward Area Language Converter), a computer which provides instant translations. If soldiers found documents during searches they could scan them into the computer to see whether they had military importance. It won't be too many years before it will be possible to send an e-mail message and specify which language(s) it will be translated into en route. Is it worth training as a translator? Think for a moment about the implications in other professions.

Mobile and home based working will become even more prevalent as words, sounds, pictures and video can be sent and received via computers and 'phone lines without the need for workers to be there - wherever 'there' might be. This could lead to higher demand for larger homes - where spare bedrooms will be converted to home offices. High-tech houses, wired to satisfy the demand for home offices are already being built in Britain. Ownership of home based computers, connected via modems to the Internet, will grow exponentially. Using company intranets (private computer networks) people from different areas of the world work together on complex time-critical projects. While one area of the world goes to sleep, another is beginning its working day. Nine-to-fivers (or more accurately eight-to-seveners these days) cannot compete with this way of working.

Millions join the Internet each and every month. Giving a figure here is pointless - it will be out of date instantly. It's no use having a telephone when no one else has one. Who would you be able to call? But when there are millions of 'phones, they become invaluable - it's the same with the Internet. The more people who use it, the more indispensable it becomes. People and computers are already working together as a team, helping us to work more intelligently. And it's only just begun. The Internet has grown more quickly than any other communications medium.

Everything on the Internet is stored on 'servers' - about 7 million of them at the last estimate. When you open a page, you connect to one of these servers. Click onto a hyperlink (a system invented by Tim Berners-Lee), where text, usually underlined and in a different colour, acts as a switch to take you to another piece of information. In doing so you could be re-directed automatically to another server - perhaps on another continent. The Internet is continuing to grow at a phenomenal rate - more US citizens are linked to it than hold library cards.

It isn't hype to say that computers will have a staggering impact on society in the next century. But so many non-users of computers still refuse to be a part of it in much the same way that millions don't want to be able to read and write. They don't see the point.

In the 21st century anyone who cannot or will not use a computer will be regarded by most employers as functionally illiterate.

They will become increasingly marginalised as everyday activities such as banking, shopping and even obtaining a 'newspaper' move over to computerised systems.

Some angrily deride the Internet, especially those with a vested interest in older, less interactive technologies. Janet Street-Porter is an outspoken TV executive who presented a television series in 1996 on the Techno-nerd. This is part of what she wrote in *The Times* on 19 March 1996 *"Every decade needs some kind of blotting paper to soak up the socially challenged: in the past it has been things like designer drugs, religious cults and colonic irrigation. The Seventies gave us the Moonies, the Eighties aura cleansing and rebirthing. Now the Nineties have spawned the mega cult of all time, the ultimate tool to keep the nerds off the streets - the Internet..... takes a disproportionate amount of time.... it's more like sitting in a traffic jam waiting for the lights to change and they don't."*

But not everyone agrees with her view. The Economist's *Going Digital* says of the Internet, *"How important this revolution will eventually turn out to be is as yet impossible to say. A reasonable guess might put it ahead of the telephone and television but behind the printing press and the motor car.... the world has never seen a technology like this before. "*

The Information Superhighway. Build it and they will come.

Contrary to widespread belief, the Information Superhighway has yet to be built. Some sceptics say it won't ever exist because of the staggering costs involved. The Internet is merely a dirt track in comparison. Question the knowledge of any one who describes the Internet as the Information Superhighway. It seems fashionable to mock and ridicule the Internet and those who use it. But companies of all sizes have already grasped the realisation that no matter who they are, where they are, how large or small they are - they can compete against the 'big guys' on an almost equal footing and at low cost. Low cost is the crucial element. This allows anyone with the necessary knowledge to open up some kind of business. There is far greater usage in the United States than anywhere else on earth, fuelled by the fact that the local telephone calls which are used to access the Internet are free there. Soon many of these manufacturers may no longer need retailers; they will sell directly to their customers.

Peter Cochrane, the leading BT telecommunications expert defines the Information Superhighway as "2 clicks and 1 second'. By this he means, any information you could ever want from your computer or interactive TV including text, audio and full motion video should be only 2 clicks of a mouse away and involve a delay of just 1 second. (This assumes the mouse will continue as a means of interacting with a computer. Voice recognition software is now so sophisticated it can perform many of today's mouse functions). This is a long way from what is currently delivered by an infuriatingly slow Internet. Anyone who has ever spent hours downloading computer software will know exactly what I mean.

42% of American parents claim their kids watch significantly less TV since they bought a home computer. According to Forrester Research 70% of US adults say they sacrifice TV viewing in favour of using their PC. Network television has peaked in importance. As the increasing number of TV stations compete for an increasingly fragmented audience and a dwindling number of viewers, each station's audience will inevitably shrink further. Under intense pressure to deliver high numbers for their advertisers whilst producing programmes which cost less and less, they will increasingly turn towards finding ways to justify programmes which pack as much 'stimulating' sex and violence into their programming as possible. It's already happening - commercial pressures dictate what is shown.

TV will continue as an electronic babysitter and company for senior citizens. Young viewers are bored by tired formats and bland programming. Raised on interactive computer games, these viewers want interactivity. If TV doesn't supply it, they will go elsewhere for it. TV companies know this. In the next 10 years television and desktop computers will merge. More computers will become TVs, more TVs will become computers. And all of them will be linked by the telephone.

The future today

On a visit to BT's research headquarters at Martlesham near Ipswich I once filmed a demonstration of technologies which have since become available commercially. Wearing a *Robocop* style helmet fitted with a video camera, microphone, headphones, and a video monitor across one eye, I was linked, via a high quality ISDN telephone line, to an operator who could have been situated thousands of miles away (he was in fact next door at the time). Using this technology I was able to assemble a complex puzzle within 20 seconds as I received verbal instructions and the help of a colour schematic diagram sent from his computer screen via the link and placed in front of my eye. This will allow for highly skilled (and better paid) individuals to achieve higher productivity by instructing less well qualified individuals to carry out complex repair work on location.

This will revolutionise remote working in many industries. It is already becoming more commonplace for insurance accident assessors to work in this way. Accredited car body repair shops are equipping themselves with the video and telecommunications equipment to look at detailed shots of damaged vehicles remotely in order to help the assessor make faster and more productive use of his time, cutting down on non-productive travelling time and minimising unnecessary delays for customers. How long will it be before insurance companies favour those body shops which invest in this technology or refuse to do business with those which don't? What's the lesson here? Become as well qualified as you can, or you could end up being the one out in the cold and wet holding the camera!

Using Computer Assisted Design software (CAD) it's easy to assemble components electronically. CAD encourages innovation. It allows designers to try out new ideas without committing manufacturers to expensive new processes. It saves money and time. Indeed an amusing example comes to mind. Using 3 dimensional CAD software, my architect friend George Young designed a specially shaped kitchen window which demanded precise measurements so that long, tall double glazed units could be slid into specially cut slots in a hard-wood door frame. The glazier looked at the gaps and declared, based on many decades of experience that the glass would never be made to fit, the clearances were too tight and the angles were too acute. He was certain. To his utter astonishment, both pieces of glass were fitted within 5 minutes! He didn't realise that the glass had already been fitted successfully on George's computer screen.

You can now walk around a virtual new home designed on computer. Sophisticated 3D computer systems are capable of creating lifelike simulations or 'virtual reality'. But more complex virtual simulations provide scientists with detailed information on the effects of their experiments. If you want to know how a new design of ship will behave in any combination of wind and sea conditions, you can create and study a detailed computer simulation first. The ship's design can then be modified and tested again and again until it is ready for construction. A £1million earthquake simulator, financed by the Engineering and Physical Sciences Research Council and designed by Bristol University is being used to help engineers create earthquake-proof buildings. The aeroplane manufacturer McDonnell Douglas together with Nasa is designing a 'super-jumbo' 'plane on computer which could be capable of carrying 600-800 passengers, travel 8,000 miles at 600mph and fly at 40,000ft, made from a light weight carbon-composite whilst using about 20% less fuel.

It's far better for airline pilots to crash a few computer-generated planes than the real thing. Similarly, doctors can perform and rehearse complex operations using computer simulations before they ever get near an unsuspecting and unconscious living patient. More ominously, when pilots returned from the first bombing mission during the Gulf War they were asked how it felt. Their answer was "Very realistic." Months of virtual reality training on simulators had distanced them from the harsh reality that they were now killing people.

The entertainment industry has been quick to adopt this new digital technology to help us escape reality - or at least to create safe visions of terror. Futuristic fiction such as *Jurassic Park* and *Independence Day* can be created electronically, but as the technology improves 'real life' images can be created from within high powered desktop computers. Computer generated images (CGI's) of tornados in *Twister*, volcanos in *Dante's Peak* and *Volcano* are so likelike it is impossible to 'see the joins' as actors are seamlessly integrated within the computer-created and enhanced scenes. The list of examples keeps growing. One of the best early examples of this technology features the actor Gary Sinise in *Forest Gump*, playing a Vietnam veteran who has his legs blown off. We see many different shots of him showing very clearly that he has no legs. He definitely does not have any legs. At the time of the film's release Sinise said he had been there and still didn't know how they had done it. His legs grew back for his next movie. Some of the stunts featured in films such as *Batman* are 'performed' by computer generated images. Crowd scenes are faked using computer images, while at least one company offers producers a virtual set, which saves studio space, and hordes of technicians, carpenters and plasterers. This can and may well be used by authoritarian political regimes to 'doctor' news coverage events in a way which would make old Soviet government controlled TV look like *Thunderbirds* by comparison.

The sight of a 'resurrected' Steve McQueen driving a brand new car in a TV commercial is a disturbing (and to me, an immoral) indicator to future possibilities. By carefully collecting old footage of the actor he was seen to drive the car. Seeing is no longer believing. Imagine what will be possible in 20 years. Most of us can't. Celebrities and their families might be well advised to seek legal protection against the future use of their images and work.

Television has created a virtual reality for millions who opt out of their own realities by tuning in to daily soap operas. For some, the characters are real. By simulating real experiences, it won't be too many years before large numbers of people withdraw into their own simulated worlds devoid of genuine interaction and intimacy. The 'birth' of millions of 'cyberpets' is just the beginning. Progress.

Machines have already been produced which can see, touch, smell, hear and speak. How many machines do you talk to each day? Shouting abuse at them is not quite what I mean. We routinely talk to answering machines and voice mail (more accurately described as 'voice jail'). Many such systems are capable of understanding you in simple ways. As described elsewhere in this book, I regularly talk to my computer which understands the thousands of words I use. Expect voice recognition systems to become even more sophisticated and ever more pervasive in society.

'Coughing up' for healthcare

Healthcare is the largest industry in the world. It is entering a new era. The days of 'trial and error' medicine (as defined by Richard Worzel) are ending. In your old age, your bank will be more likely to keep you alive than any doctor or government. Look after yourself and you may live to a ripe old age. Future rises in the cost of healthcare means that the prudent will invest in the prevention of ill-health.

The older you get, the more healthcare costs. The average lifespan of affluent people will almost certainly continue to rise. As the number of old people is likely to double in the next 20-30 years, and consume between a third and one half of all healthcare spending, it doesn't take a genius to work out that the costs of heathcare will rocket as baby boomers reach old age and spend their savings (if they have any) by clinging on to their life on earth rather than passing their cash on to their kids. Residential care facilities and jobs for carers will increase in the decades to come.

Advances in medicine and nutrition mean that we can live far longer, on average, than our ancestors. Europe has the oldest population in the world. Don't expect the government to keep you alive. Government cash will be in short supply which means people will end up going without the treatment that many believe is their right. It has been estimated that by 2031 there will be ten times more centenarians as today - 40,000 people. It won't be too many years before senior citizens will outnumber those in employment. How are those in work going to finance the pensions of those in retirement? Quite simply, they won't be able to. The existing concept of the State pension can't work for much longer. Government funded healthcare provision will ultimately collapse under the sheer weight of the demands from our greying population.

Already we are seeing a growing number of easy to use yet sophisticated self-help and self-diagnosis tests coming on to the market. The trend towards seizing back control of our lives from the medical profession has already begun. Patients are becoming more demanding and have come to realise that doctors are not Gods. Doctors do not always know as much as they make out. There will be an even greater shift away from conventional pharmaceutically based medicine as more people take responsibility for their own wellness;

holistic and Eastern medicine will become increasingly accepted in the West and will continue to be resisted by the medical establishment.

Only since the 1930's have drugs been able to kill bacteria. But how long will it be before such germs adapt and mutate so that our drugs are no longer as effective? The fight against disease is constantly shifting as germs and viruses evolve to resist chemical treatments. Some infections don't respond to treatment any more. Doctors find it easier and quicker to write out a prescription than to take a more in-depth approach - there is a growing fear that antibiotics are too easily prescribed. Antibiotics are a 20th century discovery, but if we continue using antibiotics as a first resort in clearing up a wide variety of common ailments, existing germs will mutate and develop into strains which are immune to existing treatments. One in six prescriptions are for an antibiotic. If you regularly take or are prescribed antibiotics, pray they work when you **really** need them in the future.

As the population continues to move around the planet on business and for pleasure, disease spreads more quickly. TB and malaria are becoming more common place. Medical experts fear global epidemics of new air-borne diseases.

What's in your genes?

The Human Genome Project is a gigantic worldwide project to map the entire human genetic code and find disease-causing genes. In simple terms, particular defective or mutated genes increase the possibility of certain diseases. By identifying those genes most likely to induce infectious diseases or hereditary diseases such as Diabetes, Cystic Fibrosis, Muscular Dystrophy, Huntington's, Alzheimer's or colon and breast cancer, researchers believe such genes can be 'switched off', corrected, or replaced with healthy genes. Discovery and cures for some of the 4,000 genetically linked diseases are likely within the next 2 decades. Great news for anyone at risks from life threatening diseases - and monumental profits for the pharmaceutical companies which are buying up related patents and those companies involved in this recom-binant DNA technology. SmithKline Beecham allegedly paid $125 million for a stake in Human Genome Sciences and the Institute of Genomic Research. The commercial value of exploitation rights and patents of its 35,000 databank of genes could be awesome. One of its competitors, Merck claims the SKB sponsored project restricts genetic research and has set up GenBank, an American genetic database which it has placed in the public domain. Drugs companies need new products as more and more of their past money spinners reach the end of their patents and cheaper, generic versions of those drugs come onto the market. DNA based drugs represent their future.

A desperate need for new products has led to an acceleration in genetic research. Too fast for some researchers such as the US molecular biologist John Fagan, who fears the consequences of commercialising poorly understood genetic discoveries too rapidly. No one knows how genetic manipulations will behave when passed from one generation to the next. Concerns over unintended and unpredictable consequences are being voiced but ignored, together with a whole host of other ethical questions. Should an unborn baby with a genetic defect be aborted? Should insurance companies be given access to your genetic details as a condition of cover? Money has a louder voice, but as author Herb Cohen writes, '*it doesn't always tell the truth*'.

Within the next 40 years, the technology will almost certainly exist to remove defective genes from human fetuses and to add desirable ones. Try to work out the ethics of that one! What happens when scientists identify the genes linked to longevity or human intelligence? Or how about human cloning where identical human copies can be produced? Wouldn't you be interested to see an identical copy of yourself ? Scientists certainly would - but is there a young Adolph Hitler type out there somewhere, just waiting for an opportunity to create a master race?

A computerised healthcare system - at last

The days of doctors scribbling illegible prescriptions are numbered. There is still far too much duplication and inefficiency in the healthcare industry. As costs come under ever closer scrutiny, widespread computerisation will take place. Smart-card technology will allow you to carry a card which includes all of your medical history and medication details.

Imagine a time when a computer database becomes available listing every known disease, from every corner of the globe; detailed symptoms for each, together with the most up-to-date medical research and every known pharmaceutical, herbal and holistic treatment. Will it be confined to the medical professions? Probably not. Ultimately they will be unable to keep it to themselves. This information won't replace the need for doctors, but more and more people will take an active interest in their own health. Firstly, by looking after themselves better (see Chapter 7) and secondly, by learning to ask doctors detailed questions about their illnesses. Today there is a huge amount of data and knowledge available on the Internet to anyone who wishes to carry out the research. There are electronic bulletin boards and user groups for just about every type of complaint - often administered by knowledgeable sufferers.

Doctors admit that more of their patients are taking their findings to the surgery to share with their physicians, many of whom would never be able to keep up with all the latest developments. Last year a friend with a baby girl discovered that the baby had stopped growing. By searching medical databases on the Internet, we discovered a new genetically-engineered drug that had just been made available in the United States to treat this condition. This availability of medical knowledge will profoundly change the relationship between patients and doctors.

Less invasive surgery is also being developed using computerised ultrasonics, allowing doctors to 'see inside' the patient without having to gouge huge holes in their bodies and then sew them back up again. This equipment also dramatically speeds up recovery, helped no doubt by 'living bandages' - genetically-engineered human skin cells such as those developed at the University of Akron, Ohio. See the technology chapter for more details of advances in medicine predicted for the 21st century.

How would you like to be operated on by a robot? No thank you? Created by Integrated Surgical Systems in Sacramento, California, *Robodoc* is a robot used to perform hip replacements more accurately than the best human surgeons. Medical technology is becoming so sophisticated that specialist surgeons will soon be able to use telemedicine to perform operations by remote control. The patient, perhaps a soldier on a far off battlefield, and the surgeon could be thousands of miles apart. The surgeon manipulates robotic scalpels, assisted by less qualified people in the make-shift operating room.

Money; how would you like to pay?

In many Western countries, most notably the United States and Canada, the obscene national debts will create widespread financial hardship amongst their populations in the decades to come. Canadians already 'joke' that their current tax regime means they don't start earning anything for themselves until June each year! More countries will seek to raise taxes based on consumption rather than income as politicians accept that they may become unelectable if they suggest income tax increases. This will raise the prices of many products and services. Although as Charles Handy points out in *The Empty Raincoat*, this is a much more efficient method of raising tax revenue. If tax on income is removed, you remove the temptation to evade payment and with it, the need for labour-intensive policing of the system. If tax is levied on consumption instead, this is much easier to police and also acts as an incentive to save, which in turn makes more cash available for investment in industry and commerce. Provided that a fair system of subsidies is implemented to avoid forcing more people into poverty, this system is not without merit.

We will see a return to a more simple form of life for those who do not need to worry about money. They will spend less, and save and invest more. But those without savings will eventually realise they will have nothing to live on in their old age and will be more inclined to take a gamble on their future by investing in high risk, potentially higher return investments. If such investments fail to deliver those high returns, life for these people will become desperate. At present we are free to decide whether or not we make adequate provision for our old age. Many decide not to make provision for themselves but ultimately expect the state to bear the responsibility for them. This will change. The Labour government may move to make pension provision compulsory. Expect more regulations as the population is pushed into self-reliance. Government will attempt to move society away from a dependency culture to one of individual responsibility where only the desperately poor will be helped.

The introduction of digital money looks set to transform the world of business. Electronic cash will enable money to be transferred rapidly, easily and inexpensively between individuals and organisations. Once this is achieved, the world will never be the same again.

Anyone, anywhere in the world will be able to sell anything to anyone else and know they will be paid for it. This means that customised products and services can be sold without the need for costly intermediaries such as retailers, distributors, agents or wholesalers. These traditional forms of trade will not disappear but the ability to transfer money will totally change existing business systems. Why buy a car from a car dealership when you can import a car to your exact specification directly from the manufacturer? Expect increased tension between intermediaries and manufacturers. Retailers exert enormous pressure on manufacturers, dictating what they will sell and under what conditions. Up to 20% of the price you pay for some retail goods pays for the costs of putting it on the shelf. But limited retail shelf-space and an ever growing number of high quality, customiseable products means that, ultimately, manufacturers will need to find other ways to reach their potential customers. Electronic money and improved communications technology will help them achieve this.

Banks are routinely 'getting their fingers burnt'. Massive defaulted bank loans to under-developed countries have resulted in a highly cautious approach to lending. But the banks are still getting it all wrong. A bank is less likely to agree a loan to an organisation or individual without fixed assets such as property. To a bank, your ideas are worth less than what you own. If they can't see, touch or measure something it has a lower value. But banks have lost fortunes accepting commercial property as collateral. Intellectual capital is growing in value, while physical bricks and mortar are no longer 'as safe as houses'.

Education; reading the trends

More mature students will attend university and colleges - not necessarily to work towards academic degrees but to improve their knowledge in the workplace or if they do not work, to improve their minds. Consequently universities and colleges will have to change radically or have their positions usurped by commercial training organisations using the latest computer and satellite technology. Up-to-date information and knowledge will become more available than at any time in history.

Parents, dissatisfied with standards of state education, will provide a huge boost to the educational electronic publishing industry. Continuous learning and re-training will become the norm. Those 'too busy' to learn new skills will become obsolete. Already there is a trend towards more women going to university and college than men. Better qualified females will therefore enter the workforce in the next few decades. This will represent bad news for men.

Work and business; more for less

Some of the largest and best known businesses will disappear in the next 20 years. Downsizing will continue and intensify (even though many downsized companies now realise they went too far) in many industries as staff endure the increased competitive pressures on business to remove all unnecessary costs. 'More for less' will drive many more businesses. There will be more attention to workers' effectiveness. This will lead to a shift towards more part-time, contract and freelance work. Just because you work for a large organisation, it is no longer a guarantee of success or a long career with that firm.

Full-time employment will decline for a growing proportion of the population.

This in turn will produce job insecurity at an unprecedented level for those affected. Many jobs will be performed overseas by better qualified, highly motivated, less costly individuals. Government sponsored job creation schemes will continue to fail. Governments will be too slow to persuade workers in 'old' industries to move into newer 'growth' industries.

More businesses are being financed by large financial institutions rather than individual investors. This will radically change the behaviour of business executives because individual investors tend to seek long term performance, while financial institutions are more interested in short term returns. There will be more mergers, acquisitions, alliances and partnerships. This will lead to major consolidation and probable redundancy for many of those involved in duplicated functions that can be performed cheaper elsewhere. With existing over capacity in many manufacturing industries, coupled with increased automation and advances in robotics technology, redundancies in the manufacturing sector will increase worldwide. Customers will demand ever faster response times. Those individuals and organisations who are unable to match such demands will lose business. This will lead to increased stress and pressure for the individual.

Many European and North American businesses will lose their global dominance. Far Eastern competitors with lower costs will lead the way in their home Asian markets. Western companies burdened with mandatory healthcare and pension provision will become increasingly un-competitive.

Businesses everywhere are wrestling with the problems of globalisation and integration. How do you develop a profitable business across national boundaries, different time zones and cultures, whilst successfully persuading diverse people to work together seamlessly for an equally diverse client base? That's the business challenge for the next century. It is also represents the biggest business opportunity for consultants and advisers.

More and more employees are being empowered to act without managerial supervision. People will be forced into taking the initiative to create or invent work for themselves. This involves education, self-confidence and the acquisition of self-marketing skills. Anyone without formal qualifications will risk unemployment. Those who rely on their muscle power for a wage will be under an increasing threat of extinction. The situation will not improve in the foreseeable future. Unskilled people will be replaced by sophisticated and constantly improving technology. "Knowledge work' will be where most new jobs will be found. However, those industries which rely on highly trained individuals are already finding it difficult to recruit enough high calibre people -especially in the IT industry. This problem will become more acute. The work is out there if you are prepared to train yourself well enough!

As the predominantly white, male bosses in the workplace retire or are let go, women and members of ethnic minorities will become far more influential within the workplace. More middle managers and supervisors will disappear from the payrolls of companies. Businesses will rely more on workers' ideas. Organisations will continue to strip away wastage - people and processes. However, once they have become lean, many won't then be able to cope with future growth.

Individuals and organisations will gradually move away from selling their time, instead they will be paid for the results they achieve for their employers, customers and clients. This will have a fundamental impact on consultancies, lawyers, accountants and other professions.

Older people (especially divorced women) will choose or feel the need to continue working to enhance inadequate pensions, making it even more difficult for young people to find work at the beginning of their careers. Young people already feel isolated. Many already feel defeated by the system - their numbers will increase. This will fuel the crisis for children leaving care. The rest will stay single and live at home with their parents for longer. This means a lower demand for all the goods and appliances which constitute a new home.

The detail of retail

According to *The Economist*, retailing represents Britain's single largest industry employing from 7-12% of the workforce. Retailers exert tremendous power over their suppliers and manufacturers. Retail buyers rule with rods of iron, relationships are not always amicable, but they need each other. Everyone does whatever they can to preserve their profit margins. Intermediaries add layers of costs which will be removed by many manufacturers and retailers. There will be a move towards larger stores with fewer staff. Small retailers are collapsing every week, many high streets all over the country are losing these small independent traders - often caught between the economies of scale enjoyed by the national retailers and the excessively high business charges by local authorities.

Competition between businesses is intensifying and changing. The restaurant trade is massive. There was a time when the only competition for restaurants was other restaurants - but not any more. Supermarkets have brought out high quality cuisine products at a fraction of the price of restaurant meals. So rather than spending to go out, millions have the option of dining in style at home.

With increased consumer competition and lower prices, retailers will not be prepared to pay for high quality, knowledgeable sales people unless they differentiate themselves as specialists. Julian Richer's, *Richer Sounds* hi-fi chain is an excellent example of a company which encourages and rewards its knowledgeable workforce. But in many other areas of retailing, a bad situation will get worse - sales staff will become even less knowledgeable and more unhelpful, further pushing consumers, who are drowning in a sea of confusion and conflicting information and advice, to find alternative ways to buy products and services.

In *Future Shop* by Jim Snider and Terra Ziporyn, the authors predict a growth in ICIC's - Independent Consumer Information Companies. These commercial organisations will be a bit like a highly computerised and automated version of *Which?* Magazine. They will change the most funda-mental elements of trade - supply and demand. ICIC's will not sell products (which affect 'supply' in the marketplace) but provide bias-free information on the widest variety of products and services; cars, consumer electronics, restaurants, films, financial products - the list goes on. This will radically affect 'demand' for particular products, leading to even more competition between product and service suppliers. Snider and Ziporyn believe that, in a high information society, the provision of product information will remove confusion for the consumer and save them precious time. Supplying this trusted information and knowledge will provide huge potential profits for entrepreneurs wishing to set up such information services.

The technology to deliver this information already exists. In 1995, I worked with a German client which demonstrated such technology by *Magic Link* (a Californian software company) at Telecom 95, a World Technology Fair, held in Geneva. Personal digital assistants (PDA's) equipped with sophisticated software 'Infobots', or knowledge agents, can be individually programmed by the user to search for information relating to pre-defined topics on the Internet, and to make decisions on our behalf, including sched-uling appointments and other mundane tasks.

We are moving from an era of mass production towards 'mass-customi-sation' where products can be manufactured to a high standard to the exact specifications demanded by the consumer, within a short time frame. Manufacturers in a wide variety of fields who are unwilling to comply with such requests will be squeezed out of their markets. Expect this from vehicle and clothing manufacturers (Levi Strauss already offer tailor-made jeans from selected retailers, linked directly by computer to the fabric cutting machines at their factories). This is great news for consumers who no longer have to make do with the best fit they can find. Many other products will be manufactured in this way - made to order, providing every link in the business chain with cost savings - some of which may even be passed on to the consumers!

Consumer loyalty towards well-established brand names will continue to decline as consumers question why they pay more for the name when other products seem to be just as good. Coca-Cola, the world's biggest brand has suffered very badly in the UK from the introduction of cheaper colas manufactured by the Canadian Cotts Corporation and distributed by Sainsbury's, Virgin and others. Why pay more for Kellogg's cornflakes when it appears that a supermarket's own brand is just the same? (Why we drink and eat such products in the first place is another issue altogether).

As businesses downsize and convert information into space saving electronic form, there will be a massive surplus of commercial property. Today, up to 2 floors of many 15 storey office blocks are used to store paperwork. The increasing trend towards home working will further dampen the value of office space everywhere. In London, the Royal Institute of Chartered Surveyors claims up to 15% of second hand office space is no longer required. There are an estimated 10 million square feet of office space in central London alone which the Institute predicts will never be used again. The National Audit Office has estimated that about 8.4 million square feet is no longer required by the state. Is it really a good idea for any business owner or manager to sign a long property lease?

From the 1450's, helped by Gutenberg's printing press, power and knowledge was taken away from the Church by government. Because of this, Europe was transformed in less than 50 years. In the future, global businesses using communications technology will take power away from governments. It will almost certainly take a lot less than 50 years. Few governments like it, but they can do nothing to control or censor the flow of information.

These are just a few examples of how the way we live and work is changing so radically. No book could include every future development, but this chapter has attempted to give you some idea of the massive and at times, frantic activities which have yet to trickle down into our day-to-day lives. The future has already been invented for many of us - it's just that we haven't seen it yet.

Individual predictions and trends outlined in this chapter may turn out to be true or false. But one thing is for sure - the 21st century will be very different from the 20th century and everyone will have to deal with massive changes. Some will be beneficial, whilst others may pose serious threats to your future well being, health and wealth. But what, if anything, can you do about it? The next chapter explains why there is so much change in the world, why change will increase and accelerate in the next few decades, and - crucially - what can be done about it to minimise the possible consequences to you, your job and your future.

Chapter 3
All Change

"Grant me the serenity to accept the things I cannot change. Courage to change the things I can, and the wisdom to know the difference".
The Serenity Prayer

Just when you have got used to the way things are at work - what happens? The bosses decide to change it all - yet again. They are obviously doing it to justify their own jobs. After all, if they didn't constantly change the company structure, reporting responsibilities, remuneration packages, working hours and shift patterns, they wouldn't have a job. We've all seen it - bosses disappear for days on end for 'strategy meetings' and 'brain-storming' sessions, and so are not available for the constant stream of crises you and your colleagues have to deal with as a result of the last round of their company 'improvements'. Will it ever end? In short - almost certainly not. Change is very definitely here to stay. In fact, even more change is likely. The process of change is highly demanding, requiring additional effort and more work - work which you probably do not welcome on top of growing pressure and responsibilities.

In this chapter we will look predominantly at how to handle changes at work - although as you will see in the following pages, the principles for managing or coping with change can be used in other situations too.

Why all this change then?
There has been more change in the last four years of this century than in the entire 20th Century. But how is this possible? Advances in technology have led the way. Firstly, there are more scientists alive today than in the entire history of humankind. Secondly, the phenomenal growth in computer availability and computer processing power means that these scientists are now able to record, store and distribute their findings in digital form. The sharing of scientific data, information and knowledge, throughout the world, has also enabled the rapid implementation of new knowledge. Rapid implementation is also a financial necessity within today's global corporations, which spend billions of dollars on research and development annually. This drive for achieving constant technological breakthroughs is based on the fear of corporations that if they do not innovate, competitors will seize an advantage leading to a drop in short-term results, subsequently leading a drop in their share price and ultimately death in the marketplace.

Simultaneously, businesses all over the world are looking for new innovations in order to improve their productivity and efficiency. This desire to buy into the latest technological advances is often seen as their way of getting or staying ahead of their competitors. This too is led by fear; fear that if they don't constantly upgrade their technology, they will fall behind in the corporate race to keep existing customers and attract new ones. The stakes are high and it's expensive to take part in these technological games of one upmanship.

So, how can businesses afford to compete? Some can't - more and more are going out of business or getting swallowed up by larger organisations. Take food retailing as an example; the large supermarket chains are opening more and more stores. These highly automated and technology driven money making machines will continue to put small, independently owned 'corner' shops out of business.

The larger companies which buy new technology to improve their automation processes must look around to find ways to save costs. Hence the widespread implementation of 'process re-engineering' and the delayering of corporate hierarchies over the last few years. Many more companies will be forced into making massive layoffs and redundancies.

For the first time ever, it is now possible to make anything, anywhere at anytime for anybody and in any colour. Advances in technology allow products to be made in smaller numbers, with fewer parts, manufactured and assembled by sophisticated multi-purpose robots, supervised by fewer workers. Indeed some joker once commented that the factory of the future will be equipped with a wide array of robots, just one worker, and a dog. The robot will do all the manufacturing and assembling, while the worker's job is to feed the dog. The dog's job will be to distract the worker so he or she doesn't tamper with the robots!

In manufacturing businesses, if owners can't eliminate all unnecessary waste and costs they run the real risk of becoming un-competitive. Therefore to preserve the future of the company, they must make constant changes and improvements, some of which may result in radical changes to the ways in which the company operates. As computer software becomes more sophisticated and capable of performing more complex tasks, service businesses will be affected in similar ways.

The bottom line for individuals is that most change programmes put some or a lot of people out of work. But if such changes are not made quickly enough, the consequences can be worse - the company will become unprofitable, go out of business and everyone loses their job.

Businesses have never had to deal with change on this scale before. It's small wonder that those people who are being forced into making such changes are nervous. They've never had to do it before. Those affected are sometimes terrified - and will do whatever they can to stop the process. But to no avail. No one can stop change without suffering in other ways.

Understanding change

Frederick Taylor, the grandfather of 'time and motion' studies in industry was responsible for many positive innovations in the way complex tasks were broken down into manageable and measurable chunks. However, many of the work practices he advocated so successfully, were based on the deeply held belief that workers were incompetent and had to be supervised at every level within an organisation. Today and in tomorrow's business world, the most successful companies MUST assume they employ competent people and treat them accordingly. This requires levels of trust and empowerment which many organisations have difficulty in creating. A major component of change within organisations is how they transform themselves from being perceived as the employer of incompetent people into an organisation which provides competent, skillful and knowledgeable people with the resources they need to achieve business success. This transition is nearly always painful for everyone involved.

Different people respond to change in different ways. Those in the more junior positions within companies are amongst those most open to change. Despite some understandable cynicism towards 'initiativitis', they realise how much change is needed. They hope that the real cause, rather than the perceived cause, of problems will be addressed. But middle managers are a different story. Some, not all, tend to believe that any fundamental changes to an organisation will result in a loss of their personal power and authority - therefore many tend to stand in the way of change in any way they can think up. Later we'll explore some of the reasons why we all obstruct change if we can - just to preserve the status quo.

In many ways, our ancestors were lucky - their basic patterns of life hardly changed at all - sometimes for hundreds of years. As the pace of life continues to accelerate, how we deal with change will have a direct bearing on our ability to survive and thrive in the 21st century. How do you respond to increased stress and pressure? How do you react when changes are introduced at work? Are they an annoyance? Or do you enjoy the challenge of doing new things, learning new skills, operating new equipment, reporting to different people or working in new locations?

Anyone who enjoys change is a rare individual. The fact is that most of us are 'change averse' - we're afraid to change, just in case matters get worse! There is a certain degree of comfort and cosiness associated with having a routine. We can just get on with what we have to do without thinking about it too much. When we know how to do something, we are more likely to perform the task well. But when things are constantly changing, more tasks must be attempted for the first time. And because there usually isn't a clearly defined company procedure for these new tasks and new ways of working, our superiors won't necessarily have the answers either so we are left to get on with things in the best way we can. Each new task increases the possibility that we will get things wrong. Changes increase the likelihood that we will get important things wrong - who would want that? Screw up too often and who knows if we will still have a job? You have to be prepared to make some mistakes - there simply isn't the time to ensure that everything is perfect. This is one of the key short comings surrounding the admirable concept of Total Quality Management (TQM) which ardently promotes "get things right, first time, every time". Striving for perfection is commendable but senior managers need to 'get real'. It's not achievable - get it right as often as you can and constantly learn from your mistakes is probably more realistic. No wonder people get hacked off with 'unreasonable' demands - no one wants to do a bad job, or if they do, someone must have really annoyed them.

So, it's understandable that when changes are likely, most sane people will view them with justifiable suspicion and caution - or as we will see later, it is often better to convince ourselves that the changes probably won't actually happen, if they do they won't be that important, or if they are important they won't affect us personally.

Ignoring, or refusing to think through, the personal consequences of changes in our working lives, society, the environment and international government is a well documented 'coping mechanism' for millions of people. When we don't think about fundamentally important personal issues (such as "What are you going to live on during an expected 30 years of 'retirement'?") it gives us permission to avoid feeling worried. After all, if we were to think too much, we might risk forcing ourselves into doing something about it!

There is absolutely no point simply hoping that change will not affect us in the future. No one will escape the consequences of change in the decades to come; technological changes, changes at work, in the home, in government and in society - in every area of our lives. We can run but we can't hide!

An ostrich may think it is safe by sticking its head in the sand but think for a moment how vulnerable it looks, with its backside sticking up in the air!

Understandably, people are worried about change, but you have more cause for concern if your employer is not changing. If you are particularly averse to changes in your life - ask yourself what benefits you think you get from trying to live in the past? Take a moment to think about some of the fundamental changes in your life over the last two decades. How has your job changed? What technological devices, which may not even have existed 20 years ago, do you use today at work? at home? or as part of your hobbies? What impact have these items had on your life? Positive and negative.

Think about any changes that you feared in your company or in society and then, in reality changed your mind about when you discovered that the changes produced improvements rather than the negative outcomes which you expected.

We must all learn to turn change into a friend. Throughout this book you will read examples of how change is having, and will continue to have direct and indirect effects on your life. But there is no point in understanding clearly the changes which are happening all around you, if you are not prepared to alter your behaviour to take full advantage of such changes and so get them to work in your favour. Dealing with change is potentially painful when it involves changing the way you have worked for a long time or means facing the prospect of losing your job. But the problems are not limited to these types of 'bad' change. 'Good' changes can be hell, too.

Living through the hell of 'good' change

In 1996, I was heavily involved in writing and delivering a series of conferences for the British staff of one of the world's largest manufacturers of semi-conductors. A key area for discussion was how to 'manage change'. How those individuals interpreted their situation will go some way towards explaining how we as human beings approach change, and what we can all do to 'stack the cards' in our favour for the future.

Before we go into the detail of how the topic was addressed, it is worth explaining a little about the semi-conductor industry and the context in which the staff worked. This will help you understand more fully, how change impacts us all, and how we can choose to manage it.

Try to put yourself in the shoes of those involved in the process - and ask yourself how your industry could be affected in similar ways as we move more and more towards a global economy. If you don't work in manufacturing, don't be tempted to believe that you won't be affected.

The semi-conductor industry is enjoying (or suffering from) explosive growth and will continue to do so. It is **the** growth industry in the world.

Electronic equipment uses many semi-conductors but much of the industry growth stems from the fact that more and more basic electrical products are being designed to become 'smarter', by offering consumers additional benefits and features. Examples include the refrigerator that knows when to de-frost itself, the door knob that knows if the door is open or closed, car engines that alert the driver when it requires an oil change or how about babies' nappies that alert parents when they need changing - no more holding the baby's bottom up to their noses to find out! More and more commodity products will become available in the next few years that offer these added qualities and 'smart' functions. Linked to our home computer, our appliances will talk to each other, allowing us to control them remotely. Using the 'phone, we will be able to instruct the micro-chips in our heating system to switch the heating on or off, or instruct our VCR to record a TV programme.

This is fantastic news for the semi-conductor business. If you want to work in a 'secure' industry, semi-conductors is the one.

So, on the face of it, the staff of the company I was working with have got it made in the 21st century. I am sure you know many individuals who would readily swap their own insecure jobs for such an assured career.

However, the price you have to pay for job 'security' is a high one. The staff at this factory have been through hell and back. Much of the time they were unaware of what they were facing - all they knew was that it was a truly horrible experience.

The semi-conductor industry it is not without its problems - a world glut of semi-conductors forces prices down. This squeezes manufacturers' margins, which means that businesses must be ruthless in eliminating unnec-essary costs and maximising productivity, wherever and whenever possible.

For a number of years the staff at this particular factory were told their very survival remained in the balance. The holding company said "Improve performance or we close you down." This ultimatum made them feel used, abused and under-valued. Sadly, but understandably, no one felt the need to explain the situation to those directly involved. It was one of those classic situations; senior management couldn't say too much because they were up against the unions, who only had the interests of the workforce in mind - not the future of the business. A long standing distrust of management ensured that the union representatives would refuse to see that the interests of the staff and the long term survival of the business was inextricably linked.

But the owners knew that, crucially, the future success of the company (and the workforce) depended on their ability to produce and deliver the highest quality products at the lowest possible cost and at the precise times they were required by their customers. A tall order - especially when so many of the 'workers' believed deeply that quality control was a 'management' issue - they were just there to do as they were told. If management told them to do something that was stupid - they would do it to show management how stupid they were. A good case of 'fixing the blame, not the problems.'

The owners had to decide whether to keep the factory open or build a brand new one. If they decided to relocate, it would put nearly a thousand people out of work. As a major employer in a rural area this would have a catastrophic effect on the local economy and create massive local unemployment. But the company senior management knew that if the workforce refused to deliver what had to be done - they would lose their jobs anyway, forced out of business by superior products manufactured by their competitors. In any case, why work in an environment dealing with unions which seem obsessed with maintaining the status quo regardless of the longer-term costs both to the staff and the business?

Relocating factories to areas where such unions do not exist has many distinct advantages. More and more companies - especially those in electronics, consumer appliances and textiles are moving their operations elsewhere in the world - often where labour is cheap (or cheaper) and the best available manufacturing technology costs less to buy and implement than using existing technology in the West.

As all countries in Asia are continuing to grow at explosive rates - demand for consumer products in that part of the world is rising dramatically - so it makes sense to move closer to the marketplace and the main centres of component assembly - in this case, India and Pacific Rim countries such as The Philippines, Taiwan, China, Japan, Korea, Singapore and Malaysia. This would save distribution and transportation costs whilst increasing the speed of supply and allowing the company to lower the levels of products it had to keep in stock - 'just in case' - a considerable financial saving.

The capital costs of building a new factory would be considerable but it could be built using the latest technology to exactly the specification needed, whilst ensuring and building in the capabilities for expansion. A new factory could be equipped with the latest labour saving equipment using the most up-to-date technology and there would be a large pool of available labour all of whom would be eager to work.

In some countries, annual salaries are a small fraction of those enjoyed by workers in Western Europe. There is another massive incentive to move a factory to such an area of the world - the company would not be saddled with cripplingly expensive statutory healthcare and pension provision.

Germany's healthcare costs are amongst the highest in the world - can they remain competitive in the global marketplace? Unlikely.

The temptation to relocate an international business is therefore high. But this particular company chose not to do so. The seriousness of its message eventually got through and under intense pressure, the staff and management had started to work together to improve the quality and efficiency of performance at the factory.

But morale was at an all time low. This much-needed change of attitude represented the greatest hurdle the company had still to overcome.

Their customers represented a wide variety of high quality, global consumer electronics companies. These customers were becoming far more demanding of their suppliers; every faulty component used in the manufacture of their products represented additional and unnecessary costs to their businesses. Correcting any fault on a sophisticated production line takes time, which means money, while faulty goods returned from consumers result in a tarnishing image for any manufacturer of quality products. The headaches of unnecessary shipment, dismantling, fault isolation, replacement of faulty components, re-assembly and re-delivery of the product means few manufacturers can afford to risk working with a supplier who falls down on the quality side of production. In today's competitive marketplace, product manufacturers have absolutely no room for shoddy and unreliable components.

The company knew that if existing staff at the manufacturing plant were unable or unwilling consistently to deliver products to such demanding specifications - then neither the company nor the staff had a future. It was as simple as that. This tough message was not well received at the time. However, there is nothing like a crisis to focus the mind!

Management had started to implement a variety of change programmes and initiatives which were designed to 'empower' their staff to do what ever was necessary to improve product quality, product availability and internal morale. Many of these programmes had achieved some success, but the changes were not being accepted by all staff. Attitudes amongst the workers varied greatly; from those who were embracing the changes eagerly, to staff who were effectively digging their heels in and doing what ever they could to make it clear to management that they would not cooperate. All sorts of emotions were being stirred up. As I stated earlier - there was a great deal of unhappiness.

One delegate even said during a particularly 'lively' open forum discussion that the company had 'ruined his life'. It was obvious that as far as he was concerned, they were to blame for his misfortunes in life (someone told me later he had certain financial problems - nothing to do with his company) but he needed to blame somebody - so long as it was not himself.

This example is a perfect illustration of how a situation of change can be perceived either as an opportunity or a threat. During our extended discussions, many staff were able to see that they had been given a huge opportunity, while a small, but significant proportion adamantly refused to accept the situation in this way - sadly, those people will have to be 'carried' by the others.

All businesses go through these phases of change; indifference, ridicule, abuse, oppression and respect. My work with the staff revolved around how to cope with 5 clearly defined stages of change.

- denial
- resistance
- exploration
- acceptance and
- doing it

This is better known as the D.R.E.A.D. of change. These elements have distinct qualities and a varying array of emotions attached to them. Some of them can be particularly intense and include anger, bitterness, hatred, irritation and an overwhelming sense of helplessness. Some, if not all of these emotions are experienced by most individuals who are subjected to large scale changes in their life, especially within a work environment.

One of the basic drivers of human behaviour involves the pursuit of pleasure and the avoidance of pain. Each new situation we find ourselves in is open for personal interpretation. If we suspect it will take us towards pain, we will use whatever resources we have available to us to minimise this threat, regardless of whether the pain is real or imagined.

Our personal feelings of self-confidence, self-esteem, our sense of security, how much we love our partners and want to care for them, how uncomfortable we may feel about a whole host of real and imaginary reasons, all have a bearing on how we respond to a new situation. And how we respond to individual situations has an impact on our future lives.

All our behaviours and attitudes are shaped by the information we have available to us and how we interpret that information. This is fine if we can analyse a situation accurately. However our emotions, insecurities and fears can and do get in the way sometimes.

It is worth taking a look at any 'change situation' in your life today or one which you have been through in the past. Go through it now in your mind and try to identify any of the 5 key stages. It can be a fascinating and enlightening experience.

Denial

It is very common for individuals who are presented with a situation which could represent emotional pain to respond in a predictable way. If, for example, someone was led to believe that she was about to be affected by a significant organisational change within her company and, even though there were certain indications to suggest that such a situation would occur, it is quite common for such an individual to blot it out of her mind by denying that it was actually going to happen. Ignoring changes or stonewalling may help you feel you are protecting yourself but it doesn't usually work in the long run.

As part of the denial process, individuals avoid getting involved, happily unhappy that they cannot do anything about it. Denial mechanisms run so deep in some people, sometimes they don't even know what they are denying!

A classic example of denial is the inextricably interlaced emotions associated with either being an alcoholic or having to live with one. The alcoholic may deny for years (sometimes violently) that there is a problem. For the families, they routinely choose to collectively deny that they have any difficulties at home - to the world they are just one big happy family. The children of abusive parents often grow up in a constant state of denial. Confronting the reality of their situation is too painful to consider - so it's buried deep inside them - where it is all too often left to fester and contaminate the entire lives of those affected. This emotional anaesthetic through denial and self-deception is an understandable means of self-protection. The troubles begin when the anaesthetic wears off. So, many people need to ensure that it doesn't ever wear off. They may look to alcohol, nicotine and stronger mood altering drugs - some are legal (they are the ones which generate tax revenue) and others such as heroin and cocaine remain illegal (and do not).

This denial doesn't just occur amongst individuals - large corporations, even governments perpetuate these 'vital lies' as Daniel Goleman describes in his 1985 book *Vital Lies, Simple Truths*. He quotes psychiatrist Lester Grinspoon who commented on how people *"avoid acquiring information that would make vague fears specific enough to require decisive action"*. When you have learned to deny a threat, you can allay most feelings of trauma, fear and anxiety. It's a neat mental trick. If only it worked for long enough.

In which ways do you deny the existence of potential threats to your future survival?

Resistance

By filtering out potential pain through denial, we reassure ourselves that 'everything will turn out fine in the end'. That's great if matters do improve - but what will you do if they don't? Many embark on a campaign of 'resistance'. It's the perfect alibi for anyone who is determined to reinforce in their own mind that they weren't being daft to be in denial. Resistance to change is also a well documented way people use to convince themselves that by not acknowledging or helping with the change process they have a degree of control over their situation, albeit a misplaced one.

Paul and Sarah McBride are environmental journalists who spent three years in the jungles of Madagascar. Paul and Sara organised the building from scratch of a 36 ton wooden fishing boat for their village. Their first job; to make the boat building tools - this project brings new meaning to the term 'hand built'.

Finding timbers for the boat often involved trekking for six or seven miles into the jungle, selecting a suitable tree, felling it with their primitive tools then with the help of 30 to 40 Malagash natives, literally dragging the hardwood tree back to the boat building site. For generations the villagers had physically lifted and moved such trees a few inches at a time. Moving an entire tree would take many weeks of hard, back breaking work. Paul was able to construct a simple rope and pulley system which the men pulled in unison, successfully sliding the tree trunk far faster and easier than using mere muscle power. Everything progressed well until they stopped for a break. Paul and Sara wandered off into the jungle to smoke a cigarette and returned 10 or 15 minutes later to find a native elder angrily berating the men for using the pulley system instead of dragging the timber by hand. The elder was absolutely furious because in his mind the men, by accepting this new method, had insulted their ancestors who would not have used such technology. The men went back to work - but without the pulley system. Imagine the utter frustration experienced by Paul and Sara. This refusal to use what we in a high-tech society might consider very low grade technology, is a prime example of how human beings will sometimes refuse to embrace change even if it ultimately makes their lives easier. It must be similar for executives trying to implement some new method of working, which is dismissed by those workers haunted by the past.

How people resist change is very well documented in business and represents a fascinating insight into what drives and motivates individuals. Whenever a change programme is introduced at a company it is often thought by a significant proportion of staff to be the latest monthly initiative which, like all the others which have preceded it, will not really make any difference to the way things are done. Many changes are not taken seriously. This obviously creates problems for those responsible for implementing the changes as well as those affected by them. Often, when the change programme falters, it may be jettisoned in an attempt to find something else which will be more successful. This of course, perpetuates the idea that change programmes are not important - if they were, they would be 'stuck at'. Everyone in such an organisation is responsible for such a dynamic. Half the workforce are to blame - the other half! While this management versus workers game goes on, Nero style, the business may be burning to the ground.

Resistance in all its forms is well known in business amongst middle managers in particular - especially in organisations which are flattening their hierarchical structures or down-sizing. Many such managers wield what remains of their power to do whatever they can to slow down the change process. Often this means merely 'paying lip service' to the changes, conveniently forgetting to keep key players within the organisation informed of important meetings and developments. There are a whole host of common behaviours that fit this resistance stage. They are well documented - and well meaning by those who practice the art of resistance. Psychologically, they believe they are preserving their future. In reality, they are merely prolonging their pain. Interestingly, workers in the more junior positions within a company are often those most keen to implement change - they tend to have less to lose and, being at the 'sharp end', they can see at first hand what things need improving.

Trying to maintain the status quo, is a human frailty and is the human response to a rapidly changing and uncertain world. Whenever we are asked or forced to change, our immediate thoughts are for what we will lose as a result. When ever the word change is used in your life, you may find it easier to cope with it if you try to substitute the word improvement. On many occasions you will see that this is indeed the situation if you choose to look at it in this way. Advice to executives and business owners: delete the word 'change' from your vocabulary - substitute the word 'improvement'. Why? Most people fear the consequences of change, but are often more willing (please note I didn't say 'willing') to accept and embrace improvements - even if they may need convincing the improvements for the business will also mean personal improvements for them.

When changes are being implemented it is easy to feel out of control - therefore resisting changes is one way to believe we do in fact, have an element of control over the situation. If you have ever thought that your employer has mistreated you in any way (even if they have not) you may feel aggrieved -

your resistance could be your way of getting your own back. When resisting change, people often come up with long lists of reasons why the change or changes are a bad thing for the company, the rest of the staff and for them in particular (although many resistors tend to insist that their own feelings do not matter - all they are interested in is looking after the business and their colleagues - oh yeah?!). It is also common for those who resist change to believe genuinely and deeply that their bosses are making a huge mistake. They refuse (either conveniently or otherwise) to accept that without the benefit of seeing the fuller picture, their views and obstructive behaviour is at best misguided, at worst - destructive.

For some individuals it can be particularly difficult to share the ethics or new direction of their company. This may significantly affect their ability to be fulfiled within that company. Trying to influence senior management is one option - leaving is another. Unethical companies, or more importantly those perceived to be unethical, suffer when attempting to recruit new staff. The best people shy away from unethical companies. Therefore if a business is to flourish in the future, its ethical policies will become increasingly important.

The view from the top of an organisation is often far better than from the trenches. That doesn't mean that bosses are always correct, although I have noticed more than one of my clients embark on change programmes and make a number of key mistakes - out of fear, distrust or a genuine desire to insulate their staff from the problems and pressures the business is wrestling with. After all, dealing with problems is what managers and business leaders are paid for isn't it? Well, they used to be. Today, and increasingly in tomorrow's companies, more and more staff will become involved in the business decision-making processes. This frightens the life out of many business leaders and managers. They've got to learn to change too. When people are consulted rather than presented with orders of how they will change, changes tended to be resisted less. This is usually because they all have a fuller understanding of the circumstances and the need for the changes. It is worth noting that 'consultation' is not the same as 'negotiation'. This confusion often poses a problem for both managers and staff.

Another common mistake is how executives become so obsessed with solving the crisis, they either forget, or refuse to tell anyone what is going on. They're afraid of the unions, they're afraid that staff will panic, they are petrified that it will affect the company share price (and the value of their stock options). The result? - usually more staff resistance and the accompanying stress and frustration. It would probably be easier to carry that tree through the Madagascan jungle!

Anyone who is resistant to change probably lacks confidence about their ability to cope with it. They could be afraid of losing their job or status. They'll say things to themselves like :
• "What will other people think?"
• "My spouse will think I'm a failure if I'm thrown onto the scrap heap."
• "I'll never be able to find another job at my age."

Perhaps they vaguely realise that they do not have the necessary skills to deal with the situation. If that's you, get them - quick! Improve your problem solving skills, increase your technical knowledge or develop your management and leadership skills.

You may be thinking what should someone do if faced with fundamentally negative changes in their life if resistance is as futile as I'm leading you to believe. Obviously not all resistance to changes is a waste of your time and energy. What is important however, is knowing when to resist change and fight for what you believe in and when to accept the reality and the need for any proposed changes. The answer is to explore all the options fully - this includes your personal behaviour, anxieties, needs and aspirations as well as the context in which such changes are being suggested or demanded.

Exploration

Before any change can be accepted, embraced and implemented a process of exploration is essential. By looking at your situation, whether in work or personally, you can only make a sensible decision based on the amount and accuracy of information relating to the proposed changes. By asking a series of well thought through questions in a non-confrontational way, you can equip yourself with many of the answers you will need to make it easier for you to accept or otherwise cope with changes. It is important you don't make any assumptions - or accept them from others.

Brainstorming questions could include the following;
• What are the reasons for the changes?
• What internal factors necessitate the change?
• What external factors are demanding the change?
• How can you be sure that this is the reality of the situation?
• If the changes relate to business, what if anything will be the benefits to staff and the business when the changes are implemented?
• What are the consequences to me as an individual and to the company as an organisation if the changes are not implemented?
• What is your answer based on?

- What other options have been investigated?
- Why have they been dismissed as impractical or unworkable?
- If the change is on a more personal level, what are the benefits or consequences to everyone involved?

In my experience, changes within an organisation are usually instigated for the best of business reasons. These could include the very survival of the organisation, protecting the longer term prospects for staff, improving working conditions and streamlining processes which staff find unnecessary, frustrating and time consuming. Staff have a different way of describing it; mushroom management - being kept in the dark and fed a load of s***!

If you are a manager, it is so tempting to be selective about the information you give to staff, customers or suppliers. As mentioned earlier, a 'need to know' approach from the top of an organisation often causes pain, frustration and confusion for everyone in the longer term.

This is well illustrated by the following example. I was due to interview a sales director at a meeting of his 70 sales staff. In the lead up to the event he refused point blank to discuss anything negative *"It would be bad for staff motivation and bad for business."* he said emphatically. He was adamant that the subject of the company car policy was absolutely forbidden - even though it would certainly be at the forefront of people's minds at the meeting. It had been a recurring and painful issue for him for the previous six months or so.

After sustained and gentle persuasion he explained privately what had happened. He confided that he'd even told his wife about it. Her response was hilarious - even though he didn't think so.

Finally, he agreed to talk about it in front of the staff. With his full backing beforehand I made the following opening remark *"You've got a lousy car policy, haven't you?"* This elicited cheers and a spontaneous round of applause from the audience. He then said (as agreed) that when he'd told his wife about the changes, she replied *"And what idiot came up with that idea?"* Howls of laughter from the audience. He went on to explain that all reps. cars had to be exchanged for diesels because his board had forced him to make a saving of £80,000. He had two choices - going diesel or making three staff redundant. He added that he too had handed in his Saab Turbo for a diesel. His problem of six months' standing was solved in less than five minutes.

He learned that his staff did need to know why he had made a decision which represented a big change to their working lives - anyone who knows anything about sales staff will quickly tell you what car they are supplied with means a great deal to them - any company which equips its sales force with cars perceived to be of low quality and kudos is asking for trouble. Morale instantly improved at this conference and, for the rest of the day delegates were far more open to the other challenges their highly competitive marketplace was thrusting upon them.

Trained therapists are taught that all behaviour has a positive intention, but sometimes there are negative consequences. The sales director's intentions were positive, honourable and professional (he didn't want to fire three staff) but the assumption that people need only have partial information resulted in the problems he and the staff encountered.

If you are not undergoing a process of change in your working life it is recommended that you go immediately to 'exploration'. Look at your situation very carefully. Find out where changes are most likely. Turn 'exploration' into a personal priority. What is happening in your life? What are the threats affecting your particular business or industry? Don't be tempted to provide yourself with the convenient knee jerk reaction "There are no threats." Read your trade publications. Talk to superiors, suppliers, customers and competitors. Look towards the horizon of your future. What's the weather forecast? In areas where tornadoes occur regularly, people know that if a tornado does not appear to be moving - it's either going away or its heading directly at them. Is there a tornado heading straight for you - how fast is it going? When could it hit?

'Exploration' before fundamental change 'hits' your life will open up additional choices to you, it will give you the time to prepare. Build your internal and external networks of people who could help you jump ship should you ever need to. Equip yourself with new skills and knowledge. Remember the phrase used earlier "The future belongs only to those who have adequately prepared for it." The alternative is to 'hope for the best' - and that's not a good choice in these turbulent times.

Acceptance

Accepting the need for change does not mean the same as being happy about it. What should you do if you discover that changes are on the way? What if you have grounds to suspect that the change is bad news for you? You could go back to the resistance stage, dig your heels in and make life a misery for everybody else too! (plenty of people do) It can seem like the only option - but it isn't. Karen, a friend's sister, has a high powered job in a telecommunications company which has recently been bought out by a larger conglomerate. (By the time you read this, her job could have been eliminated). Her approach is intelligent, pragmatic and the one most likely to deliver the best personal result in what is a difficult situation. She has been given the job of firing herself. Her employer hasn't actually said that but she knows what is going to happen. As part of a team she is tasked with assessing who should go and who should stay when the companies are fully integrated. This is happening everywhere as companies continue to merge.

She decided early on to learn from the experience. Realising her future employability will improve if she can demonstrate confidence when dealing with such a situation she has embraced these fundamental changes even though she is not happy about it. Karen realises that once this project is completed there will be less people to manage and more competition for the remaining jobs. Who knows, her employer may want to keep her. Fantastic - if it happens. Meantime, she's busily designing and sewing together her parachute before her plane goes into a vertical dive ... just in case!

How is your company doing? Is business performance sluggish? Is performance outstandingly good? Either way, your company could be ripe for a takeover. What would you do if your company was bought out by a larger concern? It's worth some serious thought, especially if you work in a rapidly changing and dynamic industry sector.

Doing It

This, the final stage in the D.R.E.A.D. process speaks for itself. Get on with doing your bit to implement the change. Some colleagues will almost certainly view you with suspicion - especially if relationships between staff and management are strained or there is a history of conflict, distrust and a prevailing 'them and us' mentality. How you deal with such situations depends so much on the unique circumstances within your company but the thought processes you went through and the answers you received whilst reaching the 'doing it' stage should help. Others may respond similarly if you share your new found information and insight with them. Let me stress, just because you are involved in the change process does not mean you have to be happy about it. This is often irrelevant. The wider consequences for refusing to change can be more damaging and ultimately more painful than grudgingly accepting the need for change and implementing the necessary changes. Recruiting help from colleagues can often work well. Take the initiative by helping colleagues and staff to overcome their own concerns and reservations. Recruit help from everyone affected by the changes. Organise informal discussion groups. Become part of the change programme.

Sometimes the consequences of change programmes are unpleasant for those involved. The personal consequences of any change programme produce fear amongst the least well informed. Many individuals who go through changes feel as though no one cares about their situation, when in fact those at the top of the organisation are trying to wrestle the best way they can. Many examples come to mind of working with companies who were working so hard to solve the problems associated with change that they failed to communicate these changes to their staff. This can have catastrophic results but it is often quite understandable because the managers are doing the best they can in circumstances which have no instructions! The whole problem with change is that no one - staff or executives - has all the answers.

Protecting yourself

What if all your efforts result in the loss of your job or your power, authority and influence. These are possibilities which must be considered. Physically assaulting your boss is not an acceptable option (especially for the boss!), although you may believe it is worth it. Sensible, forward thinking people will create an exit strategy whilst implementing the required changes.

- When fundamental changes are announced, speak to your superiors about your concerns.
- Find out as much as you can as early as possible.
- Make it clear that you fully understand how it is impossible for anyone to know all the answers. Some managers will be either uninterested in your feelings or could simply tell you to do as you are told.
- Seriously consider looking for a better job sooner rather than later.

A more professional manager will empathise with you - indeed he or she may even admit their own feelings of unease about the situation. Acknowledge between you the possible consequences if the changes were to have personal and negative impacts on your jobs. Work together on the possible solutions. How can you make their lives easier and less stressful? If possible negotiate an agreement with your boss which sets out the conditions for your compliance and help. Ask what the company is prepared to do to ensure that you are amply rewarded if you suspect that your position will be put in jeopardy. Why should you help? If you are a middle manager, you could be in a particularly vulnerable position. Not only could you end up with no job, but you will probably be made responsible for organising and implementing the changes. It is naive to expect cast iron promises covering every possible consequence for change programmes. Indeed, your boss may end up suffering more than you. Follow up your meeting with a written summary of what was discussed and agreed.

Keep any correspondence which applauds your involvement in the changes. These can be used as part of your curriculum vitae if the changes ultimately eliminate your job. Prepare for the worst-case scenario. Where can you get training to help with the change process? What new skills and knowledge do you need to acquire to protect your position?

Ask your customers, colleagues and clients what you could do to improve the way you deal with them. How can they change to improve things for you? What processes and systems exist which you think could be streamlined or even abolished? Julian Richer is the head of the Richer Sounds company which he has built up from scratch into a £50 million organisation. He has set up something called "the cut the crap committee" which allows and even encourages staff to eliminate stupid rules and regulations which slow the business down.

Many change programmes ultimately improve conditions and working practices - although the benefits are notoriously slow in coming. This is the nature of change within business. When tangible results and improvements are slow in coming, this creates a situation where many staff lose faith in the abilities of those involved in implementing the change. This, in turn, leads to less cooperation which slows the process down even further. Accept that changes take time. Don't fall into the trap of believing that once the current round of changes are implemented, that everything in the garden will become rosy. Change is here to stay. Get used to it.

Change and the future

With so much change happening in our lives, it is impossible to be in control of everything. But you can control how you respond to what happens. Knowing what you can control and what you can't, will make a significant difference to the results you achieve and how you feel about changes in your life.

For many middle managers in particular, organisational changes could mean the loss of their jobs. Any middle manager who is not preparing him/herself for such an possibility is being foolish and naive. Those that do not prepare for such an eventuality tend to reinforce their position as a potential 'victim'; they always seem to be waiting for disaster to strike - when it does, they can tell colleagues and spouses how unfair it was, even though they should have seen it coming. It is an example of how people reinforce their beliefs that others are responsible for their lives and destiny. After all, it is always easier to blame someone else. For some people it is more comforting to absolve themselves of all responsibility. This is a cop out. Too many employees allow themselves to become conditioned into believing that they have little say in what happens. Perhaps they believe their only role in life is to do as they are told.

Persuading others to buy your changes

One of the biggest problems I encounter with clients is the unwillingness of business people to be more realistic and candid about the challenges and problems being faced. Changes and improvements can only take place in an honest and open environment. Tell the truth, and communicate it often. Communicate the benefits of the change more than you feel is necessary. And educate those affected, by explaining the real tangible consequences if such changes are not implemented This is not another way of describing threats!

Initiate and organise visits for staff to other non-competing companies which exhibit good practices. When workers can speak to people in other companies which have undergone such changes, it allows them to see their own roles in a different light. Return the favour by inviting companies to visit you once you have implemented changes. The success of the Department of Trade and Industry's *Inside UK Enterprise* scheme is based on this sharing of knowledge, problems and solutions amongst the hundreds of participating companies.

Many organisations fall into the trap of failing to communicate - they get so wrapped up in trying to sort out the messy problem, they don't realise the demoralising effect of the message they are sending to staff who only see countless rounds of secretive and confidential meetings. So, communicate regularly and in detail. If some of the information is thought too commercially sensitive to share with staff, you have a trust issue which must be solved before the changes are eventually implemented. Ask yourself "Why don't we trust our people?" You and your senior team must learn to change too. Your fears and insecurities will hamper the change process.

Helping clients improve their internal communication often requires a fundamental change of approach for senior managers and executives. They are not always keen to do so. This is good because once it is explained that their reluctance to change is precisely how their staff will think, the executives usually take a deep breath and 'go for it'. Most if not all the time, they learn from the experience and discover that the process is rather enjoyable instead of emotionally painful.

Dealing with change requires courage backed up by knowledge and strategic thinking. The highest performing companies realise the need to capture the knowledge, insight and different perspectives of all their staff; those at all levels and across all sectors including gender, race and other minorities. Learning to deal with change involves finding more creative solutions to your problems - do not try to address them all purely on your own or within your management teams - shielding others from the truth is often well meaning but misguided. Acknowledge that you need help - it will often be forthcoming. Then have the confidence to listen and, where appropriate, act on the advice you receive - regardless of where it has come from. The solution is more important than where a person resides within the hierarchy.

A wonderful example of this occurred at a conference in Monte Carlo. Bay Networks, the third largest computer networking company in the world, brought me in to help them improve the communication with their top 400 European Partners. Peter George, the European VP knew they had to change their approach and relationship with these partners. It demanded bold and decisive action. Dave House (formerly number 2 at the Intel Corporation) had been CEO for just 100 days, he'd brought Dave Shrigley with him to become the new Executive VP Sales and Marketing. Peter wanted me to 'rip apart' him and his new bosses in front of these important partners. He knew some of the issues would be difficult and there was a risk of personal humil-iation and even retribution from superiors. Peter explained his rationale *"We have an internal set of 'True North' values* [Dr. Stephen Covey explores the need for values which remain constant through good times and bad in his books *The Seven Habits of Highly Effective People* and *First Things First*] *which we all had a hand in creating. These values do not shift but remain constant and demand straight talking, facing up to business challenges and going past the point of pain. In short, it means doing the right thing regardless of short term consequences."* Honesty like this requires supreme courage.

Most people don't have it. Fear, internal politics and pressure to deliver short-term results moulds the behaviour and therefore the values of too many organisations. How many companies espouse the concepts of 'customer care' but only ever speak to customers in the last few days of a financial quarter?

House and Shrigley rose to the challenge. During the conference I taunted and cross-examined these executives with unscripted and unrehearsed questions. Once or twice they and other colleagues were hit with my unfair and barbed questions. This was a change for me too, but I had to remember that Bay wanted me to give them my worst shots. But how serious had they been about this? Were they going to cut me dead afterwards? As the audience's 'conscience' I asked the difficult questions everyone was thinking but were too polite to ask. Audience feedback confirmed the response Bay had hoped for - the audience realised that the company was serious about dealing with everything head on, without painting pictures which might be perceived as being too optimistic. As for Peter George, his courage to change paid off. His bosses knew what was at stake, and supported him. But no one could have known for sure beforehand. All Bay Networks' executives were happy with the result (although somewhat relieved when the ordeal was over!).

The most enlightened leaders realise that you can no longer say one thing and do something else. They too must change. The most successful companies in the future will be those which create an environment in which staff are rewarded for doing the right thing. Indeed, there is growing evidence that the best people choose not to work with unethical organisations. Ethical and successful individuals know that it takes years to earn a reputation for integrity but only moments to lose it. Keeping and attracting the best people is fundamental to the success of any business. Ultimately we have choices but in too many companies, business managers instantly resort to the FIFO management tactic; Fit In or F*** Off!

What would need to change in your organisation to retain your most trustworthy and value driven staff without such strong arm behaviour?

In summing up, changes to the ways we work and live will accelerate in the 21st century. Kicking against change may feel like the best approach - it rarely is. When enduring the effects of change, it is easy to imagine that you are the only person going through the emotional stress or trauma. By learning to identify and understand how and why you are responding in the ways you are - whether in denial, resistance, exploration or acceptance, you will be able to adapt to even the most fundamental changes.

Chapter 4
Learning
- The Key to Your Future

"Change" and how we deal with it in the decades to come will influence the results we each achieve in our lives. As we discovered in the previous chapter, there are many stages we go through before accepting and embracing change. By understanding these clearly defined stages and responding to them in a positive way, we can all increase the influence we have over our own lives.

This book is about learning to look at our lives through different eyes; to anticipate future trends and then to act on the information, so that we can insulate ourselves from the possible negative effects of such change. The prizes will go to those individuals and organisations who have chosen to acquire the most appropriate information and then convert it into knowledge, so it can be applied to their particular industries or circumstances. Those who convince themselves they are already too busy to learn about the latest developments in their sectors will almost certainly suffer.

A key measure of our potential for survival and success in the 21st century is the degree to which we are prepared to learn new skills, new technologies and to develop new sets of behaviours.

At my seminars and conferences, I am often asked what I believe to be the secret of success. Without doubt, if there is one secret, it has to be making a personal commitment to continuous learning. This is a vital key. Unfortunately, it is not the instant solution so many people are constantly seeking.

The secret to your future success is a personal commitment to continuous learning.

Continuous learning

If it is as simple as that - then why isn't everyone doing it? The obvious answer is that it involves effort. Most workers already feel overstretched and under mounting pressure to improve their productivity and efficiency. Why volunteer for extra work? Not only that, 'learning' and 'training' is only for people who are lousy at their jobs - if they were any good, they wouldn't need the training. Right?

Wrong.

Training is all too often seen as an extension of an individual's job and something an employer must pay extra for. They fail to realise that the more they know, the more they can do and the more choices they have available to them. However skilful you may be, the more tasks you can do well, the less reliant you will be on a poor employer.

In the immediate and longer term future, unskilled workers of every race, colour and gender will suffer the most because of their lack of knowledge, skill and education. More and more businesses feel the need to squeeze out every unnecessary cost. Some of these employers see their workers merely as a cost or commodity - and will find any way they can to justify lower pay, longer hours and poor working conditions. In these industries the labour unions constantly battle for even the smallest concessions. But all too often the frustrations result in walkouts and strike action which rarely produce the hoped for results - even though unions are always keen to put a positive spin on any action they initiate.

What has this got to do with learning, you may be asking yourself? Simply, the scenarios outlined above invariably ignore one crucial option. They presuppose that low paid, unskilled workers have no choice but to stay with a rogue employer or one that is unable to pay more or offer better working conditions to its workforce. Almost any worker of average intelligence who decides to improve his or her knowledge and skills, will increase the possibility of a better job elsewhere. Low paid and poorly educated people tend to be less willing to relocate to another job. Fear of ending up in a worse position paralyses them into accepting a bad deal. The most highly skilled, better educated people are more likely to relocate to a better job.

Trade unions have a problem; on the one hand they need to attract and keep members in order to have sufficient strength in numbers, whilst on the other they must look after the interests of their existing members. But what if the interests of their members would be better served by helping them find better paid jobs in other industry sectors? This could be achieved by instigating training programmes in transferable skills for union members, to help them to move on. Should such a programme be successful, employers would find it increasingly difficult to keep staff - and would have to raise salaries in line with the most basic laws of 'supply and demand'. It is a fact that most businesses have come to realise that it's usually the people who leave who are those they want to stay, while those who won't move, are often the staff they most want to lose!

But what union leader would be brave enough to advocate anything that would guarantee fewer membership subscriptions, when they are already losing members as more and more workers are made redundant in the older 'smokestack' industries? An interesting conundrum. The idea outlined above might be thought too radical a suggestion, except for the fact that one of the original roles of trade unions was to provide members with skills and literacy training.

Trade unions are changing - in some cases quite radically - but there is still an 'old guard' of militant members and leaders who maintain a contempt and loathing for business owners, who they see to be exploiting workers by controlling what Karl Marx described as 'the means of production'. The only problem with this as a valid argument is that the 'means of production' is changing too; 'muscle slaves' are being replaced by workers who use their brains. More and more workers now possess the 'means of production' themselves - it's the knowledge inside their heads. A worker's knowledge is less easy to replace. The result is that individual workers are more valuable to employers and have much more power than ever before. They are able to dictate working terms - often without recourse to a trade union - in ways in which the highly interchangeable workers of the past were not.

The benefits of learning

There are many things that stop millions of people from accepting the need to learn. We'll look at the obstacles to learning a little later but first ....

As technology and communications continue to make the world a smaller place, more and more businesses are forced into competing in a global market. This increases competition drastically. In not too many years time, a high tech factory in (say) Bracknell will have to compete with a higher tech factory in Beijing. The Job Centres in Britain and other countries are full of well qualified candidates who are willing to accept lower pay just so they can work. How could you be affected when more and more people want your job? What are you prepared to do to ensure that you maintain and enhance your value to an employer or client in order to keep your job? Learning new and additional skills on a continual basis will provide you with the necessary tools.

Learn more, earn more

What would it take for you to become a world expert at what you currently do or what you would choose to do? This question was posed to the training manager of a pharmaceuticals company which was 'rationalising' its staff. No one knew if they would have a job for much longer. This question flicked a switch in her head. Her job insecurity seemed to melt away as she described what she would do to establish herself as an industry expert. By focusing her attention in this way, she would be able to create a unique position in her industry. How could she be so sure it would be that easy? "No one is doing it at the moment - it gives me a window of opportunity which I didn't know existed," she replied. As a professional trainer she fully understood the value of learning for others, but had never thought to apply its principles in a proactive way to herself thereby increasing her employability elsewhere, if the need should arise. How could you benefit in a similar way?

Since I decided to embark on continuous learning a few years ago, my knowledge about how I function as a communications consultant has grown substantially. My interest in a growing number of related subjects is constantly fuelled by the realisation that my earnings have more than trebled. The more I learn, the more I seem to earn. Earning more enables me to take off more time in order to learn. This in turn increases my knowledge which again increases my income. But earning more is only a part of what learning contributes to my life. The rewards are many fold; more choices, a real sense of being alive, and the mental stimulation derived from learning provides regular mental workouts.

To me, learning is not work - I really enjoy it. This is fundamental to the idea of continuous learning - learning is enjoyable when it is done 'properly'. Millions of young people are introduced to learning as a compulsory activity which creates resistance - not necessarily to the learning itself, but to the methods by which it is taught. My head may constantly be in some non-fiction book or I may invest hours scouring the Internet looking for information, but I am not working. I have a voracious appetite for new information and knowledge. I get a huge 'buzz' from it - but this has not always been the case.

The turning point came a few years ago when, after many months of nervously exploring the possibility of going back to a classroom for the first time in 18 years, I finally decided to enrol on a three month part-time training course. My work schedule was busy, time was scarce - I had to be mad, especially when the assignments involved long and detailed written course work in subjects in which I had little or no prior knowledge. On the first morning, with a dry throat and sweaty palms, I took my place in the classroom. Was this really such a good idea after all? Should I give up before making a complete fool of myself?

My fears were well founded - much of the material went straight over my head!

So, why had I decided to learn to be a hypnotherapist when I had absolutely no desire to become one? Well, I earn my living by helping companies to improve the communication between senior management and their staff in order that they can all better understand how their company is performing, what the challenges are internally as well as the external competitive ones and to help people to see what everyone within the organisation needs to do together to improve their results.

In order to do this more effectively, I needed to add some new tools to my 'professional toolkit'. Years as a BBC radio & TV journalist had given me the knowledge and ability to ask pertinent and probing questions, whilst being able to absorb new information and make sense of complex subjects. But I was missing something - a much deeper understanding of the human psyche - but there were no courses called "How to Improve your Perceptiveness as an Interviewer."

If I could understand business people better: their deeper motivations, their anxieties, fears and emotions in a business environment which is traditionally highly stressful and shall we say "not always conducive to openness, honesty and directness", then I knew they would benefit. The job involves working as a business therapist without ever calling myself one - few CEOs would willingly agree to be referred to a therapist by their marketing manager!

When I interview executives in front of their staff and peers, I must address the real issues on the minds of those in the audience, whilst always being conscious of what the interviewee is thinking and feeling; The challenge is to make the interviewee look good but at the same time to represent the interests of the audience.

The 'in your face' confrontational interview style adopted by many broadcast media interviewers has very little to offer the corporate world. It certainly does not foster an open and honest environment.

During my training, not only did I meet a group of fascinating people from widely differing backgrounds, but the skills I learned added, enormous value to my work - and I now know some really good therapists if you ever need one!

How and why our education system has screwed up so badly

All human beings need stimulation. Adults need physical, emotional, sexual and mental stimulation. Anyone who offers us stimulation will attract our attention. Children crave it. If they are not stimulated at school, they will focus their attention elsewhere. Television and video games offer what they want because TV and software producers understand this basic rule of life. We want to be stimulated. They need to attract advertisers, viewers and customers. They give us the excitement and stimulation we want - so we buy what is on offer. In this context it is irrelevant that this stimulation is largely unproductive.

Any professional salesperson will tell you that no one buys any product or service unless the customer can see for him/herself the value they will receive from it. If a young pupil does not see the value of their education - they will not choose to learn. These young customers have not been sold the benefits by the educational system sufficiently well for them to want to buy. More and more young people get 'turned off' by learning. There are many reasons. It would be all too easy to point the finger of blame at the most convenient scapegoats - the teachers - but this would miss the target. Teachers teach what they are told to teach, where and when they are told to teach it. So, it must be the government's fault. Not really. Although it is only the government that can sort it out.

As Michael Stoten, former Director of Education for the Royal Borough of Kensington and Chelsea, has commented *"one must look at the National Curriculum as a force for good or evil in schools. Whilst the curriculum rightly addresses the needs of the mainstream, it excludes those at either margin."'* Following the introduction of the National Curriculum for England and Wales, many of the extra-curricular and vocational studies that students had enjoyed, were pushed out of the timetable to make way for the demands of a highly prescriptive and test-laden curriculum. Rab Butler's 1944 Education Act has only been partially realised. Whilst children are educated according to age, and usually ability, the important duty of educating according to aptitude has been ignored almost entirely.

In John Holt's *How Children Fail* he wrote *"We must ask how much of the sum of human knowledge can anyone know at the end of his schooling? Perhaps a millionth. Are we then to believe that one of these millionths is so much more important than another? Or that our social and national problems will be solved if we can just figure out a way to turn children out of schools knowing two millionths of the total, instead of one..... Since we cannot know what knowledge will be needed in the future it is senseless to try to teach it in advance. Instead, we should try to turn out people who love learning so much and learn so well that they will be able to learn whatever needs to be learned."*

Holt wrote this over 30 years ago. An education system which is primarily equipped to ensure examination success will rarely succeed at instilling a love of learning in young people.

Your attitude to learning, good or bad, is based on how well you responded to the often rigid and 'one size fits all' learning system you endured during your youth.

It's worth looking briefly at how our schooling has evolved and why most of us were taught in the way we were. Historically, an education was provided only to men in the Church or the wealthy nobility. Very few women were taught to read and write in the middle ages - cooking, cleaning, farming, making and repairing clothes and having kids didn't require it! (Indeed, even today, religious leaders in third world countries deny the most basic education to many millions of women). The Church had developed highly ritualised and authoritarian methods of teaching which reflected the hierarchical structure of the Church. There was no place for 'learning as fun' within the Church establishment. Today's Church-run schools are direct descendants and are still known (and feared by children) for their highly authoritarian methods of teaching. Sunday schools began their lives as a means of teaching children to read and write on the only day they were not working.

In turn, our state education system evolved from the Church's methods. The Industrial Revolution had begun with its highly regimented ways of working. Rows of desks, harsh discipline, a dehumanising, non-collaborative regime where everything was learned by rote - a perfect way to prepare young people for boring, repetitive factory work! Utilitarian education - students being stuffed with facts, was a new concept in the Victorian era. The role of stimulating the imagination and creativity of children was subordinated in favour of preparing individuals for work by equipping them with 'standardised knowledge'. Education was corrupted by the notion of the educators of the time that the absorption of facts equalled education. In earlier times, "Renaissance Man" had a broad knowledge of many subjects, all of which were thought of and seen to be interconnected. Context and meaning tends to disappear when subjects are taught in separate, isolated boxes by different teachers. There is growing disaffection in today's schools, where a significant minority of young people see little purpose and relevance to their lives and futures in these 'boxed' subjects.

There have been many advances in teaching methods in the past 30 years. Sadly, few have been accepted within mainstream education. The education system is shamefully slow at adapting to changes. This inability to respond to the demands both of students and the workplace will ultimately destroy the state education system as we know it. In the future, each and every one of us must learn to learn quickly and effectively. Mainstream education is often more focused on the process than the results produced by the learning. No one is suggesting that we should turn children into 'academic slaves' as happens in education obsessed Japan, where 'triangle' teenagers attend school up to six days a week, attend crammer classes and take home large quantities of homework in order to gain entry to the best schools. The pressure is intense, leading to chronic fatigue and a lack of physical fitness amongst a significant proportion of Japanese children.

Future learning must be fun and stimulating, and must generate on-going, tangible benefits to justify the time invested. If we are to remain competitive as members of any workforce, we have no alternative. This means the methods of teaching in schools and business must improve. Business learning is no longer tied to outdated classroom methods. To the more enlightened 'learning organisations', 'chalk and talk' is either already dead or is being killed off and replaced with far more effective alternatives.

Our schools are continuing to fail our children. In 1995 there were 15,000 permanent expulsions from our schools. Expulsions of children as young as six are at an all time high. Four out of five of these children are known by the social services to be the offspring of parents who neither know nor care about what their children do. A survey in the same year by the UK's largest union, Unison, found that more than 800,000 children admitted to truancy. More than 80,000 rarely bothered to go to school. Their main reasons? - boring lessons and being bullied. According to Home Office figures, children convicted of assault rose from 1,800 in 1981 to 2,900 in 1994. Alarming increases in other areas of crime and drugs are also being noted.

Myth: learning is work, not fun

When we are young children, learning is not perceived as work - it's play. If you ever watch very young children in a classroom their enthusiasm for learning is awesome. Most kids love it - they are learning machines, constantly questioning, experimenting, tasting, feeling, listening and exploring. You were almost certainly like that once. But what happened? Perhaps you have lost your curiosity? It may have been squeezed out of you. Could it be that your attitude towards teachers, classrooms and learning is based on a negative experience whilst at school, college or university? Do yourself a huge favour - rekindle that enthusiasm, curiosity and zest for learning.

Anyone with children will know that they have an insatiable capacity for learning. How many parents cringe when they hear the word "Why?" which seems to get asked hundreds of times a day - every day! Children will keep asking questions and learning from the answers they receive until they get the message that asking questions will illicit the following response "I haven't got the time dear - go and watch television instead!" Eventually they may learn that asking questions simply isn't worth it any more - they will probably get rejected.

Just because some parents muddled through and did adequately with few or no formal qualifications, it does not make this a sensible approach for a future based on knowledgeable workers.

Children are curious, they want to learn. This constant demand for knowledge tries the patience of even the most supportive parent. But parents who despised school, or achieved little by way of academic qualifications, can only pass on their loathing for or lack of interest in education to their children. Often these kids become disruptive in class - they are bored and fail to see the purpose or value of learning - after all, their parents (and some teachers) have told them they won't get a job anyway! Low expectations and boring lessons are a powerfully destructive recipe for too many individuals. They take these conditioned responses towards education with them through their lives at huge personal cost both to themselves and often the state. For the sake of our children we must start to view education in a wider context.

We humans are naturally curious 'learning machines' or 'intellectual sponges', soaking up information wherever we go. From our earliest days we watch, imitate, experiment, chew and explore everything we come into contact with. My parents still insist that they once saw me in our garden holding a half eaten slug! May be this is not the best way to discover that slugs and jelly babies are different, but I learned!

As we become a little more mobile, our curiosity includes prodding, stroking and memorising everything in our paths. It is common for very young children to know the lyrics of many many songs, they know the dialogue of their favourite videos inside out, they have memorised their favourite stories. To them learning new things is fun. It's exciting. It's a normal part of their lives. No one has to tell them to do it.

In any junior school - ask a question of a class of young children and their hands will shoot up into the air, everyone eager to tell you the answer. But ask a class of 16 year olds a question and only the 'swots' or 'creeps' will offer an answer, no doubt accompanied by murmurs of disapproval from the remainder of the class. In these short years the state education system succeeds in removing our innate curiosity and thirst for knowledge. As young children we have no concept of why it is bad to make mistakes. Making mistakes is a natural part of the learning process, but we become afraid of making them. When we get something wrong, people laugh at us. We are made to feel stupid. We finally get the message that if we ask too many questions we annoy our parents and some of our over-stressed teachers. We learn eventually that it really doesn't make sense to stick our hand up to ask a question or offer an answer.

Children are being taught subjects of questionable value to their future lives.

Young people are often being prepared for careers in industries which either no longer exist or are in massive decline. But the biggest crime in the education system is its success in crushing the innate desire to learn. How many people do you know who don't want to learn? Are you one of them?

Just take as an example how we are often taught a new language - for my generation, learning French in school was a nightmare. French is a living language but it was taught as though it was as dead as Latin. Being drilled with Latin and French grammar, the very thought of conjugating French verbs still fills me with dread. Many of my classmates felt the same way - our confidence was at an all time low. Learning that there was so much to know was the best way to convince us that it wasn't worth learning. We rationalised our non-interest in French by agreeing amongst ourselves that we would never want to go to France anyway. Without being immersed in the French culture, hearing it spoken on a regular basis or seeing it in context, we were abstracted from its real meanings and richness. And I went to a good school.

Perhaps you had similar experiences with some school subjects? If so, is there a specific teacher, a memory or a piece of information that you still remember very clearly because it inspired you? Take a moment to recall the particular circumstances surrounding that incident. Close your eyes if it helps you to remember more clearly. Can you picture the scene? How did the experience make you feel at the time? How was the information presented to you? The combination of your experience at that time prompted you to learn something new. To improve your learning, re-create similar circumstances and you will learn more effectively.

Our schools and colleges are churning out young people with an aversion to learning. Business relies on computers, and telecommunications. Schools have been very slow to turn to these technologies. Hopefully this will change dramatically with the commitment from Prime Minister Blair to equip all schools with the necessary technology. By using technology intelligently, it is possible to learn new information much faster and more efficiently. We are approaching a situation in which there is almost instant access to information, much of which is stored on a myriad of computer databases located all over the world. Much of this information is already available to those with the know how (and the technology) to reach it, whether this is via existing telephone technology and the Internet or through accessing CD-ROM. We are swimming in new information. By knowing how to filter and prioritise such information we will be able to make the most of this knowledge explosion.

Head of Research at British Telecom's Research and Development centre at Martlesham, near Ipswich, Peter Cochrane described his school as an oasis of learning, a vast resource of books and knowledge, while home was a desert, a place devoid of learning. He notes that the opposite is now true for a growing number of families. Most young people know more about technology than their parents and teachers. Although not universal, high powered home computers are becoming commonplace. They are equipped with interesting, entertaining and educational CD-ROMs and access to the largest library on the planet - the Internet. (Apart from those who cannot afford the equipment, it's only people who don't know where to look on the Internet who say it is full of rubbish).

This is more than a shame, it is a crime.

A University graduate colleague admitted that he had not picked up a book since he left university six years before. "I can't face the prospect of ploughing through another book," he said. He has had enough of learning - it was only a means to an end. He regarded 'graduation' as an end to his learning. There was a time when school and college prepared you for 40-50 years of work - not any more. In some sectors, knowledge is becoming obsolete every seven years. This time frame is shrinking. It does not necessarily mean everyone should go back to school or college - although for many this would be a good choice. However, millions of people all over the world are filled with dread and loathing at the prospect of sitting in a classroom - it reminds them of years of boredom.

The great news for those who believe learning is not for them is that learning can be an 'organic' process of self-development. You don't have to follow topics and qualifications pre-set by educational institutions.

As we will explore later, each of us has our own preferred style of thinking and behaving. What do you most enjoy doing? Which senses do you use for those activities; sight, sounds, touch, or the way it makes you feel? How could you see yourself enjoying the process of learning new things?

Schools should ask themselves why it is that so many pupils do not want to stay on at the end of their courses? Schools, colleges and universities complain they do not have enough money and few resources, but they could earn a great deal of additional income from every past student, if only they would create an environment which encourags a life-long relationship with learning for every student. Some British universities are starting to do this, but it is still the exception rather than the rule. All business owners know that one of the first rules of building a successful business is selling to past customers on a continual basis. Could this be an answer for education? It won't be, until teachers learn to accept the need to develop partnerships with business. The teaching profession is notoriously suspicious of business - so few teachers understand it (and this is often passed on to their pupils).

Teachers who feel uneasy about business "interfering with education" will have to come to terms with reality. Every business requires a steady input of well-educated people. If schools and colleges can't or won't supply them, corporations will either turn to technology to eliminate the need for staff or take on the responsibility themselves for re-educating their future workers.

On a plane from Madrid, I once sat next to a senior executive from Motorola, the electronics giant. We had been working together at a conference for their European staff. He told me that Motorola was finding it increasingly difficult to recruit people of a sufficiently high standard. Because of this, the company built its own Motorola University to ensure their staff were sufficiently well educated and trained. Some staff children were also being educated by the company in a bid to provide staff with additional reasons to stay with the company. Revenues have soared since on-going training became such a high priority at Motorola.

Many of the largest companies spend hundreds of millions of pounds annually on training. It is linked to productivity and business growth. Businesses would not spend this money if it did not deliver commercial advantages. On a personal level, individuals strengthen their job security and position by improving their knowledge. They learn transferable skills. Companies must then look after those staff if they are to keep the best.

More learning takes place in business today than in all the country's schools and colleges. Business learning is growing thousands of times faster than state-run education. In the future, schools and colleges will be competing with business to educate our children. This will involve a fundamental re-think for mainstream education. There are few signs that schools are responding well to this challenge. If they don't, state run schools will end up educating the poor and those least likely to join the workforce. In their book *The Monster Under The Bed*, Stan Davis and Jim Botkin predict that those schools which learn to become more business-like to improve their performance will not only teach the 3 R's (reading, writing and 'rithmetic) but they will also add six new R's: risks, results, rewards, relationships, research and rivalry.

The learning organisation - a case study

The most forward thinking companies are creating a learning environment throughout their entire organisations. As individuals become more knowl-edgeable, they are capable of making more decisions for themselves. This means that senior management can devote more time to strategic thinking, confident in the knowledge that employees can be trusted to solve problems without supervision. This is a profound change for many companies. When people share problems and work together to provide solutions, trust within the organisation increases and people feel they are part of the solution, working towards making tangible improvements to the company. Their own personal development improves and they see at first hand the satisfaction it brings to their customers.

Few British companies have such an enlightened view of learning and education as the motor parts manufacturer and distributor, Unipart. In 1994 the company spent over three million pounds building its own internal University, known as the Unipart U. The company's Chief Executive Officer, John Neill, has strong views on the value of learning and the consequences for individuals and corporate organisations which fail either to take personal responsibility for their own learning or to create a learning environment for their staff. In a recent interview for the charity Business Wise he told me,

"Sir Christopher Ball once said to me - 'When you are born, your first instinct is to breathe because if you don't, you die.' Your second instinct is to learn because if you don't learn you also die. The minute you have stopped learning you have given up on life."

"People are being made obsolete by the rapid changes in technology. What choices does a company have? It can make its people obsolete by getting rid of them every few year's - that does not seem like an agenda which many people would sign up to. Or you can try to help people understand what they, as individuals and we, as a company, are facing, and then create an environment which says, "It is very important for you to take responsibility for your own learning" and then make it possible for people to do so. We are trying to create in Unipart U an inspirational environment for people - many of whom have been working for 20-30 years and the last time they experienced learning, it was not a particularly happy one. Our job is to try and create a set of conditions - particularly for those people - whereby we make learning a pleasant and fulfilling experience. For some groups of people we want to ensure that what they learn in the morning they can apply at their job in afternoon."

"Learning does not have to be a major capital investment, it is more an attitude of mind. Even if you do all the right things there is no guarantee of survival [in the decades to come] but one thing is sure if you do not try to do the right things, then you won't make it."

Unipart has seen the need to train everyone. John Neill routinely attends training courses to equip himself with new business skills. No successful business can function by training only certain groups of individuals - it has to be for everyone. In contrast, the European President of an engineering company told me their people were the companies' biggest asset and training was the key. I ask when he had last attended a training course. This was met with silence - apart from another board director who burst out laughing - I think that director is still with the company. You cannot engender a learning culture if the most senior people do not invest time in attending classes themselves.

Technology to the rescue

Unipart's library (*The Learning Curve*) is equipped with powerful laptop computers which staff are encouraged to borrow, and used to learn anything they wish - even if it is not directly related to their job function. Alongside *The Learning Curve* is a computer-packed room known as *The Leading Edge*. Here you will find just about every type of computer, fitted with a massive range of software - comprising commercially available packages as well as bespoke programs used within the Unipart Group of Companies. You've never used a computer? Or surfed the Internet? No problem - a team of people are there to show you the ropes. Technology outside schools is redefining education and learning. When Gutenberg's printing press was first invented, it destroyed the Church's monopoly on education. Computer technology is already removing the state's control of education. Rightly or wrongly education is moving into the realm of business.

Developments in learning technology are progressing rapidly. In Chapter 2 I recalled the time when I demonstrated a system of 'search agents'. These are sophisticated software programmes which act as your personal 'software agent' by repeatedly scanning countless databases, retrieving articles and information on whatever subjects you have told it you are interested in. These software agents work away tirelessly on your behalf, squirreling out information wherever it is. Even at its most basic, the possibilities for learning are phenomenal. As more and more knowledge is stored in electronic form, students all over the world will, for a fee, be able to access it.

Just suppose you are interested in anything to do with new ideas and infor-mation on providing customer service. Whenever something new becomes available on this subject and anything related to it, the search agent will find and deliver it to your electronic mailbox. This means you will be able to learn from the most knowledgeable individuals and organisations from all over the world. Search agent technology alone has the potential to change education radically. By selecting a range of subjects, would you ever need a newspaper again? Would you need a teacher? How will the teacher's role change?

Anyone who refuses to embrace technology as a learning tool with both hands is making a big mistake - regardless of their reasons or motives. 'Chalk and talk' is a thing of the past (and has been for a long time) but many teachers still stick with it!

Obstacles to learning

I mentioned earlier that there are a number of things that prevent people from wanting to learn, and we have seen how most school systems are failing to prepare young people for their future lives. If you feel incapable of learning something new, it is likely that this feeling springs from deeply rooted self-beliefs based on difficulties you experienced in school. If you don't currently invest time in continuous learning you may find some of the deeper reasons for your reluctance to enrol on training and learning courses below.

Do you have the 'wrong' intelligence?

When you were at school it is highly likely that you were taught in a way that the teacher was trained to teach, or felt most comfortable teaching. If you were able to deal with that, you probably did well at school. However, over the past century, millions of pupils have been judged on the way they responded to one particular style of teaching. Just because teachers or parents may have said you were a 'slow learner' or 'stupid' - they are not necessarily correct. Sadly, it's a human trait to accept such 'put downs' if we hear them often enough.

It is now known that there are seven distinct intelligences which can be further divided into twenty varieties. Based on research by Howard Gardner at Harvard University the following have been identified: linguistic, logical mathematical, visual spatial, musical, bodily kinaesthetic, interpersonal and intrapersonal intelligences. We each possess all of them, although one or two will be dominant. Below is a brief description of each one.

- Linguistic intelligence - good at using words, enjoys reading books, writing down information
- Logical mathematical intelligence - attracted to science, problem solving, computers, puzzles
- Visual spatial intelligence   - likes art, architecture, using diagrams, colours, patterns
- Musical intelligence - a composer might benefit from using baroque music to accompany learning
- Bodily kinaesthetic intelligence - responds well to touch, practical exercises, using hands, likes to get involved, prefers experiential learning
- Interpersonal intelligence - drawn to communicating and interacting with people, a team player

- Intrapersonal intelligence - likes thinking quietly on their own, thinking things through, being reflective, independent, a self-starter

If you are predominantly 'Bodily kinaesthetic' but you are taught using 'dry' lecture-based 'Logical mathematical' methods (i.e. those used almost exclusively in our schools), you will almost certainly not do as well as a 'Logical mathematical' student. This has nothing to do with your own ability to learn. Conversely, a 'Logical mathematical' student will not respond as well to practical, experiential and other 'Bodily kinaesthetic' methods. Gardner's research cast doubt on the validity of IQ (Intelligence Quotient) tests used so widely to determine the intelligence of students. Originally, IQ tests were formulated using predominantly linguistic and mathematical criteria. These tests were used to determine the so called 'intelligence' of millions of people and consequently how they were 'streamed' within the education establishment. Such tests are flawed and do not acknowledge a person's true intelligence(s) or ability to learn. For example, IQ tests do not take into consideration Gardner's 'Interpersonal' and 'Intrapersonal' intelligences. These intelligences reflect our ability to interact with others and to deal with the non-academic aspects of our lives. The education system does not value such qualities - but they are the very factors which often determine our ultimate success in life.

We all have these seven intelligences and use them with varying degrees of proficiency. Historically, equal importance and respect was given to each of these intelligences, even if they were not defined in the way Gardner expressed it. How many people do you know who are regarded as very intelligent but behave as though they are a complete 'klutz'? Some of the 'brightest' people are unable to relate to others, or look after themselves in all but the most basic ways. Academics determine our intelligence based on their narrowly defined terms. If you do not conform, you will be dismissed as someone who is not intelligent. So many people have gone through life burdened by the mistaken belief that they are not 'bright' just because the system was unable to measure their particular types of intelligence. Their inferiority complexes and the self-limiting beliefs they now foster are largely a result of how our mass market, conveyor-belt education system treated them when they were young. This, I believe, is yet another significant factor determining an individual's reluctance to learn after they leave school.

Daniel Goleman redefined intelligence when he wrote his book *Emotional Intelligence*. He claims that our emotions have a far greater role to play than our IQ in the way we think, make decisions and interact with others. This goes some way towards explaining why people with a high IQ do not necessarily achieve any more success than many with a lower IQ. Being 'emotionally intelligent' requires a level of self-awareness - how well we know our own emotions, possess self-motivation, are able to control our impulses, anger, lust and the desire for instant gratification, how well we demonstrate empathy and our ability to calm the emotions of others, understand and notice more about others, manage intimate and business relationships by becoming attuned to the moods of others - it's what Goleman describes as being proficient at 'emotional judo'. People with high emotional intelligence are capable of achieving great things irrespective of what their IQ's are judged to be. The best news is that emotional intelligence is not fixed at birth, but can be learned. This in turn helps to build the neural pathways or 'circuitry' within the brain. As Goleman writes *"... Our emotions destine the way of or enhance our ability to think and plan, to pursue training for a distant goal, to solve problems... they define the limits of our capacity to use our innate mental abilities, and so determine how we do in life."*

Emotional intelligence is a life skill for which women seem better prepared. Their upbringing includes the discussion of emotions and the ability to articulate them more accurately. Many boys are encouraged to suppress emotions - any such exhibition is perceived as a sign of weakness or being 'girly'. For girls, the answer is co-operation, for boys, it's competition, even when it's inappropriate.

Ask yourself, "What is stopping me from learning?" What attitudes do you have which justify not learning? Think back to good learning experiences in the past (not just those confined to a classroom), and find ways to learn using your preferred 'intelligences' - the more appropriate learning methods for you.

'New learning' is about self-development and acquiring skills, it is not about testing the acquisition of facts. You can determine your own pace and methods from books, training courses, TV and audio programmes. You can have full control of the timetable.

Stress

Stress is increasing as the pace of life continues to increase. Learning to deal with a life of increased stress is dealt with more fully in a later chapter. Most people do not respond to it well. Stress dulls our ability to concentrate. You cannot learn effectively when you are under stress. So what happens at school? We endure years of tests and examinations that almost guarantee a poorer result for those who are not good at handling stress. An individual who receives a low test score because 'nerves' got in the way, will be most likely to build up a chronic fear of examinations which triggers even more stress in the lead up to and during future tests and exams.

Perhaps your inability to deal with stress is one of the biggest hurdles to your future learning. If you are prone to stress, you will be more likely to avoid situations which induce it. Therefore you will be unlikely to seek opportunities to learn. You are likely to avoid attending any training course which incorporates examinations despite the fact that the increased knowledge and skills acquired during such training may improve your self-esteem and how you perceive yourself , your skills, knowledge and future abilities. These in turn would help move you towards more formalised learning and training. One approach to overcoming this problem would be to go initially for a course in something in which you are interested but does not involve tests or examinations.

Fear of failure

Closely linked to stress, fear of failure is another major hurdle to learning new skills. Why put ourselves into a situation that would reinforce what others may have told us about our inability to learn? So, if we don't bother to learn - we cannot fail. Nor can we win. The only way you will fail is by not attempting any learning at all. All new learning involves stepping outside our 'comfort zones'. It goes with the territory. Yes, you might fail, but you could succeed. You have no idea how many otherwise intelligent people I know who refuse to learn to ski because they are afraid of falling over or looking silly to others who have already learned. What they forget is that everyone who has learned to ski has been through the learning process. Fear of being laughed at is laughable! No one laughs at learners - because everyone has been through the falling down stage - repeatedly in some cases! Every skier learns that falling flat on your face in the snow does not hurt. You only break bones when you try to do too much too soon. It is the same with many other types of learning. We all fell over plenty of times when we were learning to walk - it's just that we weren't self-conscious about it at the time!

Earlier, I described my own experiences of going back to a classroom - there are times when everyone feels uncomfortable about putting themselves into a potentially challenging environment. Don't let it stop you from learning. Any disadvantages are far outweighed by the advantages.

Fear of success

No one likes to be seen to be a 'swot'. This throw-back to school days may be responsible for ensuring a 'learning-free zone' in your life today and for many years to come. If you have a low self-esteem, or lack self-confidence, part of a reluctance to learn could stem from the fear that if you succeeded, you would attract attention. Are you afraid of someone mocking you or not wanting to be a friend if you 'bettered' yourself? Such cycles of limiting self-belief paralyses many into maintaining mediocrity in their life. Is this you?

Family contempt for learning

In Danny de Vito's excellent children's movie *Matilda* based on the Roald Dahl story, the young Matilda has a love of books and asks to join a library. *"What do you want books for, you've got the TV!"* says de Vito's father character - as the camera reveals a mindless game show to which the rest of this dysfunctional family are glued.

Children are sensitive and impressionable. Anything and everything can be turned into a stimulating learning experience. If surrounded by a family or friends who show no interest in learning - or show a distinct contempt for it - children are more likely to adopt similar attitudes. For too many children, learning stops at the school gates - for some it's on the way out, for others it's on their way in! If you lived in such an environment, how much of your present attitude towards learning is a result of family history?

Too old?

It's never too late to begin learning new things. The saying "You can't teach an old dog new tricks" is rubbish - unless the dog is unwilling to learn. In the next decades more middle aged people will be made redundant from their jobs - this, as we explore in a later chapter, is a clearly identified trend within the workplace. If (or when) people are affected by this, their future employability will be severely restricted unless they can demonstrate an ability to adapt to new conditions within business. Anyone who relies on what they see as their 'years of experience' will be disappointed to hear that much of this experience will not be valued.

At the turn of the last century, there were countless highly skilled horse whip makers. But when the motor car put them out of work, their expertise and experience was no longer required. They had a choice; battle on trying to persuade people to employ them as a horse whip maker, or learn something valuable about motor cars. For many people, learning something new is frightening. If this is you - face this fear, start enrolling on re-training courses now or suffer years of frustration and bitterness until you retire. Employers will want people with a more 'entrepreneurial' approach - supervisory management experience is becoming less relevant in business. Employers want people with more leadership qualities. You can add this type of value to your employment tool kit by learning it now.

Learning to learn

Hands up if you were ever taught how to learn at school? Probably not. Most of us muddle through our learning. The most valuable lesson of all - 'how to learn' is rarely if ever taught. Learning to learn is almost certainly the single most important skill you can acquire to stack the odds in your favour for a successful future. Learning becomes easier when you know how to learn. We all have an innate ability to learn but the learning methods we develop are often slow and ineffective. Remember how easily we learned when we were very young. The inappropriate, uninspiring learning methods many of us adopt from our school days must be jettisoned and un-learned. To become more flexible and adaptable in the future we need to learn to absorb and apply new information, knowledge and skills quickly. Learning how to learn is the first step towards becoming a fast, productive learner.

How the brain absorbs, stores and accesses information has been studied extensively in the past few decades. Research into how the limbic system functions within our brain, has further helped scientists to better understand how information is transferred from short term memory into long term memory. This is obviously crucial if we are to remember what we learn. For example, it has been discovered that we tend to learn best at the beginning and end of each learning session. Therefore the most skilled trainers deliberately build into their learning programmes, a lot of short learning experiences - therefore increasing the number of 'beginnings' and 'ends'.

Much of the research into learning has shown how conventional teaching methods inhibit rather than promote speedy and potent learning. The best learning takes place in an environment which encourages playfulness - in other words a non-stressful environment. When we are kids we experience joy, excitement and stimulation. To learn more effectively we need to find ways to recreate these feelings. When young children learn, they use their eyes, taste, hearing, touch and smell - in fact whatever it takes to get the job done. Learning anything new by using just one or two of our senses makes the process more difficult than it needs to be. While at play, we become lost in the experience. Time flies, it doesn't feel like learning.

I often work with a team of trainers headed by Chris Howe. They produce large scale inter-active business games for large corporations. It is fascinating to see how senior executives respond to the idea of a 'game' at work. Some are locked into believing that if it is fun, it cannot have a business value. But Chris and his team show repeatedly that by engaging hundreds of staff in a common experience, they will learn far more, more quickly than using conventional lecture based learning. During such experiential learning sessions there's a lot more going on than it may appear. Participants build relationships with colleagues as they work on a common problem. Sessions are often deliberately designed to ensure participants make mistakes. And by forcing everyone to believe there is a time limit, they undergo a carefully choreographed period of stress. This brings out the best (and sometimes the worst) from the group. Much of the time individuals are so wrapped up in the game they do not even realise what they are learning. The learning is sub-conscious.

It is only when a skilled trainer de-briefs such an experience that the participants gain a clear understanding of what they learned. Indeed, the best trainers facilitate a structured discussion with the participants so they tell each other what was learned. The trainer acts merely as a conduit. This is often so much more effective than a teacher or trainer spouting forth in a lecture based lesson.

As we grow into adults we become afraid of looking foolish or making mistakes. But making mistakes is an integral part of the learning process. Find more ways to make mistakes within your learning - not less. You will learn more. Make the mistakes in a safe environment. Learn from other students - increased collaboration is a marvellous learning tool. In school it was called cheating! So steal with pride.

Accelerated learning

Dr. Georgi Lozanov, a Bulgarian psychologist conducted extensive research over 30 years ago into sub-conscious learning and super memory. He successfully developed a system for what has become known as 'accelerated' or 'suggestopedic' learning. Learning language is particularly effective using his methods which involve listening to classical (predominantly Baroque) music to help accelerate the learning process. Three types of music are recommended to specially prepare the mind for an optimum state of relaxed alertness. The rhythm of the second music selection is then used to accompany a reading of the material to be learned. This is known as the 'active concert' stage of the Lozanov method. Finally, to baroque accompaniment, the 'passive concert' provides a background while the material to be learned is read again, facilitating its transfer into long term memory. The learning material comprises illustrated picture book stories, with the English story text written alongside the foreign language being learned. For more information on this fascinating and widely acclaimed method for learning, read *Learning in the 21st Century* by Colin Rose of Accelerated Learning Systems.

NLP

No serious discussion of learning would be complete without reference to NLP (Neuro Linguistic Programming). NLP has been described in many ways; from being the 'martial art of communication' to 'psychological skills for understanding and influencing people'. It is an invaluable aid to learning. Developed by Richard Bandler and John Grinder in the 1970's they set out to find and define ways to reproduce at will through copying (or 'modelling' as its known in NLP terms) the qualities shared by the most successful individuals in all fields. NLP provides individuals with the knowledge to model excellence in others. It is particularly powerful in helping people to understand how they and others perceive their respective worlds.

In simple terms, NLP research shows that everyone interprets their life in predominantly either an auditory, visual or kinaesthetic way. What does this mean? Well, an auditory person will interpret a situation based on what they hear, while a kinaesthetic individual will process the same situation based on their gut feeling or their instinct. Someone who is predominantly visual, trying to communicate with someone who is predominantly auditory will be on a different wavelength. Just imagine the confusion between a husband and wife if the husband was visual while the wife was kinaesthetic. To show her affection she will want to hug and be cuddled - while he may find this uncomfortable; he just wants to step back to enjoy the view. He will want to show his love by buying her things and taking her to interesting places. She won't be impressed - all she wants is affection. To show her affection she will want to get close to him - to hold him. This will make him uncomfortable - especially if it takes place in a public place!

It does not follow that all men are visual and all women are kinaesthetic. For example, I am predominantly kinaesthetic while Frankie, my wife, is auditory. I know that when I want her to feel loved, flowers won't mean as much to her as a good conversation. When explaining this to friends, someone quickly pointed out that she couldn't be that auditory because she would always prefer a meal in a good restaurant. True - she doesn't over eat but loves good food. But to her, a meal in a restaurant represents a perfect opportunity for a long and meaningful conversation.

The person who can switch at will to match the preferred method (or 'modality' as it's called in NLP) of understanding used by the people they are communicating with, can raise his/her communication skill and rapport to a much higher level. You can see (if you are visual) how important it is to understand how you and others think. By understanding these fundamentals, you will be able to develop the most appropriate ways for you to learn.

If you want to know more about how to identify these fundamental differences between people and learn to communicate with others at a far deeper level, NLP skills are invaluable. What has just been described, represents just one tiny aspect of NLP - it is a fascinating subject and worthy of further investigation. Some useful books are listed at the end of this book.

Preparing to learn a new skill or subject

In *The Experiential Learning Theory of Career Development*, authors Kolb and Plovnick defined an effective cycle of learning; thinking and understanding, deciding, planning, doing and reviewing. This leads you back to more thinking and understanding and so on. This book can't tell you what to learn, but if you are setting out to improve your enjoyment or employability, it is worth investing some time in deciding what to learn before jumping headlong into a learning programme. This can be done by answering the following questions;

- Ask around, find out what you should learn.
- Is the subject itself becoming obsolete or are the available courses sufficiently up-to-date?
- Why do you want to learn?
- How will you benefit from this knowledge? What are the tangible benefits you will gain from your new learning? Be as specific as you can.
- How can you picture a successful outcome to your learning?
- Define a timescale - how long will it take you to learn the new skills?
- Write down what you are setting out to learn and why that particular knowledge is important to you.
- Gain a clear understanding of the larger picture of the subject.
- What do you already know about it? Write it down.
- Make a list of who you know who can help you understand more about the subject. List teachers, librarians, Internet websites, usenet groups.
- Which books are available from work, your local library or bookstores?
- Where else can you look for information?
- Find others (friends and colleagues) who are also interested in learning more about your chosen subject. Collaborate with them as much as possible.
- Organise informal meetings to share information.
- Who runs courses on your subject?
- How much of the subject will be taught and at what depth or level?
- Learning is about asking questions. Take a tip from professional interviewers; ask as many questions as possible about the subject. Initially, write them down as quickly as possible. Then invest some time thinking about more questions. Keep adding them to your question list. When

you think you have covered the subject with your questions delete, edit and rearrange them before setting out to find the answers. This technique is great for putting you in an inquiring frame of mind.

- Try to imagine how you would teach the information and knowledge to others.
- Spend just a few minutes recapping and summarising after a learning session to gain the best effects of learning. Re-visit the material the following day, a week later and a month later.
- Make an appointment with yourself by entering the above task into your diary or day planner.
- How can you organise your life to incorporate sufficient time for learning?

If you are still not sure what to learn, then start with becoming computer literate. Find out how to use professional word processors, spreadsheets, databases, design and publishing software, image and text scanners. Learn how to copy and move files to and from computers. Become proficient at sending and receiving files via the Internet. And last but not least, invest time in learning how to find useful and valuable information on the Internet and online databases. Your familiarity with the tools needed to find relevant information will become a key skill in the decades to come.

If you have never used a computer and are afraid of the technology for what ever reason, you MUST overcome it. Your fears are as groundless as someone telling you they are afraid to learn to read or write. Computer literacy is essential for anyone who wants to be employable in the 21st century.

Next, focus your learning in areas such as how to work better as part of a team, how to be a leader (there are already too many people on the job market who know how to manage, the trouble is, fewer people need to be managed). Anything that teaches you to communicate more effectively in written or spoken form is worth an investment of your time; so consider business writing, public speaking and presentation skills training. Don't limit yourself to skills training which is of direct use to you today - think ahead and assess the value of such knowledge in one, two or five years time.

If your employer will not pay for all your training, try to negotiate a contribution. Perhaps you will have to pay for it yourself. But your training is your responsibility. If you have little or no money, volunteer to help those with the knowledge you want on the condition they will share their knowledge with you. Don't assume someone will refuse such a deal. Think creatively about how to gain new knowledge. If you cannot afford to buy books on your chosen subjects, don't forget your local libraries.

Learning from books

Based on recommendations from others, find the three best books on your subject.

Skim read first; use the contents pages to gain an over view of the subject. With any non-fiction book, only read what is relevant - be selective. Look for the broad ideas and concepts. Unless you have the time or are completely gripped, you don't have to slavishly read every word, page by page in a linear fashion. If the book belongs to you, forget what you may have been told as a child and write your own notes in it - make it your own by using a coloured text marker to highlight the most valuable ideas and information. Make notes in the margins and develop your own coded notes to highlight particularly important information. At the end of each chapter summarise what you have learned. Re-visit the book a few days later and again a week later to re-read your text marked notes to refresh your mind and so improve the likelihood that the information will transfer into your long term memory.

Before buying 'how-to' or non-fiction books give it what I call 'The three paragraph test'. Select three paragraphs at random throughout the book - if any of those paragraphs merely tell you the obvious and do not go on to explain in full detail what you must do to initiate a change or improvement - move on to another title.

Start a company library

Does your organisation have a reference library with books, multimedia packages, audio and video taped programmes on all aspects of your industry sector? If not, persuade your superiors to create one. Even the smallest of businesses are putting together small business libraries - it need not cost much. Training courses can be expensive - the cost of good books is substantially less.

How to read more effectively: 'scanning & skimming' versus 'word by word'

How are you reading this book? Are you reading every word, line by line? Can you hear an internal voice saying each word? Or are you scanning and skimming each page for the most useful and interesting nuggets of information, just like when you read a newspaper or magazine? If you read everything word by word - you are a slow reader. Typically you will read at 200-400 words per minute. An 80,000 word book will therefore require a time investment of 3-6 hours. This is how we are taught in junior school - for many people they never un-learn this method. However, if you chose to read this book by skimming and scanning you would finish it far more quickly. But would you understand it or derive as much interest or pleasure from a book if you read it quickly? Probably not, but there are many letters, reports and publications which do not justify a slow and time consuming reading method. By learning to differentiate between what to read slowly and what to skim, you can increase the amount of material you read.

Learning how to increase the speed of your reading whilst still capturing its meaning is an essential component of 'learning to learn'. Word for word reading has severe limitations for anyone seeking to improve their learning. Active learners develop ways to read and retain information quickly. We read a wide variety of materials; some are more important than others. Reading at one speed for everything is not the best use of your limited time.

Don't get me wrong, I don't want you to skim through every page of this book - but I reason it's better for you to do that than not read it at all. The table of contents contains a detailed description of how you will benefit from reading each chapter. The text has been designed to include isolated quotes to stimulate and attract a skim reader's attention. Numerous sub-headings further break up the overall appearance of each page, which helps the reader to pick up the gist of what it is about without having to read all of it. Speed-reading instruction books and software manuals, almost guarantees you will either not understand it or you will miss vital information. Read such material very slowly!

Where to find learning time

We have only so much time in which to learn new things. Learning is too often fitted in around what seem to be more immediate and pressing issues. This is why learning time is being built in to many high grade jobs. Global consultancies which sell knowledge have come to realise the importance of training. Companies such as Arthur Andersen & Co. invest 6% of their annual revenue on training - that's an estimated $300 million each year.

Travelling time is a perfect opportunity to learn. Whilst researching and writing this chapter, I made a point of trying to study what people did whilst travelling on trains and the underground in London. Only a tiny minority were using the time productively. Most sit or stand silent and motionless, in a near-hypnotic state, staring blankly into space - with or without musical accompaniment from a Walkman. Most readers, tend to have a newspaper - my theory is that this is more a way of 'filling their time' rather than learning about the news. Buying a newspaper becomes a daily habit - a national paper on the way to work, the evening paper on the way home. They will invariably watch or listen to the news before leaving home and settle down to TV news when they return - that's a hell of a lot of daily news! Some of that time could easily be devoted to learning new skills. But not if it is perceived as work.

This is a crucial point. Most people feel that they work too hard as it is. When they travel to and from work, they just want to switch off. Use your travelling time more productively - reading a book while driving is not recommended! But there is a huge choice of material on audio tape.

Mentoring - a case study

High performing athletes cannot achieve greatness merely through working and training on their own. They need coaches and mentors; people who can provide them with guidance, encouragement and inspiration to achieve superior results in their lives. The value and power of a good coach or mentor is awesome.

Few doubt Linford Christie's prowess as an athlete. Winner of the Gold Medal at the Barcelona Olympic games in 1992, he reached the pinnacle of his athletics success. But why is Linford Christie so successful on the running track while his brother, Russell Christie, was murdered for being involved in crime and drug dealing? Is it simply talent or is there more to it? For Linford, overriding ambition and a devotion to fulfilling his childhood goal has played a significant part. Christie says, *"Ever since I was a child, I wanted to be the fastest man on Earth. My ambition has always been to be the greatest athlete Britain has produced."* This is, I'm sure, an ambition shared by many athletes, but he has guaranteed a place in history by making his dream come true. He has won more medals at international championships than any other male athlete in Britain. He has been honoured as Sportsman of the Year.

Christie has a reputation for being incredibly self-focused in his approach to winning races. Television pictures of him in the last few minutes before the 100 metre final in Barcelona showed a man who was totally oblivious to what was going on around him - his steely concentration was so intense that it was said at the time that he was "stoned on adrenaline". Nothing was going to distract him. In his mind he had won the race even before it had started. The prospect of defeat was unthinkable. Everything he had trained for culminated in what he was about to do. His determination was unmistakable. Any runner in that race could have won, but Christie controlled the intense pressure and channelled it in a positive way. All too often in other areas of human endeavour, what makes the difference between outstanding achievement and mediocrity is the way a person handles the pressure of the moment. After all, everyone gets butterflies in the stomach during such times - the secret is to get them to fly in formation.

After the race he talked about his "tunnel vision", concentrating only on the running lane in front of him.

Frank Dick, the British National Director of Coaching, has stressed the importance of mental power saying that the quality which separates winners from losers "*... is what goes on behind the eyes*".

It was Christie's attitude which made the difference and gave him the winning advantage over his rival athletes. Having programmed his mind to "visualise" a successful outcome, he was in control of the situation.

But it was only six hundredths of a second, or less than the blink of an eye, which stood him apart from Leroy Burrell of the United states, who came second.

Later that day, Christie summed up what really made the difference by saying, "*Without Ron I would never have achieved what I have achieved today*". He was talking about Ron Roddan, his coach and mentor for the previous 13 years. He would not have achieved such fame, adulation and income had it not been for Ron's work.

On many occasions since his victory at the Olympics, Christie has commented about the time Ron persuaded him not to retire after coming only fourth in the World Championships in Tokyo in 1991. If he had given up then, he would never have won the Olympic gold. Roddan successfully instilled in Christie the need to train. Christie's now believes "*If you don't train, you don't perform,*" but it hasn't always been like that for him. "*My problem was that I thought I had all the natural talent in the world and did not need to train*" he went on to add "*If Ron announced a long or tough session, I would simply not do it. I would go to Mick's cafe near the track and play dominoes.*"

It took a written ultimatum from Roddan in 1985 to jolt Christie into taking his sprinting more seriously. Apparently the letter told Christie that if he wanted to keep him as his trainer, he had better buck up his ideas and start serious training. It worked. The next year, in Madrid, Christie won the Gold Medal at the European indoor 200 metres. The show down obviously proved to be a turning point in Christie's career.

Roddan says, "*I have been successful with Linford because of the many years I have worked with him. I have got to know him better than he knows himself. He sees me more than he sees his mother or father. I know what he wants from himself, so if or when things go wrong, it's human nature to doubt yourself. It is my job to re-convince him that he can achieve these goals. You have to believe in yourself, and have faith that you can do what you set out to achieve. I trained Linford to learn to think he was running in a* tunnel. *He was not allowed to think about anybody or anything else. He moved on a specific stimulus, which in that case was the sound of a gun. All his training in the past five to ten years is geared to that. It isn't something you can learn overnight. As in life, if you start to doubt yourself, it is like a cancer - it just burrows its way into you, ultimately destroying an individual. But it's also essential to remember not to focus just on your work. Linford still has a good social life - athletics is just one part of his life, albeit an important part."*

Christie learned the hard way that success is only possible if you are willing to put in enough time, commitment and effort to achieve your goals. It is so easy to forget that, although he has experienced failure and dealt with massive disappointments, at each setback he has picked himself up and trained even harder to fulfil his overriding ambition.

How many people give up when the going gets tough in their own area of work? They all want the personal success, the rewards and the acclaim, but are so often unwilling to put in the effort required to achieve the desired result - if indeed, they have clarified in their minds the specific results they actually want.

Christie says *"I came to Britain as a West Indian immigrant to become captain of the British Athletics team and that is the greatest achievement one can ever make. When I win, I win for my country."*

Linford Christie MBE has inspired millions to achieve more in their lives. Simultaneously he has made a major impact on improving racial integration in this country. Ron Roddan said *"Everyone needs someone who they can trust whole-heartedly. Some agents and managers work purely for money. I don't believe it's the best way to gain the greatest longer-term benefits for someone. For me, I'm satisfied if any athlete I coach achieves a PB (a personal best). It doesn't matter what standard they are, if they perform better than they have done in the past and feel they can do better in the future, I'm happy."*

If someone with Linford Christie's talent needs a coach and mentor, surely that is a strong enough argument for the rest of us finding one? We can all benefit from having a Ron Roddan to coach us through life. Find one for yourself and reap the benefits.

Finding a coach and mentor

More and more individuals are turning to mentors to help improve their performance. But how do you go about finding a coach and mentor? Actively seek advice from knowledgeable people. Who are the people who stand out as experts in your field? Who are your closest friends and colleagues? Perhaps you had a close working relationship with a former boss? Re-connect with that person, if you have not spoken to them in a while.

In the unlikely event that mentors cannot be found from these sources, ask individuals to recommend others who may be prepared to help you. You do not need to limit yourself to one person.

Most people respond well to a professional and courteous request for help and advice. However, be aware that consultants earn their living by sharing knowledge and expertise. Do not abuse them by seeking 'free' advice. A growing number of experienced consultants are becoming professional mentors to business executives. Some describe themselves as 'reflective agents'. As a detached third party, they are used as sounding boards on subjects and issues which, because of their confidential nature, cannot easily be discussed within an organisation.

The best mentors do not get physically involved in tasks - their function is to guide, question and support you when you need it. You can learn from their behaviour, ways of working and where they find information. In return, find ways to add value to the mentor; and become a mentor to others.

Who you get advice from is one of the keys to your future success. There is little point in listening to those people who have never made it themselves. Indeed, listening to the wrong people will hold you back. Don't choose a mentor who does not 'walk their talk'.

By constantly soaking up useful and specialist knowledge, anyone can increase their value to clients, employers, family and friends. In the next decades you can amass valuable knowledge. Everything you learn is constantly added to your databank of knowledge. Invest the time in learning things your employers perceive to have a high tangible value, and you need never go hungry or unemployed. Every individual with average intelligence can benefit from deliberately increasing their knowledge in 'high value' subjects.

Think of your formal education as the bare minimum required to equip yourself for future success. Past failure does not ensure future failure. Likewise, past success does not guarantee future success. Gathering and applying specific information and knowledge will provide you with a significant advantage in an increasingly competitive workforce. Find and invest the time to learn new skills on a continual basis.

I don't have anything against academia, but our education system must transform itself to stop churning out batches of students who are not fully equipped to deliver the needs of the workplace. Teachers and professors are often skilled at teaching what they know, but what's the point if society needs something else? It's the same as a manufacturer producing large batches of products no one wants to buy. Ploughing more and more money into improving the production process to deliver more products (or students) is going to be a waste of money if customers still don't want what they have on offer. If a company insists on such behaviour, eventually it will go out of business. If the education system does the same, the country will collapse.

This is my challenge to government, the education establishment and teachers: Any school, college or university which turns out a student with no desire to continue his/her learning has failed in its professional duties. Until the educational system inspires students to adopt continuous learning as a lifetime skill, it is both failing our students and our country.

Chapter 5
Your Money and Your Life

Money isn't everything:
usually it isn't even enough.
Anon

If anybody ever tells you that they are not interested in money, don't trust them - because if they will lie about that, they will lie about anything! For some readers, this chapter may be the most important in this book. Which readers? Well, I'm writing about you if you find the subject of money uncomfortable, unduly stressful, or feel that you're too busy to learn about it.

In this chapter we will take a close look at our complex (and often emotionally highly charged) relationship with money. We've never earned so much - but never have we saved so little. The myriad ways we currently earn, spend and invest our hard-earned cash will be covered, as well as the likely impact new technology will have on the way we receive and spend money in the decades to come.

How millionaires do it

For over 20 years, Thomas J Stanley and William D Danko have researched and studied the habits and lifestyles of America's millionaires. The overriding characteristic shared by most wealthy people is that they tend to be frugal. They spend less than those who just try to appear to be wealthy. Genuinely wealthy people have little to prove. Some of Stanley & Danko's findings from interviews with five hundred millionaires for their book *The Millionaire Next Door* include:

- A non-ostentatious lifestyle totally at odds with the "wealth myth" perpetuated by television and glossy magazines
- People with high consumption lifestyles tend to have few if any income generating investments
- More than 80% of the millionaires they interviewed have created their own wealth and live within their means
- Most are not into "social status" and expensive "toys"
- Many of those who live in large, expensive houses, with luxury cars parked in the driveway, are not actually that wealthy
- Wealthy people tend not to live in "expensive" areas. They save money by living in cheaper areas and use the savings to increase their investments

- They are not necessarily more intelligent, but possess self-discipline, perseverance and a focused approach
- Wealthy people are committed to planning their finances, the authors noticed a strong correlation between the amount of financial planning and wealth
- About 65% are self-employed
- Each and every year, they invest about 20% of their income
- Most are in what the authors describe as "dull-normal" industries
- Each has built up a reserve fund so that they do not need to work for the next 10 years or more
- The majority set short, medium and long term goals
- They budget for food, holidays and clothing etc.
- Only 25% own a new car

Stanley and Danko's findings are not particularly glamorous. Rather than "get rich quick", they discovered that successful people prefer to "get rich slowly". You can't be a high spender and become a millionaire at the same time. Who is better off? A high earner who spends it all each year, or someone who earns less, but invests some of it wisely? It isn't the first person.

The message is clear: if you want to be financially secure in the 21st century, spend less than you earn and learn to assume full responsibility for your own spending, saving and investments. This can only be achieved by studying money. Get into the habit of asking lots of questions of people who really know about money. Listen to many people. You'll probably discover that some of the 'experts' you listen to aren't actually that knowledgeable. Ask around for recommendations of books on financial subjects of particular interest to you. The first book you should get on this subject is the US bestseller *Your Money or Your Life* by Joe Dominguez and Vicki Robin. It's fantastic.

Ask your financial adviser lots of dumb questions. If you don't have an adviser, find one and choose him/her carefully. Refer to "Choosing an Adviser" later in this chapter.

Does all this learning about money involve effort? You bet! It's certainly easier not to bother. And that's precisely why most people don't.

Canadian futurist Richard Worzel describes six stages of adult life;
1. Entry into the labour force where young workers earn little money, and start to take out small loans
2. Home buyers in their late twenties to early thirties who earn more but take on mortgages and other debts
3. 35-45 year olds who pay off debts and borrow less and start saving more.

4. Heavy savers 45-55 year olds at the peak of their earnings. They start to get ill, but devote attention to retirement planning. Some inherit money.
5. Pre-retirement 55-65 year olds. Saving as much as possible.
6. Retirement 65+. Incomes drop significantly.

Live long and prosper

How would you or your family cope if you end up living too long or die too soon?

For the first time in history, with existing medicine, healthcare and technology, you are likely to live to a ripe old age if you look after yourself. According to official figures, our life expectancy is increasing by 2 years every decade. In 1900, a baby boy at birth could expect to live until the age of 45.5 years, a baby girl - 49. In just 20 years time, the average life expectancy for men could increase from the current 74 to 78, while women could increase from 79 to 83. When 'baby boomers' born in the late 1940's and 50's reach old age in the next 10 to 20 years, there will be too many of them for whatever government is in power to be able to afford to pay out their pensions. Today and in the years to come, there will be fewer young workers. This means that the pension money invested by these younger workers will not be enough to pay for the pensions of those reaching retirement. Millions could end up being cheated out of their state pensions because there isn't enough cash in the 'pot'.

So just because your parents and grandparents didn't save and invest is not a good enough excuse for you to ignore the subject. Many of our ancestors didn't live long enough to worry about it!

Those approaching old age today will probably get caught during the forthcoming transition period. Without adequate financial planning many are statistically more likely to run out of money before they run out of steam - so instead of your parents leaving you an inheritance, they are more likely to use it all up and look to you for financial help in their old age. How could you refuse? But where would the cash come from?

No government can afford to pay pensions to individuals who live too long. Present state pensions are woefully inadequate, and the situation will continue to deteriorate. Anyone who expects to live off a state pension in their old age can expect to live out their final years in dire poverty. This is not the fault of government but a result of a healthier population. As the baby boomers, who represent approximately nine million Britons now aged between 32-52, will start collecting their pensions over the next few decades. The costs of care for the elderly will also escalate significantly. It has already started to happen with a 20% increase in the number of social workers from 1990 to 1995 (794,000 to 964,000), mostly caring for the elderly.

Extension of the retirement age to 70 is already being discussed. For women, it has already been increased from 60 to 65. Schemes to make saving or a secondary private pension compulsory are also being explored. Chile and Australia already have compulsory savings schemes. This would lighten the crippling costs of pension provision, but think for a moment about other consequences if old people have financial problems. When they cannot afford to 'retire' they will need to continue working. Older and more experienced (and therefore more expensive) workers are already being 'let go' by companies and replaced by sophisticated technology operated by less people, most of whom are younger and less experienced, and therefore cheaper. What will happen to those older people who are unable to keep their jobs, but who have to wait to qualify for the pension they have paid for all their working lives? And what about the young people who find it so difficult to find a job in the first place? With older individuals being forced to cling onto their jobs for longer, opportunities for younger workers will become more scarce. Unemployment benefit is being reduced, and whilst inexpensive healthcare is expected by an ageing population, the actual cost of providing it is increasing. There will be more old people in society, therefore they will have more influence over politicians. Young people will miss out - again.

Since about 1948, when the modern welfare state was created with the formation of The National Health Service, successive governments have tried to protect those who are old, ill and unemployed. And rightly so - to a point. As a consequence we have created today's dependency culture. The provisions of the welfare state have extended far beyond the original intentions of the safety net described in the pre-Second World War Beveridge Report. In the decades to come, politicians will be compelled to find ways of encouraging or even forcing more individuals to become less reliant on the state, even if those same people deeply believe they are unable to cope. Some who genuinely cannot cope will almost certainly suffer even more as a result. Opposition parties and the media will inevitably 'find and display' individuals who are 'unfairly' suffering at the hands of what they will describe as an unsympathetic government. All the better for the media if the government in question is a socialist one, who will be derided for not caring enough. We are entering a radical period in our history. It will involve financial pain for many many people. Financial self-reliance is the only answer.

These problems are largely unknown in Asia where people have to fend for themselves. Asian governments are either unable, or refuse to assume the role of 'parent'. Western governments are slowly realising that they too must pass responsibility back to the individual. The present Labour government has an onerous task ahead of itself. How can any socialist government be seen to reduce benefits to individuals who now regard such pay outs as their 'right'? Being a British politician in the next 20 years will be particularly difficult.

So, what will you live on in your old age? Or do you think you are too young to worry much about it? Perhaps you suspect you have already left it too late? With so many opportunities for 'fun', a huge array of consumer goods to choose from and with living expenses representing a high proportion of their often meagre earnings, it's a rare (or as some perceive, a boring!) young person who actively saves and invests from an early age. But boring or not, future wealth and financial security can only be created by spending less, and saving and investing wisely. This requires knowledge and a fundamental re-think about how we all earn, spend, save and invest our money.

Money and emotion

Money is one of the most important subjects in our lives. However, whenever there is talk about it, we respond as individuals in a wide variety of emotional ways. Most people do not understand enough about what money can, and should provide them with. Your parents' views on money are likely to have influenced yours. Many people have a 'bad' relationship with money and feel uncomfortable about it. This often means that whenever anyone starts to discuss money in a detailed way, they switch off. They do not want to face a situation which makes them feel even worse about money.

For anyone who is serious about surviving the 21st century, looking after yourself financially is a crucial topic; a subject which we tend to learn about by trial and error - if you are like most people, mainly by error! Learning the intricacies of what money can do is something which few of us are ever taught.

Charles Dicken's book David Copperfield was written over one hundred years ago. Mr. Micawber said,

"Annual income twenty pounds, annual expenditure nineteen pounds nineteen and sixpence, result happiness. Annual income twenty pounds, annual expenditure twenty pounds ought and six, result misery".

The size of the sums involved may have changed dramatically but the concept remains accurate today. Spend more than you earn and you will suffer. Spend less than you earn and do something useful with the balance and you are more likely to live a debt and stress-free life.

Earning

You are what you earn. No salary, you are worthless. A low salary means you are inadequate. You can only be successful and powerful if you are paid a high salary. What crap! We know and reject this on one level, but we accept it on just about every other. If we do not receive money for our labours, that work is usually dismissed as unimportant. What we earn is perceived as important; to others and to ourselves. We believe it provides us with a clear signal about our 'worth'. Countless women (and a tiny but growing number of men) do not receive any money, other than through state benefits for bringing up their families. Therefore it goes unrewarded. Merely telling a spouse that it is appreciated means nothing. Partners who really value their spouses tend to create saving plans which they put in the non-earner's name.

Less than 10% of women have pensions in their own right. With an increasing number of marriages ending in divorce, women who do not protect themselves financially risk potential hardship, even disaster. Women who work full or part time and spend most if not all of their earnings on 'the family' are making a grave, albeit well meaning mistake.

Dr JS Hughson once delivered a radio sermon on why he would choose to be an insurance salesman if he was not a minister. He said *"Every time a young man comes before me at the altar to marry I feel like telling him of the many benefits to be derived from Life Insurance ownership. A young man has no right to take a girl from a position where she may be earning her own living and tie her down with a family that would make it difficult for her to earn a livelihood again - unless he can give her adequate protection and security if anything should happen to him."*

According to money expert Steve Crowley in his book *Money For Life* most people are only three pay cheques away from potential bankruptcy. Are you?
*   If your income stopped today - how long would it be before your regular on-going weekly or monthly expenses cleared you out?
*   How much do you earn (apart from 'not enough')? If you are in full time employment it is relatively easy - just look at your pay cheque and sigh or cry! Self-employed people are rarely able to answer this question.
*   How much do you earn per hour? This is not the same as how much you 'charge' per hour. It should be based on the total number of hours you work - including commuting time, overtime, 'compulsory' business related hospitality and the time spent travelling on business. Divide those hours by your total take home pay - you will discover that your real hourly rate is far less than you think - and certainly less than you believe you are worth.

Time is money, but what's the value of your 'life energy'?

One of the most powerful concepts in the book *Your Money or Your Life* is how money is provided in return for what the authors describe as your 'life energy'. We are all given life energy during our time on this planet. How much 'life energy' are you prepared to give away in return for money? By calculating the value of each unit of your life energy - each hour of your life which is devoted to paid employment - you can learn its value to you.

Everything is paid for in 'time'. What you receive for your time is used to purchase the results of the time invested by product manufacturers and service providers. When you are persuaded to buy something you are effectively swapping the money you have received in return for your time.

Survival in the 21st century for men and women requires a totally new way of thinking about the money which flows in and out of your life. Instead of constantly thinking and worrying about your income it is highly recommended that you shift your focus towards how you spend your income rather than what you earn. Obviously, this does not mean that your income is not important! To create a financial future - it is essential to be fully aware of how money flows into and out of your life. Think of the money you spend in a conscious way. Here are some points to get you thinking:

- How much would you have to earn in order to stop worrying about money?
- If you want to become financially secure, what are you prepared to do about it?
- What do you need to do to improve your knowledge, and therefore confidence about dealing with money for your longer term financial security?
- How much money do you really need to earn to feel that it is enough?
- Enough for what?
- Are you only working to pay for more material possessions?
- How much have you earned from the very first penny you received as pocket money?
- What have you got to show for it?

We have been fed on the myth that the more money we earn, the happier we will become. This is a vital lie. Think about the last time you were really happy, the chances are that money had little to do with it. It is only when you have enough can you be happy. But what is enough? If you do not know the answer, or are unable and unwilling to find out, you can never truly be happy.

Many people will never earn 'enough' even though their salaries may be high. We lay great emphasis on the size of our salary, although in reality its size is not that important - it's how much of your salary you retain which counts.

Your life as a leaky colander

Perhaps you and certainly millions of others have lives like a huge leaking colander - constantly pouring money into the top to see so much of it pour out of the bottom into the buckets of everyone jostling for position below, making more for those who already have more than you! The lives of millions of people are focused on earning the money to pour into the colander. A 21st century survivor will plug up many of those holes. It is easy to see how sensible this is - but it's not so easy when it comes to doing something about it. We'll look at simple and effective ways to do this in a moment.

Sadly, in society we tend to describe ourselves or get described in the context of what we do, rather than who we are and our salary is closely linked to this. Western society focuses on how much you 'earn' - what you pay into the bank is described as your disposable income. In Asia and the Far East, you are taught from an early age to save regularly and invest the time to learn about money. Savings are described as 'discretionary' rather than 'disposable' - a subtle but big difference.

Conventional wisdom states: If you have a low salary you cannot be rich - if you have a high salary you cannot be poor. But this is not true. If you earn a great deal but are up to your ears in debt you can easily be worse off than someone whose earnings may be more meagre by comparison, but who lives within their means.

Spending

In the 1960's, psychologist Walter Mischel conducted a series of behavioural experiments on the campus of Stanford University. Groups of four to five year olds were given a choice; if they were prepared to wait for up to 20 minutes (and we all know how long that is for someone so young), they would be given two biscuits. However, if they chose not to wait, they could have one biscuit immediately - but they wouldn't receive a second one. These same kids were interviewed about 14 years later. There was a fascinating result. Those individuals who had been willing and able to wait for the second biscuit were more successful and had higher grades at school and college. They were generally happier and less stressed. How easy do you find it to delay gratification?

How we counter the intense and sustained efforts of society to 'give in' to our impulses will ultimately influence our longer-term happiness and financial security. We are constantly sold the idea "Those with the most toys - wins!" Buy that bar of chocolate. Buy those designer clothes. Buy that new car. Buy that bigger house. We are surrounded by advertisements and peer pressure to spend our money on products and services which promise to make us happier, feel more fulfilled and satisfied. Everything is geared towards instant gratification. Buy now - don't deprive yourself, you deserve it now. Go on. But will it really do you any good in the long run or make you feel better?

Notice how many advertisements implore you to act immediately. If we spend our money on these material things and we do not feel happier or more fulfilled - it's obvious what the problem is, we didn't spend enough!! Get out your wallet!

The birth of dissatisfied consumers

In the 1920's, for the first time, factory production in the United States outstripped real demand. The population had to be persuaded to buy more so those factories could operate at full capacity and make the most profit. What began was the development of the dissatisfied consumer. Until this time, home produced food, clothing and furniture was common place. A great deal of pride was attached to many of these products. A friend, Christine Johnston, remembers as a little girl wishing that her family could have 'proper frozen peas' like her friends, instead of those boring ones in pods that her dad grew in the garden!

Manufacturers and advertisers deliberately set out to make people feel dissatisfied if they did not own factory produced articles. Advertisers have systematically conditioned people since into believing that unless they owned new, factory-made products they were, by definition, failures in life. No one who was successful would ever make something when it could be bought. They were taught through consistent advertising to 'keep up with the Joneses'. If they didn't, their standards of living would not be as good as their neighbours - and that would NEVER do! To pay for all these new consumer products everyone had to work longer hours, thereby minimising the time available to make their own goods - so even if they wanted to be frugal, they no longer had the time. So began a pattern of business around the world that still continues; use whatever it takes to persuade potential customers to hand over their money. Children are routinely targeted to demand the latest toys and fashionable clothes from their parents. It doesn't seem to concern certain manufacturers that this creates untold stress and financial hardship for those they have identified as potential buyers.

Youth culture in particular demands the latest fashionable clothes and 'sports' shoes. It is sad to see so many young inner city teenagers caught up in what is the most vicious and cruel con by clothing manufacturers. Kids from poor families insist on wearing top designer brands - which inevitably involves paying well over the odds for the 'privilege' of wearing the manufacturer's logos on any part of their body large enough to show it. For some, it leads to the theft of such articles, or stealing money to purchase them. Intense pressure within schools to 'outperform' classmates by what they wear often puts untold financial pressure on parents. This is further fuelled by callous manufacturers who hike the prices of their goods, or introduce specially created brand names for this market. In order to maintain their high profits and so-called 'exclusivity' of their top brands, they create cheaper, but over-priced versions. Indeed, you can tell how exclusive a product is by the size of the logo. **The larger the logo - the less exclusive.**

One way you can create financial security for yourself is by refusing to buy any clothing which features a company logo. Incidentally, many of these clothes and shoes are manufactured in 'sweat shop' conditions in under-developed countries such as Indonesia where workers are abused, exploited and forced to work long hours for meagre pay.

You, a cash crop

Farmers prepare the ground, feeding and watering the land; investing their time and energy in order to reap their harvest. Responsible farmers ensure they never deplete the soil or harvest the crops too soon. But this is not always the case in the wider commercial world.

Herculean efforts go into surrounding us with advertising (it is, after all some of the most expensive and carefully produced manure in the world and costs British consumers an additional £10.9 billion a year). This advertising is drip fed to us through the complex and expensive irrigation system called 'the media'. At the first signs of growth of our financial fleece - in other words as soon as we have some cash in our pockets - snip! snip! "We'll have that, thank you very much!", they say.

Throughout our lives we are cultivated like a cash crop. We are all 'harvested' of our cash on a daily, weekly, monthly and annual basis by those who claim to have a stake in our lives. If others choose to spend money on cultivating us with their ideas, products and services, irrespective of what we may feel about them, they will do what ever they can, for as long as they choose, to extract a return on what they consider is their 'investment'.

Ridiculous? How can you seriously think that we can be compared to a piece of fruit, an egg laying hen, a sheep or a vegetable? You are right - it is ridiculous. But it was the advertising industry which coined the phrase "couch potato" when describing habitual TV viewers! Logically we are all aware of just how much effort goes into persuading us to part with our hard earned cash. It's better not to think about it - so we don't. We work to spend, which means we must continue to work. It is a vicious and costly circle. Shopping is actually regarded as a leisure activity by many. An estimated 4% of the population would describe themselves as 'shopaholics'. How often do you go for a 'look round the shops', shopping for nothing in particular?

We just muddle through, trying not to look at our bank and credit card statements for too long. As for the remaining balance on our mortgage - that's enough to send us into deep depression - we might even be tempted to go out shopping again, to make us feel a bit better. It's jokingly called 'retail therapy'.

The advertising industry learned a long time ago, through its constant and expensive research, that people spend more when they feel unhappy. It therefore makes commercial sense for advertisers to make you feel bad about yourself. Advertising agencies know that if they bombard people for long enough with images of affluence and beauty, they'll make people think about why they don't have all those things or look as good as the flawless models used to promote such products. Making us feel bad, or helping us to realise that we do not feel good, is part of a tried and tested method of inducing us to spend more. Make the potential buyers feel bad about themselves and then provide them with the answer - the product. Sales people describe this technique as 'hurt and rescue'.

"Spend yourself to happiness," is the promise. It's a lie. More and more people are regularly spending more than they earn. This includes governments as well as individuals and it's a recipe for disaster. According to *The Economist* in 1997, The United States has the highest GDP (Gross Domestic Product) in the world ($8431 billion) followed by Japan (at $4545 billion). But the United States has a deficit of $103.9 billion for its 258 million inhabitants. The US has been over-spending to an alarming degree. But the US government is great at its own public relations and appears so affluent. A former Republican Congressman recently told me that the level of debt is nearly $180,000 for each American citizen!

Owning more is not the answer if you want to be a survivor in the decades to come. You can spend less and feel better about yourself. It is the key to creating a more financially secure future for yourself. The secret is finding a way of doing so without feeling deprived. A sense of deprivation will almost inevitably guarantee falling back into old 'shop till you drop' ways. But wait a minute - how can you possibly be happy by consuming less? This goes against everything we have ever been taught.

More and more people are coming to realise that the more possessions they have, the more it costs to keep them. They need to be stored, cleaned, maintained, protected and insured against theft. Such costs are rarely considered while we get swept away with the excitement of buying our latest 'grown up' toys. But the additional costs can be significant. More and more people are uncluttering their lives - selling off and throwing out all those items which 'seemed like a good idea at the time'. I wonder what you own which comes into this category? Might you benefit if you sold off or donated to friends and charity all those clothes and gadgets which you no longer use or have never used, but which clog up your wardrobes, cupboards, attics and garages? Probably. Our lives are constantly filled with every form of clutter imaginable - noise, media (posters, shop fronts and hoardings have been described as 'colour pollution') and inconsequential busyness - the combined effects distracts us from what is really important in our lives.

What do you spend your money on? We tend to fritter it away without fully realising where it goes. Keeping a notebook to log every transaction is the best way to identify rampant or unnecessary spending patterns. When I first tried this, I was afraid it would be a tiresome chore. Far from it. Within a month, I noticed particular spending patterns. By adjusting my spending accordingly, I was able to reduce my monthly expenditure without any feelings of deprivation. Try it. It works.

One of the best pieces of advice I ever received was *Pay yourself first.* This does not mean you should stop paying your creditors. Invariably we pay everyone else's bills first and promise to save what ever we have left over. The only trouble is; there isn't usually anything left over. Therefore we do not save. Without savings we have no capital, and without capital we cannot earn an income from it.

If you seriously believe that you cannot afford to save just 10% of what you earn, you are almost certainly spending money in ways which you do not realise. Hobbies, eating in expensive restaurants, smoking and drinking are common areas where people spend more than they think. It is easy to cut this expenditure back by 10 or 15% without suffering.

Here are some questions that should help you identify attitudes that encourage over-spending.

- What unnecessary expenditure can you identify and minimise or even eliminate?
- Look around your home in your cupboards, wardrobes, the attic and your garage. What products do you own which 'seemed like a good idea at the time' but are now unused and ignored?
- How much money could you raise to invest in a savings plan by selling them?
- If you were to look at everything you spend your money on, which

expenditure gives you the most happiness and why?

- What items do you buy through habit?
- Each time you spend money, ask yourself the following question "Will this purchase really make me feel better about myself- and is it worth the time I spent working in return for the money?"
- How many clothes do you buy?
- What do you spend your money on to impress others?
- Why do you need to impress them?
- Does it mean that you are unable to impress them with anything else about yourself?
- What would happen if you chose to delay the purchase of a replacement vehicle for another year?
- How much money could you put aside in that intervening year to reduce or eliminate the need for a loan?
- Do you gain fulfilment and satisfaction from those grown up toys you were so excited about purchasing?
- How much of what you purchase goes to waste?
- Do you buy too much food?
- How much is your rubbish worth?
- What do you own more than one of?
- How often do you discard or throw away items which still have a use?
- When things break down, do you repair or throw them away?
- How much time will you have to spend merely to repay the interest on a car loan?

"Anything you buy and don't use, anything you throw away, anything you consume and don't enjoy is money down the drain, wasting your life energy and wasting the finite resources of the planet. Any waste of your life energy means more hours lost to the rat race, "making a dying." Your Money or Your Life by Joe Dominguez and Vicki Robin.

Economic growth seemingly demands increased consumption. Individual long term financial security demands spending less. Who will win?

The media routinely reports on the health of the economy by talking of 'consumer confidence' and 'the feel good factor'. It is crooked thinking based on the flawed notion that if we are prepared to spend and go into debt we will, by definition, be happier!! Most people would be happier if they had a substantial cushion of money available. If the worst happened, such as redundancy, a long term illness or the death of a family member, they could cope financially. If people spend too much, they don't have savings for the future. In other words, they will be poor - and when people are poor they generally rely on the government to bail them out. But government can't afford to do that. The entire economic system depends on business growth and increased consumption. Business demands it. But what would happen to 'the system', if we all reduced our spending? It will never happen if business has its way.

3 money secrets
- Spend less than you earn and do it for a long time!
- Save the equivalent of at least six months' salary and keep this safe and accessible.
- Get out of debt and stay out of debt!

How we are strangled by debt
Everyone encourages you to spend more. As far as the business community is concerned, you cannot spend enough. If you don't have the cash - someone will almost certainly lend it to you. Getting into debt is easy - getting out of it is more difficult. Being offered a loan is a compliment, it makes you feel good about yourself - for a while at least! Do you owe money or do you own money? According to Ron Blue, author of *Master Your Money*, "*80% of Americans owe more than they own... Repayment of debt consumes 25% of all incomes today, not including mortgage debt.*"

In 1994, Visa alone processed $643 billion in goods and services. It represents about half of all credit card payments made world wide. For many millions of people, credit card debt eats up a significant proportion of their earnings. It creates untold stress in millions of households throughout the so-called civilised world. Banks, mortgage providers, and increasingly car dealers, furniture and consumer electronics retailers will offer you credit terms.

Refusing to step onto the debt treadmill and eliminating debt from your life will have the most positive impact for your long term financial security. Most credit cards charge about 20% in interest. Paying for such credit is the same as working for five days but allowing your employer to pay you for only four!

If you use credit cards, clear the balance every month. Organise a monthly direct debit through your bank. Most credit card companies offer this option but don't always tell you about it. By using your 'plastic' in this way, you retain your cash for slightly longer, thus earning something in interest if it's held in an interest bearing account. The credit card company earns less from you, and you benefit from their 'free' insurance on goods you have bought. It's worth pointing out the following myth "You don't pay interest for a month from when you buy something using a credit card." In reality, this is only true if you always clear the credit balance on your card each month. If there is an outstanding balance owed and you buy something else, you pay interest from the date of the new purchase - on top of the other interest you are being charged. It is easy to get into a situation where you are still paying interest on money you borrowed up to two years after buying an item.

Anyone who is in debt is not in control of their life. Their behaviour is dictated by the demands of creditors. Being in debt costs far more than merely the interest you have to pay back. Think about the extra time you must work to pay back this additional money and the interest your cash could be earning you if it were not being handed over to your creditors. Learning to use credit intelligently can have a huge impact on the sums of money you can save for the future. Sadly, instructions for controlling your inflexible fiend (sic) are not as easily obtained as the numerous opportunities for debt creation.

Astonishingly, the education system does not regard it as part of its role to educate young people about money management. In any case, how can we expect poorly paid teachers to educate young people about something they almost certainly don't understand themselves!? Yes, I am being deliberately contentious. It does not seem in anyone's best commercial interests to educate young people to spend less. The banks almost certainly want to continue their efforts to offer cash loans to young people as early as they can. They know that the sooner they can persuade people to go into debt, the more money they will extract from their largely unsuspecting quarry. Our education system itself is rapidly moving over to 'education on credit'. The current proposals to charge tuition fees in higher education 'outlets', together with the 'borrow as you learn' methods of financing study, mean that it will be very easy for graduate students to end up starting their working lives with debts in excess of £20,000.

Work out how much debt you repay each month. You may get an unpleasant surprise. For many readers, the risk of an unpleasant surprise will guarantee that they do not make this sort of calculation. Sadly, the level of debt will not go down if you do not investigate it.

How we live in one home but pay for two or even three

Take our mortgages (please) as an example. An average 25 year mortgage for £50,000 will cost almost £150,000 to repay. At 10% per annum, a £1,000 loan over 25 years costs £2,727 to repay without tax relief or insurance. The same loan over 15 years costs £1,935 to repay. In other words, when you buy one house you can end up paying enough in interest for three. Mortgage companies rarely point this out to their borrowers. I wonder why? Obviously, the longer the mortgage period, the more you pay - but we are seduced by the 'good news' of lower monthly repayments if we extend the mortgage for a few more years. How kind. A shorter term mortgage may cost a little more per month, but the total repayment figure for a twenty year mortgage can cost substantially less. No wonder we are rarely encouraged to go for the shorter option.

And who says owning your own home is a good thing anyway? Many millions of people already regret buying one. It is fascinating to see why widespread home ownership has become so common in Britain. Home ownership is certainly not such a national obsession in other countries.

It is worth realising that much of this originated in the early to mid-1980s, when British industry practically ground to a halt as trade unions tried to take on the government by instigating a widespread series of labour strikes. In 1980 11,964,000 working days were lost through industrial stoppages. By 1985 this figure was down to 6,402,000, and by 1990 the figure was nearer 1,903,000. By 1994 only 278,000 days were lost. How was this achieved? Through mass manipulation. The Conservative government skilfully manoeuvred millions of people into a position where they no longer chose to go on strike. How? By encouraging blue-collar workers (those thought most likely to strike) to buy their own properties instead of paying rent to local government. In so doing, a more stable workforce was created - a worker with a mortgage debt and at risk of losing his home if it is not paid, will think twice before swapping a full wage for strike pay. Simultaneously, the government was able to rid itself of very costly property, much of it in need of major repair. A very smart series of moves don't you think? Unless, of course, you lost a packet. The government had persuaded these people to buy property by appealing to a combination of our basic human needs: providing our own privately owned 'shelter', implying that there is more 'security' in owning your home, appealing to our inherent 'greed' by hinting that if you own your home you will make a lot of money from it in the future (as the old saying goes, 'you can never go wrong with bricks and mortar' - it's not true any more). And finally they sold individuals on the idea that if they bought their own home, it was proof of their success in life - no longer were they just lowly workers - they were 'property owners'.

The housing market enjoyed a boom, prices soared and everybody was happy - that was until prices plummeted, leaving many of these new homeowners with houses that a) they could not sell, or b) had dropped in value to a level below the amount they were mortgaged for. When mortgage interest rates rose, these helpless individuals, caught in the 'negative equity trap', had to work even harder to keep up payments - and therefore they were even less likely to go on strike.

Do you really need to own your home in the 21st century? In today's and increasingly in tomorrow's work climate, the shackle of a mortgage often reduces work mobility.

If you did not have debt hanging around your neck like a noose, what could you or would you do with your life which would be different?

Eliminating all debt from your life.

If you have a mortgage, try to pay more than your required monthly payments. If you increased your payments by just 10% you could end up paying off your mortgage many years sooner, thus saving thousands of pounds in additional interest. Check beforehand to make sure that your mortgage lender does not penalise you for doing this.

Pay off your most expensive debts first. If you use many credit cards, get rid of most of them. Credit card companies know that people spend more if the buying process is simple. This is why it is possible to buy something by merely swiping a credit card through a machine. I sell various products and services - my sales went up when I started accepting credit cards using such a machine!

Wherever possible, pay off any overdrafts, loans, outstanding balances on credit, and charge & department store cards, as well as hire purchase agreements. Stop using credit cards altogether unless you only use them for convenience and pay off the full amount each and every month - preferably by direct debit. Most credit card companies rely on a proportion of customers paying additional interest when they forget to pay their bills on time.

By eliminating debt from your life, you can free up more of your time and reduce your stress. The confidence that comes from the knowledge that you owe nothing to anyone and that others are paying you interest on your capital, can fundamentally improve the way you feel about your life.

Saving and investing

Recently I saw an advertisement outside a DIY chain store. It said "Spend and Save". This is a bit like putting up a notice at a swimming pool which says "Drown & Swim." Or its the same as "Fighting for Peace." Notice how the word 'save' has had its meaning altered over the years. It used to involve keeping your money. Not any more; saving has now been linked to the process of spending by those who desperately want to convince you to part with your cash. If you spend immediately, you won't have to pay so much. To save is not the same as being given a discount.

Once you have been able to find 'spare' cash in your life by limiting your spending without experiencing any feelings of deprivation, you will be in a better position to build up a cash sum. Saving at least 10% of your income, by 'paying yourself first' and doing this for a long time, you will be doing what most others 'never get around to.' Saving regularly and from the earliest age is one of the secrets of long-term financial security and independence. When the interest on your savings is compounded over time, your money will grow and grow and grow. Compound interest has been described as the 8th wonder of the world. However, if inflation is higher (as it so often is), these accumulated savings may not be worth more. Inflation is the most fundamental of financial risks - it erodes the value of your money in real terms. The "Rule of 72" states that if inflation is running at 10% per annum, then the value of your money will be halved in just 7.2 years.

To survive the 21st century, your first priority must be to build up a sum of money which represents 3 to 6 months of your salary. Certainly save more than this if you wish. In my regular *Secrets of Successful Freelancing* seminars, delegates are shown how this approach can so dramatically improve the way they feel about their work. They can be confident in the knowledge that they do not have to accept every work assignment which is offered. This is sometimes referred to as an "FU Fund" (or more politely described as a 'screw you' fund). It ensures that the freelancer does not feel the need to accept poorly paid, and often time consuming work which they would not choose to accept if they were not desperate for the money. Building up one of these funds is invaluable in improving your self-esteem and reducing your stress and worry about money. No matter how young or old you are, or how much or how little you may earn, creating one of these funds is very highly recommended.

Deposit some of this cash in the highest interest bearing, instant access account you can find. This fund should not be used to dip into to pay for holidays and other luxuries. The rest should be deposited into a notice account so that it cannot be accessed on demand, perhaps to pay for 'a whim'. This account will take time to build up, but having eliminated debt from your life, savings in interest you would otherwise pay to creditors should allow you to build it up sooner.

From today, put aside at least 10% of your earnings. All financial experts agree that the secret of financial security is saving regularly and using that money to generate additional cash.

The next stage towards achieving financial security and independence involves using savings to create a series of investments. It is outside the scope of this book to advise on particular investments (indeed any investment advice would be illegal without a full understanding of your own unique personal circumstances). As someone who is not a certified or accredited financial expert I am not allowed to (nor do I wish to) give you financial advice - this is survival advice - nothing more, nothing less.

However, wise investors study their options thoroughly before creating a financial portfolio. Putting together such a portfolio involves a mix of investments which balance low return and low risk to your capital with a potentially higher return but a higher risk. When most people think about investments, they immediately think about the Stock Market. This is just one way (and a potentially very risky one at that) to invest your capital. Financial products exist which allow for a low or no risk investment in the UK and worldwide stock markets, but one thing is for sure, leaving all your money in a bank or building society will provide you with a very low return on your money.

"Canny investors watch the tide, not the waves." Anon

Pensions are boring but...

Earlier in this chapter, the subject of pensions was raised. Mention pensions and most people's eyes glaze over. Let's be honest about it; pensions are boring. However, give serious consideration to your pension provision - even if you are young (or are trying to convince yourself that you are). According to the charity Age Concern, in 1995 there were 10.6 million people over pensionable age representing 18.2% of the population. This number will increase by almost 1 million by 2010 as baby boomers reach retirement age. This will put huge financial pressures on which ever government is in power at the time.

Many older people who have worked hard for decades have little or no savings, many of them do not have enough money to feed themselves or heat their homes. They were too busy earning a living or spending money on the wrong things to have the time or knowledge to provide adequately for their old age.

Learn from their experience - prioritise. **To survive in the future do not rely on the state pension.** To begin with, do not assume you will be entitled to the full state pension. To qualify for a full pension (prior to the retirement ages for men and women being equalised), men must have made full National Insurance contributions for at least 44 years of their 49 year working lives (the government deems a 'working life' to be from age 16 until retirement). Women must have made full NI contributions for at least 39 of their 44 year working lives. This is a major problem for many people, especially women who may have a long gap in their 'working history', when raising a family.

Female financials

If you are a woman, you are statistically more likely to live longer than a man. Women are very poorly provided for in old age. If married, your own independent provision for old age should be a priority. Only 16% of women qualify for a state pension in their own right. If you do not work and you live with a man, do not assume any rights to his property or money if he dies or if you split up. Even if you are married you may get nothing if he dies.

Anyone reaching old age in the 21st century without a pension and/ or a regular income other than from the state could find themselves in dire financial trouble.

I meet a large number of self-employed people. It is frightening how few have any pension provision. Far too often self-employed people believe their small business is their pension. This can be a fatal mistake because it is rarely worth what the owner thinks it is worth - too many such businesses are merely a personal 'job creation scheme' for the owner. If you are employed, your company may provide you with a good pension. However, it is worth finding out if that pension can be transferred, should you wish to or if you are forced to leave that employer.

If you have not investigated the creation of an investment which guarantees a regular income for yourself in your old age, imagine the following; two hands have jumped out from this page, they are loosely gripped around your throat, I am looking deeply into your eyes and asking you to find out what you need to know in order to protect yourself against poverty in your old age. Thank you for your attention.

One of the most common reasons people give for not making this a priority is the fear that they will make a costly mistake by going with a financial institution which rips them off. This has been a real problem amongst some unscrupulous pension providers. They seem to find a whole host of ways to deduct 'administration and commission charges'. At the time of writing, the government is seeking ways to curb such practices and introduce its own private pension plans. In any case, seek professional advice from a number of different sources before making any decisions.

Choosing an adviser

Your ultimate aim for future survival is to become your own expert, although as saving and investing is becoming increasingly complex, it is impossible to know everything about the latest developments in all financial areas. This applies to advisers as well as investors. The financial world is full of charming individuals who expertly hide their 'vested interests'. So beware.

There are good advisers and bad ones. Ask friends and colleagues for the names of those they may know and feel comfortable about recommending.

- Ask which financial regulatory bodies and/or professional association they belong to.
- Ask how much commission they earn from the sale of the products they are selling (You now have a legal entitlement to this information).
- Be particularly wary of any financial sales person who insists that you pay anything immediately.
- Beware the sales person who telephones you without having been referred by a friend or colleague.
- Beware the salesperson who has not worked for his or her company for very long. The financial services industry is well known for a high turn-over of sales people. You need to be fairly sure that your adviser is a 'stayer' and will be around in the future.
- Don't assume that your local bank will provide you with the best financial deals. Many banks provide advisers who are paid on commission only to attract additional business. Some do not actually work for the bank full time. Expect them to recommend their own tied 'in-house' company. This does not mean 'tied agents' should never be used.
- Always ask how 'independent' your adviser is.
- If you ever seek a loan, do not go ahead with it if the lender is only prepared to do the deal if you take out a life insurance policy too.
- Do not believe what you read in the press. Some of it is inaccurate, biased story-mongering written by people who are often without training, accreditation or regulation, and on whom you have no come-back when they give poor advice.

Future money

Money is money. Right? Not quite. There's the metal stuff which wears holes in your pockets, the paper stuff (which incidentally is not 'paper' as such - it is made not from wood fibre but fabric fibre - and some 'paper' currencies are actually washable plastic), we can write cheques, use cash cards, debit cards, credit cards or smart cards. There have never been so many options when answering the question "How would you like to pay?" And there's another way on the horizon; a fundamentally different type of money is being developed - electronic money or "e-cash", "cybercash" or "digicash" as it is being called. This new form of money is set to have a more profound and far reaching impact on our lives, more even than credit cards, which have only been in use since the 1950's. Digital money will almost certainly eliminate hundreds of thousands of existing jobs.

'Rolling and folding' cash is expensive to manufacture and transport. It wears out and has to be replaced. An army of cash counters weigh and lug around bags of it from the Royal Mint to banks, to users, from users, back to the banks. Unless, of course, this process is 'interrupted' by individuals with more immediate investment plans and a shot gun! What a waste of time, effort and money. Less actual cash is being circulated as more and more people pay by cheque, credit and debit cards. Less people are therefore required to count it. So it's goodbye to them. As the processing of money becomes more and more automated, even less people will be required to handle, count and distribute it. If your work involves handling money in any form, you will be affected by these ongoing changes. Processing cheques and handling credit card vouchers is time-consuming for everyone involved and therefore adds costs to all businesses. It's thought that up to 15% of time and money is wasted in some businesses just counting, fetching and carrying the stuff. More businesses are moving to electronic terminals which allow the swiping of cards into the system - eliminating unnecessary time and paper, speeding up the process and allowing businesses to get their hands on your cash much faster. In 1986 there were 451 million Visa and Mastercard transactions in Britain. Only eight years later there were 817 million transactions. Their value increased from £13.2 billion to £37.8 billion in that same period.

Already, a growing proportion of the 39 million people with e-mail addresses are buying products and services using their credit cards via the Internet. I have done so myself many times. Earlier today, from my PC here in the heart of the Burgundian countryside in France, I purchased eight books for $99 from the world's largest on-line book store to be delivered to my home in London. It was quick, simple and fully automated. I was the only person involved in the transaction at the ordering stage. No one was needed to answer their phone or write or type in the details of the books I wanted. Would it be totally unrealistic to suggest that a proportion of each transaction could be diverted automatically to the Inland Revenue or Customs & Excise in the form of E-Tax? This would eliminate the need for so many accountants, civil servants and tax collectors. Perish the thought.

Sending credit card details via the Internet is deemed by some to be risky, but it is no more so than giving the same details on the 'phone. Indeed, it's said to be about as risky as someone finding your credit card details in your rubbish bin and using the information to go on a spending spree. It's possible but highly unlikely.

The number and value of Internet transactions is increasing dramatically but still represents a tiny proportion of overall credit card trade. For 1994, the credit-card company Visa, estimated there were $200 million worth of Internet related credit-card transactions worldwide. Only 1 year later it was estimated at $30billion.

The introduction of systems such as EFTPOS (Electronic Funds Transfer at the Point of Sale) and SWITCH have already led to widespread redundancies in the banking profession. These are just the beginning. The 'how quaint' Switch advertising campaigns persuaded millions to apply for debit cards. Their rapid take-up and widespread use further accelerated redundancies amongst bank employees. Each of these developments has eliminated unnecessary costs in the supply, distribution and processing of financial transactions. E-cash is the next step towards a cashless society. And it's not that far away.

A licence to 'squirt' money

E-cash has the potential to change the very concept of money throughout the world. It could even provide multi-national cash rich corporations to by-pass government-issued money altogether. Inhabitants of Swindon, Wiltshire have taken part in a trial in which goods and services can be paid for using a Mondex smart card. They can load the computer chips embedded in these plastic cards with cash from their bank accounts and swipe the card to pay for goods and services from participating retailers. People no longer need to carry cash. If the smart card is stolen, no one else can use it. It is extremely convenient when paying for small transactions - buying newspapers, drinks, food etc. - and this is where its potential is so enormous.

Once E-cash becomes widely available (as it almost certainly will), you and millions of others will be able to 'squirt' your money from computer to computer as easily as picking up a cup of coffee. If an electronic payment system is very simple and safe to use, millions of people will certainly use it. Unlike credit card and cheque transactions, E-cash is anonymous. Sending and receiving secure and untraceable digital money via computer networks will therefore appeal to criminals too.

Large or small sums can be transferred around the globe within seconds without any risk of the money being intercepted by third parties. Governments have already realised that they could lose millions in tax revenue if people and organisations using E-cash can receive or transfer funds anywhere in the world anonymously.

Sophisticated encryption is the key. The US government, as paranoid as ever, has even investigated a law abiding citizen, Phil Zimmerman following the development of his encrypted code Pretty Good Privacy, or PGP for short. It is thought to be so impenetrable that agencies such as the FBI don't think they can ever crack it - therefore he is prevented by US law from exporting his technology because, in the wrong hands, it could undermine US national security.

Digicash, an Amsterdam based company has also developed a system for transferring money electronically. According to the company, instead of giving you bank notes, you are given digital coins which software can store on your PC's hard disk. When you want to make a payment, you simply confirm the amount, payee and description of the goods, with a mouse click you instruct the E-cash software to transfer coins of the correct value from your PC direct to the payee. Merchants (ranging from casual participants in the global Internet bazaar to mega-retailers) can then deposit the digital coins into their accounts. WorldPay is a secure multi-currency micro payment system developed by National Westminster Bank plc and is already in use.

At the moment, transferring electronic and digital money is confined to large financial institutions and global corporations. According to David Brown in *Cybertrends*, for every dollar spent or saved in the real economy, an estimated $30-50 is circulating in financial cyberspace.

But what impact will this have for you and me? At the moment, it's impractical to buy and sell all products and services electronically. Credit card transactions already take place but tend to be used only by a tiny proportion of Internet users. The widespread use of E-cash will radically change world trade by opening up mind-boggling opportunities for some and pose significant threats to the incomes of others. It also renders virtually meaningless the heated and emotional arguments against a 'single currency' in Europe on the grounds of loss of sovereignty.

The crucial point about E-cash is that it is the 'cheapest' type of money. Because E-cash relies so heavily on technology, few if any people are involved in each transaction. This means it can be transferred around the globe very inexpensively. For the first time in history, millions of people all over the world will be able to find and buy products and services very easily and at the best prices. The actual processing cost for each transaction is tiny - far smaller than for debit and credit cards. Credit card companies typically charge retailers 2- 5% for each transaction, as well as charging interest to each borrower. This means 'micro payments' will be possible for the first time. You will be able to buy things for say 1p, 2p or 10p. This may not seem like a big deal at first sight, but imagine if you could buy useful information for a fraction of its value to you. Newspapers and magazines cost a lot to produce, distribute and sell. If you and many others chose to buy the information, but did not need the paper it was printed on, your local newsagent could be out of a job. Publishers could afford to do this because the actual costs of allowing customers to buy their information would be very low. They could make more money without having to print anything. Think of the people in the printing, distribution and retailing sectors who would no longer receive an income. Indeed, take this train of thought a little further - would you need publishers at all? Any writer could generate a more lucrative living by marketing directly to the end user. If you and tens of thousands of others liked one particular writer, each paying just 10p to read their latest articles, the writers could earn far more than they were paid by any magazine or newspaper publisher.

But don't limit this to writers, what about musicians, and software and movie producers? Using the same E-cash technology, you could pay just a few pence or pounds in return for downloading the latest digitised albums, computer applications and movies onto your ultra-high powered computer hard disks or recordable CD-ROMs or DVDs (Digital Video Disks). Why go to your local video shop when you can access any movie you want (without the possibility that it is 'out' and therefore unavailable) via much cheaper 'phone lines, for a fraction of the price you would pay at Blockbuster Video? Some products will never again need to be sent via 'snail mail' as computer users call the conventional postal service.

Distribution is expensive. Moving products around, warehousing, displaying them on shelves, holding products in stock, the profit margin demanded by the wholesalers and retailers - each element adds more cost to the consumer. By using E-cash and the technology to transfer words, pictures and sounds as computer data, entire distribution channels could be eliminated. If you are a manufacturer, why would you need to sell your products in a retail shop at all, if you could reach the consumer direct? In any case, as many manufacturers know to their cost, distributors exert enormous power over them. The relationship is often described as 'the tail wagging the dog'. In many cases, distributors refuse to accept product lines unless manufacturers agree to pay substantial sums merely to obtain shelf space. E-cash could enable manufacturers and producers to bypass existing distribution channels.

Distributors are already aware of this - especially in the computer industry. They can see very clearly that companies such as Microsoft may not need them in the future, if consumers can pay for products using E-cash technology. Why should the likes of Bill Gates at Microsoft allow others to make a profit from his products, when it could be argued that 'the channel' as its known, adds little or no value to the equation. There are some very worried software distributors in the world. On the other hand, until E-cash technology is widely available, manufacturers cannot afford to upset the distributors. What will happen? Who do you know who works in distribution?

When E-cash achieves widespread usage within the next decade or so, the world will change very quickly. In the 1950's, some banking experts declared that credit cards would never catch on because people didn't need them. This time, the banking industry is not so sceptical. Extensive research and millions of dollars are being invested into developing this technology. Nor is it confined to conventional banking businesses. Sainsbury's and Tesco, the food retailers, have already moved towards becoming banks, other businesses with large numbers of regular customers are following suit. Why? Quite simply, they can make even more money. Perhaps one day more than by selling their existing core products. This technology is opening up massive money making opportunities for large and small entrepreneurs.

E-cash is going to be big. How could you or your employer benefit from it? And what could you do over the next few years to minimise its threat?

Without doubt, in the 21st century, the ways we spend, manage and transfer money will change dramatically. But unless people radically change their money habits, poverty in old age is more likely. Living for 20-30 years after we retire may sound idyllic, but not if you have nothing to live on. Develop the habit of limiting your spending (without inflicting austere deprivation on yourself - let's be realistic here). Use those savings to generate an independent income for yourself and do it for a long time.

Even so, no one can guarantee financial success; if the technology driven world financial markets collapse as it's thought they might, everyone will be in the 'do-do', but one thing is sure(ish) - you will be far better off than anyone who tries to spend their way to happiness.

Electronic money may be in its infancy today, but, as we will discover in the next chapter, massive and rapid developments in technology, will lead to even greater changes in the ways we live and work.

Chapter 6
Technology - Threat or Saviour?

Q. What do you call a 'nerd' in 15 years time?
A. The Boss.

Nerds may become millionaires almost overnight but we like to reassure ourselves that most still can't get a date!

If anybody said at the turn of the last century that man would fly heavy mechanical contraptions, faster than the speed of sound in the 20th Century, or if Neil Armstrong's grandparents had been told he would set foot on the moon in July 1969, who would not have laughed? What other examples of technology can you think of which didn't even exist 50 years ago? Here are just a few; personal, laptop and palmtop computers, audio cassette and CD players, colour TV, mobile phones, velcro, satellites, space ships, the Internet, digital watches and cameras, photocopiers, bar codes, microwave ovens, camcorders, credit cards and 'hole in the wall' cash machines. The list is endless. Advances in technology are remarkably fast; Armstrong and his fellow astronauts used slide rules to get them to the moon. Today even many of the poorest people in society own or use the latest electric and electronic gizmos and gadgets.

A hell of a lot has developed in just the last half of the 20th century, but we now take so much for granted. Caught up in the ever increasing pace of life, our attention span seems to grow shorter and shorter. As our expectations rise, it takes more and more to impress us. When we see reports of new discoveries and inventions, which seem to happen almost every day, we're too busy to pay more than passing notice. When was the last time you devoted even a moment to truly marvel at the technology which seamlessly links our lives. Yes, as today's "Sophisticated Skeptics" (as defined by Paul & Cox in *Beyond Humanity*) proclaim, technology does go wrong. Sometimes on a large scale. But most of the time our everyday lives are enhanced by increasingly powerful computers and electronics. I haven't sworn at this PC for at least a couple of weeks! Whether used for business or leisure, technology continues to improve the quality of our lives in ways our ancestors could never even comprehend. As my 79 year old Great Uncle George Abbott declared at Sunday lunch recently *"When I hear people talk about the 'good old days', I think, no they bloody weren't. Life was hard. Work was very tough. We didn't have enough food, and medical treatments weren't that effective. And during the war, Gracie, my wife had to work with lesbians in the munitions factory!"*

Millions of VCRs around the world flashing 00:00hrs demonstrate the population's true interest for technology. People are almost proud of the fact that they don't know how to use things. We're too busy to learn about what we perceive to be the overly complex features we are so keen to purchase. Equipment manufacturers, through extensive research have discovered that a high proportion of consumers don't bother to read instruction manuals. They are too difficult to understand. Or is it we are too impatient to devote time in finding out what our 'stuff' can really do? At my seminars for freelancers, I often ask the audience how many own a computer. Invariably 90-95% shoot their hands in the air, proud of the fact that they own a PC. But when I add, "How many know how to get the most out of it?" Most hands go down. I tell them, "Anyone who uses a computer in their work and does not make money from it, isn't using it properly". High powered, relatively low cost, sophisticated but simple-to-use computer technology is widely available in business today, allowing even the smallest business to compete against the largest corporations. However, only a small proportion of users devote enough time to discover how this technology can be used to its fullest capacity, streamlining their work, increasing their productivity and ultimately their employability. We allow our short-term frustrations and fears to undermine the longer-term benefits they can provide.

Do you tend to use technology to perform simple functions? So many people use word processors in exactly the same way as they used manual or electronic typewriters. Learning even the most basic word processor functions radically improves a user's effectiveness and confidence. If you want to survive in the 21st century, consciously decide to become proficient at operating a wide range of computer applications and learn to understand fully their many features.

Techno kids: 'zombies' or intellectual athletes?

Unimpeded by the slower paced, unstimulating environment they so often find at school, millions of children could be preparing themselves for the next century without even realising it. Far from wasting time, new evidence seems to indicate that a child's computer proficiency leads to improved mental agility. Such kids develop their ability to think rapidly on many different levels simultaneously. It appears that linear thinking is just for old folks. Parents and teachers have for many years worried about the consequences of the prolonged use of computer games. Even though there are still some concerns (primarily relating to excessive cyber-violence), experts are starting to realise that, through computer games, kids are actually improving their concentration and memory, literacy, co-ordination, their information processing ability and become better at solving complex problems; qualities of great importance for their future employability. Kids are rewarded for their computer game success by being set more daunting challenges, which stretch their concentration and ability even further. However, it is worth noting that research by Dr. Alan Durndell, a psychology lecturer at Glasgow Caledonian University, suggests that young girls may be turned off computers for life because so many computer games are too violent or too immature for them.

Overcome your technophobia!

Anyone who is afraid of technology for whatever reason should get help or therapy as soon as possible. Ask your kids. If you don't have any, borrow some. Young kids take to technology so quickly; their innate curiosity, playfulness and the fact that they have yet to learn to take mental 'short cuts' in their logic, provides them with the necessary tools for learning technology. Grown-ups, on the other hand, take it all far too seriously and get annoyed and frustrated when a piece of equipment doesn't 'think' the same way they do. Widespread aversion to technology is not helped by the inability of those who develop it to show users exactly how they will benefit from it. It's those incommunicative nerds again! You know, those spotty kids (almost exclusively male) who live on Coca-Cola and pizza, blink for hours on end at the Internet, download pictures of their favourite silicon-implanted bimbo and constantly pore over pages from technical magazines and computer manuals.

No wonder so few people want to be seen to be too interested in technology.

If you suspect you do not derive the maximum benefit from the technology you own today, dig out all the instruction books and manuals for every appliance (you did keep them didn't you?). Over the next few weeks, take one manual or booklet to work with you each day. Dip into it on the train or during your coffee/lunch breaks - preferably wrap it in something like a popular newspaper or magazine to conceal your nerdlike behaviour. By learning something new each day and applying it, your knowledge will increase.

Alternatively, put them in the privacy of your bathroom to read in a 'quiet moment'. I guarantee you will find yourself saying, "I didn't realise it could do that." Greater familiarity begets increased confidence. Once you achieve confidence, you will find yourself becoming more adventurous with technology. This is exactly the same process we all go through when learning to read and write.

Things you really SHOULD know even if technology bores you

In the future, most if not all information will reach your home via a telephone cable rather than by an antiquated TV aerial mounted on your roof. Try to imagine what it could mean to be able to dial up any video programme or short snippet, in any language, on any subject, at any time. You could choose from just about every movie ever made from the earliest silent movies to the latest blockbusters, news from any country in any language, education programmes of every subject at any level, opportunities to view demonstrations of every product and service. This may sound like science fiction but companies like BT are working to turn this into a reality. It's what computer guru, Nicholas Negroponte calls *'anything, anytime, anywhere television'*. Once the formidable technical challenges are overcome, the provision of high quality video via telephone, to the entire population, will radically change the face of world communications and represents profit potential beyond belief to those who own the means of distribution - namely the 'phone, electricity or cable companies.

Today you can deliver any audio or text based message almost anywhere in the world via the telephone and a modem linked to a computer, for a fraction of what it used to cost. The next step is widespread distribution of high quality moving video images. This is already happening, but the digital ISDN technology is expensive and is therefore confined to business users such as broadcasters, designers and advertising agencies. But not for much longer.

Since the earliest days of the Industrial Revolution, power has resided with those who control the roads, railways, seas and skies. Once video can be delivered to your home via telephone lines, companies such as British Telecom could become the most powerful organisations in the world.

Once this technology becomes available (the technical obstacles are quite considerable and get worse when more people want it, because additional strain is put on the telephone system) it will become what is known in the computer industry as a 'killer application'. In other words, just about everyone will want it. This is what happened when mobile 'phones were introduced in the early 1980's - and who benefited? Those 'phone companies again.

With so much at stake, the telecommunications companies are laying thousands of miles of optical cabling every month. Optical cable is capable of carrying vast amounts of digital information; hundreds of thousands of telephone calls can travel down these high-tech cables simultaneously. Marginally thicker than a human hair, optical fibre cables represent the 'A roads' (but not the motorways) of the information super-highway. Before they reach our homes, telephone calls are switched and re-routed at the telephone exchange onto the equivalent of a 'B road' or dirt track via the copper "twisted pair" telephone lines running into your home or office. It's these last few hundred metres to our homes which are causing all the frustration. The human voice can be transmitted along this type of wire without too many problems, but sending high quality digital video pictures is a different matter.

Existing technology cannot send the vast amounts of computer data needed for high picture quality video through an ordinary telephone wire. Engineers have two choices; replace all this old cabling with optical cable which can carry this wide 'bandwidth' information at a prohibitively high cost or find a way to use the existing cable by compressing (squeezing) the information to fit through the pipe, and then decompress it when it reaches your TV or computer. The second option is being pursued with vigour and a massive capital investment.

It's worth taking a moment to understand the impact it will have when it becomes possible to deliver video to people's homes via the 'phone lines. TV broadcasters currently decide what goes on the airwaves and they exert tremendous power over those individuals who create the programmes. But why would you need a TV station if you can persuade enough people to dial up to see your latest production? High quality video production equipment is becoming so inexpensive and user-friendly that almost anyone can film and edit their own programmes. Whether anyone would pay to watch them all is another matter, but that is not the point. Virtually anyone who can create video material will be able to gain access to anyone they choose to target and, using the electronic cash systems currently under development, they will be able to receive payment on-line. Oftel, the telecommunications regulatory body has made it difficult for 'phone companies to offer video services in competition with TV broadcasters, but inevitably this will change. When it does, anyone will be able to send video programmes to those who have the equipment to receive it.

This is just one of the problems facing the television industry. Another major problem facing them is the need to fill airtime with programmes which cost less than the revenue they can generate for showing it. By early 1998 up to 200 digital satellite and cable channels will be launched in Britain alone, followed shortly afterwards by up to 30 digitally based terrestrial TV channels.

As audiences continue to fragment and decline, hourly programme budgets are being squeezed harder and harder. Afterall, the programmes are what TV companies choose to give away, unless you are paying a monthly subscription to view movies or sport. At the time of writing, some programmes broadcast via satellite cost less than £2,000 per hour to produce. This is pitifully low and can only result in poor quality programmes. Computer based video-on-demand does not share the same problem; stored on a computer server each programme can be seen at the precise moment the individual consumer wishes to view it. In theory it can be viewed by an infinite number of people. It turns on its head the traditional means of broadcasting , creating what has been described as 'narrowcatching'.

Ian Pearson's telescope to the future

Ian Pearson at British Telecom Labs has assembled a comprehensive 'technology calendar' by looking into what research laboratories are up to throughout the world. Below are just some of those developments. Remember, these are not science fiction, but deliberately conservative predictions for the implementation of these new (and mostly, already existing) technologies.

More details can be found on the Internet at http://www.labs.bt.com/people/pearsonid. Ask yourself how such technological advances could affect your life - positively as well as negatively.

BT Technology Calendar 1997

	Earliest	Expected	Latest
Artificial pancreas	1998	1998	1999
Artificial blood	1999	2000	2001
Artificial ears	1999	2000	2001
Artificial heart	2007	2010	2014
Artificial lungs	2010	2015	2020
Artificial kidneys	2010	2015	2020
Artificial brain cells	2012	2017	2022
Artificial liver	2015	2020	2025
Artificial legs	2025	2030	2035
Artificial eyes	2025	2030	2035
Brain 'add-ons'	2028	2033	2038
Artificial brain	2030	2035	2040
Determination of the whole human DNA base sequence	2003	2005	2007
Devices roaming within blood vessels under own power	2007	2010	2014
Genetic screening widely used	2007	2010	2014
Direct pleasure production	2008	2012	2016
Prevention of cancer	2009	2013	2017

	Earliest	Expected	Latest
Genetic links of all diseases identified	2010	2015	2020
Many new forms of plants and animals from genetic engineering	2015	2020	2025
Extension of average lifespan to over 100	2015	2020	2025
Artificial brain implants	2020	2025	2030
Global electronic currency in use	2003	2005	2007
Paper and coins largely replaced by electronic cash	2003	2005	2007
Integrated taxation in all transactions	2010	2015	2020
Automatic text summarisation and abstracts	1997	1997	1997
Distance learning in virtual universities	1997	1997	1997
Life long learning is the norm	1999	2000	2001
Real time language translation for print and voice	2002	2004	2006
Machine use of human-like memorising, recognising, learning	2008	2012	2016
Human knowledge exceeded by machine knowledge	2012	2017	2022
Space solar power stations	2025	2030	2035
Effective prediction of most natural disasters	2007	2010	2014
Deep underground cities in Japan	2015	2020	2025
IT literacy essential for any employment	2001	2003	2005
Widespread VR use for recreation and training	2003	2005	2007
95% in advanced nations computer literate	2007	2010	2014
Go-anywhere personal numbering	2001	2002	2004
Odour and flavour sensors comparable to human	2003	2005	2007
Odour and flavour sensors comparable to dog	2015	2020	2025
Machine recognition of body language and gestures	1997	1997	1997
Wall hung high definition colour displays	1999	2000	2001
Electronic newspaper	1999	2000	2001
Home shopping, using bar code scanner or tablet	1999	2000	2001
Speech dialling	1999	2000	2001
Positioning sound at any point in space	2000	2001	2002

	Earliest	Expected	Latest
Video walls - single screens 2m across	2003	2005	2007
Full voice interaction with machine	2003	2005	2007
Voice synthesis quality up to human standard	2003	2005	2007
Portable translation device for simple conversation	2004	2007	2010
Household access by facial recognition	2007	2010	2014
3D TV without need for special glasses	2008	2012	2016
3D video conferencing	2010	2015	2020
Thought recognition as everyday input means	2020	2025	2030
Full direct brain link	2025	2030	2035
Use of nanotechnology	2010	2015	2020
Smart skin for intelligent clothing and direct human repair	2015	2020	2025
Production, storage and use of antimatter	2020	2025	2030
1 Terabit memory chip	2007	2010	2014
DNA storage device	2007	2010	2014
1 Petabit memory chip	2012	2017	2022
Computers which write most of their own software	2003	2005	2007
DNA computer	2008	2012	2016
AI technology imitating thinking processes of the brain	2013	2018	2023
Parallel computer with 1000 million processors	2015	2020	2025
Robotised space vehicles and facilities	2003	2005	2007
Fire fighting robots that can find and rescue people	2004	2006	2009
Totally automated factories	2004	2007	2010
Autonomous robots with environmental awareness sensors	2005	2008	2011
Robotic security & fire guards	2005	2008	2011
Housework robots - fetch, carry, clean & tidy, organise etc.	2005	2008	2011
Artificial brains with ten thousand or more cells	2007	2010	2014
Robots for guiding blind people	2010	2015	2020

	Earliest	Expected	Latest
More robots than people in developed countries	2020	2025	2030
Various forms of electronic addiction will be a big problem	2001	2003	2005
On-line voting in UK	2004	2007	2010
Replacement of people leads to anti-technology subculture	2005	2008	2011
Electronic shopping dominant	2007	2010	2014
Near Earth space tours	2010	2015	2020
Use of human hibernation in space travel	2025	2030	2035
Cars powered by hydrogen fuel cells	2003	2005	2007
Video recorder capable of being programmed by adults!	2013	2018	2023

Reproduced with the kind permission of Ian Pearson at BT Labs.

Author of *Technotrends*, Daniel Burrus has identified the following 20 core technologies as those most likely to make the biggest impact on society in the future; genetic engineering, advanced biochemistry, lasers, fibre optics, microwaves, superconductors, high-tech ceramics, new polymers, thin-film deposition, fibre-reinforced composites, distributed computing, advanced computers, artificial intelligence, optical data storage, digital electronics, advanced video displays, micromechanics, photovoltaic cells, molecular designing and advanced satellites. Hands up who knows what they can all do.

Each of the above technologies will impact our lives, but it is worth focusing on how such developments will affect the food we eat, the treatment of disease and the ways we work.

Slaves to the silicon chip

The technology we routinely blame for its unreliability and high cost is still more reliable and less expensive than even the most hard working and competent human beings. Look around most high-tech factories these days and what do you find? A distinct lack of people for one thing. Advanced robotics already produces highly complex, quality products faster and at a lower cost than can be achieved using people. And as yet, robots don't gather around the coffee machine for a chat, but work constantly without holidays, pensions, health insurance or sickness benefits.

'Phones & Computers; the techno-marriage of the decade

Mobile 'phones and personal computers - neither existed less than thirty years ago. Take a moment to think about how just these two items have so radically changed our lives. In many ways our lives have been enriched, but in other ways we have become slaves to machines which can now function far, far quicker than our human brains. Have we become slaves to the silicon chip? The boundaries between work and leisure have been smashed. The portability of technology makes it easier to stay in touch, even when we may prefer to be left alone. Sadly, travelling on the train is no longer a refuge. Mobile 'phones distract and disturb passengers. More 'phone free carriages please!

The size of mobiles and PC's have shrunk (and continues to do so) while their power has increased dramatically following major advances in battery technology and ultra-low-power consumption circuits. These developments alone have opened up a multitude of new uses, benefits and opportunities to millions of people. They have also fundamentally changed the way people work. Ignoring or refusing to use such technology makes workers less productive than they must be in today's increasingly competitive marketplace. Companies which cannot afford to, or refuse to harness such technological advances are heading towards oblivion.

But are they really? Increased productivity cannot be guaranteed. Some commentators have concluded that productivity in real terms has not been improved since the introduction of technology. Technology providers have successfully seduced businesses into buying technological answers which do not always deliver the time savings, productivity and competitive advantages which they promise so enthusiastically. Many businesses are conned into believing that technology offers all the answers. But it's difficult for a CEO to refuse the latest technological solution to the companies woes. What if the competition gets hold of it and it does deliver on its promises? The excutive cannot risk being seen to be a Luddite, or worse, being seen to make a mistake.

Selling; techno-style

Most businesses cannot survive unless a sustained and concerted effort is put into selling - attracting orders for the products or services which the business provides. Let's take an example of how selling itself has already changed, and the implications these changes are having on the workforce and the ways business is already changing dramatically.

With the rapid and increasing convergence of mobile computing and telecommunications, it is now possible (and easy) to connect your mobile 'phone directly into a hand held computer to send and receive faxes and electronic mail literally at the press of a couple of buttons. What if you are a salesperson and need to find out the latest information about the products you sell? With your prospective customer sitting opposite, you can call up your company's product databases providing the latest prices and discount structures with the most up-to-date details of how your products can be customised to suit individual needs and delivery dates. By offering all the relevant information in an instant, a sale can be completed quickly, efficiently and at a much lower cost to everyone concerned. It eliminates unnecessary visits and meetings, 'phone calls and faxes.

But it's not all good news for the salesperson. Amongst the larger and more enlightened companies, when a sale is confirmed, using technology called EDI (electronic data interchange), the information about the sale is relayed back to headquarters. The electronic data automatically gets routed to the sales department, where the sale is logged. Then, in a matter of seconds, this same information is relayed to the accounts department, where an invoice is raised and simultaneously sent to the manufacturing plant as well as to the suppliers of raw materials. By electronically linking every part of the business process, shortages, delays and production bottlenecks can be avoided. This technology is not particularly new and is already widely used. Those organisations which do not are becoming increasingly disadvantaged. When every purchase is recorded electronically in this way, retailers and manufacturers are able to monitor and predict demand for all their products, whilst minimising costly inventories and the possibility of running out of their most popular product lines. Small operators cannot compete against this technology.

Sales people on the road are a very expensive overhead for a business. EDI is eliminating the need for sales people to visit customers and take orders. The EDI computer system raises the orders itself automatically when and if the customer's stock level drops below pre-agreed levels with little or no human intervention.

Large retailers rely on information technology in every part of their enterprises. Sophisticated scanners allows them to know exactly what is being bought, in which stores, even at what times. When they link details of your loyalty card, it is relatively easy for a retailer to know exactly what you buy and how often. Anyone who knows what you buy can build up a remarkably detailed profile of you and your family. The analysis of this information is invaluable to any retailer - and even more valuable to product manufacturers. At the moment, the retailer earns money from the products you buy, as well as the detailed information you provide them with each time they swipe your loyalty or discount card through their system. That information is worth big money to a retailer. They get it for free. It is used to help them work out the best ways to get you to spend more each time you shop. Filling in question-naires may not be in your best long-term interests, although this helps them streamline marketing costs and can send you mailings about products and services you are more likely to be interested in and respond to. With more supermarket chains offering services such as banking, they can know far more about how you live than any conventional bank which does not have details of your buying habits. It was John Sainsbury of the supermarket chain who is credited for coining the phrase "retail is detail".

You would think sales people would want to know all about these techno-logical developments - but 'no'. A couple of years ago I was a key note speaker at a conference for a professional sales organisation. Before I took to the podium, another speaker gave a talk on the impact of technology in the selling environment. I was shocked and saddened at the response to her talk. The audience laughed at her. This predominantly white, middle-aged male audience mocked the young and attractive female presenter as she clearly and professionally outlined the latest developments in portable computing and telecommunications, CD-ROM technology and customer/contact tracking software. As far as they were concerned, what could she tell them which would help them 'close more sales'? What could she tell them about selling? Why should they listen? It was obvious to them that she did not have the many years of selling experience that they had accumulated. The problem is - she did tell them, but they were blinded and deafened by their denial. Such deeply held opinions and prejudices will cost them dearly in the years to come. For many, by the time they cotton on to what is happening around them, it will be too late. Increased sales will go to those open-minded professionals who welcome and embrace new ways of working and future technological developments.

In these politically correct days, it would be outrageous to suggest that an attractive young woman should not have been chosen to deliver this type of message to an audience of this age and profile. Sad to say, they probably wouldn't have laughed quite so much if the messenger was male and their own age, or even older. That audience not only refused to accept new technology, they couldn't or wouldn't accept that a woman, in their man's world, was capable of adding value to their working lives.

Time to mock

Here's another example of how dangerous it is to laugh at new developments in technology. Only a few decades ago, at a worldwide trade show for clock manufacturers, a firm of Swiss watchmakers displayed an electronic watch using new LCD (Liquid Crystal Display) technology. They didn't consider it a threat to their livelihoods - so it was shown as an 'amusing' novelty. They foolishly believed that no one would turn away from the high-priced precision engineering which had established Swiss-made watches and clocks as the best in the world. But it took only a few years for the Japanese to decimate the world market for mechanical timepieces. They instantly grasped this new technology with both hands - seeing it as a massive business opportunity. It cost the Swiss watchmaking industry dearly. Thousands of highly skilled craftsmen were no longer required.

The printing revolution

In the last few decades printing, too, has gone through the most fundamental changes since Gutenberg created moveable type in the 1450's, and the processes and skills required by those who work in the industry have altered dramatically. Almost overnight, the skills which took years to acquire and develop, setting hot metal printing plates, were made obsolete - those working were no longer required unless they re-trained using computer-based desk-top publishing technology. Today a 12-year old can do what it previously took talented crafts-people decades to acquire the necessary skills.

The highly unionised printing industry did everything in its power to stop or slow the implementation of such computer technology, but to no avail. I recall a colleague telling me about a training course which he was holding for a number of these highly skilled typesetters to retrain them to use desk-top publishing equipment. Many of these men were in their forties and fifties. Etched on his mind was one particular man who gazed in disbelief at the speed and accuracy of the computer to complete in seconds what it had taken him 30 years to learn. His look of disbelief turned to deep sadness as the significance of this technological development started to sink in. He slowly shook his head, aware that he was attending the funeral of his much cherished craft.

He and his other colleagues were prepared to grasp this new way of working - but so many others refused to accept that their skills would no longer be required. They convinced themselves they did not need to re-train. Depending on which experts you choose to listen to, it took dinosaurs thousands of years to become extinct - most hot-metal typesetters were made extinct in less than a decade.

This book is a relic of the past too. Compiling information, squirting ink onto paper, binding the pages and distributing it to bookshops or by mail to the reader is antiquated. Once a method of electronic payment is widely available, many books will be produced electronically via computer networks, to be printed out by the user or on CD-ROM as already happens with encyclopaedias. Who would want a dust-laden shelf full of heavy books, when more up-to-date information using colour pictures, audio and video clips can be seen on a computer? Updated information can be made available by including special text links which go straight to the latest information update on the Internet.

Books won't disappear for quite some time, if at all - there's something so intimate, tactile, practical and portable about holding a book and flipping its pages. However, Nicholas Negroponte in *Being Digital* , describes a medium-future replacement for the rigid computer screen where the 'display' is in the form of a self-contained, thin, flexible and almost indestructible sheet of material, remarkably like paper in its feel and texture.

Book publishers have exerted enormous power over most of their authors (celebrity and best-selling authors are treated somewhat better). They dictate terms, content, promotion and distribution. This power is sliding away from them as the cost of book publishing and the means of distributing books has already begun to change. *Logica Views*, a book self-published by the global software integrator Logica gives the example of a frustrated author of popular medical books, with 800 pages of high quality text on the prevention and alleviation of back problems. Her publisher only wanted to print 200 pages on the subject. The author has since published independently, a 500 item questionnaire on the Internet instead. The 'patient' fills in the details over a period of time. Once completed, the respondent can either request a free personalised summary of their condition to take to a physician, or purchase a customised book which details how to treat his or her specific back problem. Who needs a publisher when you can do that?

This book is also the result of a frustrating past relationship with a publisher and represents how the structure of many businesses, and publishing in particular, will change. It has been produced using the latest technology and a team of self-employed, highly professional and knowledgeable freelance specialists, most of whom work for conventional book publishers too. The 'virtual' team has been assembled specifically for this book project, the team members will move on to other projects when it is completed. Working in this way, massive savings have been possible at nearly every stage of its production.

Most of the words you are reading on this page have not been typed into a computer. Instead, wearing a headset with a microphone, I am dictating these words directly into the word processor programme, Microsoft Word.

By using IBM VoiceType, the latest in voice recognition hardware and software, I am able to dictate at up to one hundred words per minute without getting sore fingers. With an overall accuracy of better than 95%, any incorrect words are identified and replaced from a menu of alternatives. The more the system is used, the more accurate it becomes. Although the first day I used it, I wanted to impress Frankie by looking into her eyes and saying the words *"I love you"*. On screen, the words I had dictated appeared. They said, *"I love Graham"*. She wanted to know if there was anything I needed to tell her! Thankfully, dictation accuracy is far better these days. However, my PC has been called Graham ever since.

As each chapter of this book is written, the text is edited and improved using the keyboard in a conventional way. The text is sent via the Internet to the virtual team, some of whom live in different countries, for their comments, suggestions and improvements. They are returned in electronic form.

The book cover has been designed using relatively inexpensive desktop publishing technology, and similar computer software will be used to typeset the finished text, by copying and pasting text rather then re-keying every word.

When my first book was published in 1986, the proofs were liberally littered with typos that were not present in the original computer-generated text; a thoroughly time-consuming, costly and inefficient system.

Because such technology is now so widespread and continues to drop in price, the 'cost of entry' to publishing has been lowered dramatically. This has led to a massive growth in magazine titles aimed at small niche markets. In the old world of publishing, the costs involved would have been so high that such small-circulation magazines would be uneconomical.

Authors typically earn an 8 to12% royalty; the lion's share goes to the publisher, distributor and retailer. They control the distribution chain but this has changed and will continue to do so. Most books take at least 12 to 18 months to be published by conventional methods. Much of this delay is down to the rather slow buying process of book stores. They plan which books they will stock far in advance, and like most retailers, this will represent only a small proportion of the number of books actually published. Obviously, if a book cannot be bought, sales will suffer. Most books do not sell in large quantities because so many, even good ones, are not given the distribution needed to generate a high level of sales. As an author who has written a number of books, it is fair to say that the book publishing industry is old fashioned, averse to technology and ... a bit of a shambles.

A business/self-help book of this genre, would often be given an initial print run of just four thousand copies, best-seller status would follow if sales reached about 20,000 copies. By writing, publishing and distributing it yourself you may sell far fewer books but still make more money than working through a publisher. Distribution is the key; for many, the Internet provides an excellent route to customers. It is easy to give away sample chapters or, in the case of software authors, provide it free of charge for would-be users to assess its usefulness. If they like it, they send a small payment to the author. It's a system which used to be confined to small companies, but software empires such as Microsoft now routinely give their products away for free too. And they make money doing so. When large numbers of people are persuaded to use new software, it quickly becomes an industry standard which can attract millions of people who are prepared to pay for it. The original users are highly likely to pay for future upgrades. The rules of business are certainly changing.

My role as a seminar leader puts me in direct contact with many delegates and client companies who are likely to buy this book - either for themselves or bought for the staff by a company. Therefore, the distribution of this title has already been arranged a long time before the book has been printed. This approach does not appeal to all book or software authors, but those with a more entrepreneurial attitude who are willing to invest time and their own money in selling their products can do well.

More and more individuals are setting up their own highly professional self-publishing and recording facilities at a fraction of the price it would have cost only ten years ago. Computer based audio recording and editing is already commonplace and affordable. High quality video, traditionally requiring very expensive equipment is also showing signs of 'affordability'. Broadcast quality video cameras can cost £40,000. Digital video cameras are already for sale for about £3,000. More and more of these cameras are being used by the professional broadcasters. We will see massive growth in DTS (Desktop Studios).

When desktop publishing began, the creative quality of many documents dropped for a couple of years as unskilled people tried the DIY approach to designing brochures. But the technology spawned a massive DTP industry, although many of these newly trained designers are already losing business to a growing army of multi-skilled secretaries who are no longer required purely for typing duties. When it becomes possible to buy high quality video equipment at low cost - thousands of skilled television technicians will be discarded for exactly the same reasons highly skilled technicians in the printing industry were jettisoned at the beginning of the DTP era.

In the future, it is highly likely that many professional performers and writers will simply bypass conventional publishers and record companies.

George Michael's costly legal dispute with his record company, Sony, illustrates many performers' dissatisfaction with their distribution agents. How long will it be before you will be able to visit his website (http://www.aegean.net/) or that of any other performer, pay a small electronic fee and make the highest quality copies of their latest musical offerings onto low cost recordable CD machines? Another performer famed for his contempt of record companies, distributors and retailers is 'The artist formally known as Prince', who is already selling his music directly to fans.

Inteco, a market research company, forecasts book and music distribution is most likely to shift towards Internet distribution in the years to come. There will be no need to pay what are often described as obscene profits to overly greedy record companies and music retailers. We have been listening to the record companies' transparent 'justifications' of ever-increasing retail CD prices for years now, when the actual production costs of the disks has been going down. Musicians do not have to suffer the refusal of record companies or retailers to support them either by signing them up or providing shelf space. The fans will love it because they will save money buying music this way, whilst the artists could earn significantly more by charging less.

Simultaneously, for the first time, the artistes will know exactly who their customers are. The more entrepreneurial musicians and writers will be able to develop an electronic relationship by tailoring specially recorded work or live events to their most valued customers. Henry Ford once said "Only half our advertising works, the problem is, I don't know which half." This is one of the key reasons advertising agencies and the media make so much money. Traditional marketing is frighteningly expensive and precludes anyone without deep pockets from playing the game. But Internet marketing is not so expensive, which means that the point of entry is far lower, allowing more entrepreneurs to take part. For example, even the tiniest florist can become an international player. Indeed in the US, one company claims to have doubled its business by selling flowers in this way. It is now feasible to operate a small scale business, aimed at a relatively small number of customers (or fans) and still make money. As discussed in the previous chapter, the widespread use of digital money will encourage the power shift away from publishers and distributors, back to the 'creatives'.

Computer technology looks set to transform the music industry's distribution channels within the next 20 years. This will require millions more computer owners, but only thirty years ago, only a small proportion of people had colour television sets. Now look - over 99.5% of homes have at least one.

There are other considerations which have yet to be ironed out relating to copyright and other intellectual and creative rights. Making original, high quality copies of just about anything in its digital form is very straight-forward. There is huge potential for fraud, although technology exists such as SCMS (Serial Copy Management System), which copies digital markers or 'fingerprints' from an original to the digital copy. Anyone who attempts to make another copy from a copy, rather than the original, will not be able to do so. These telltale digital markers also exist if partial copies are used to create other products. However, it is both cheap and perfectly legal (provided you do not use them to infringe copyright) to buy 'code strippers' which will remove SCMS protection codes on audio media. There are several legitimate situations where such 'strippers' are needed, but the fact that they are available at all means that, inevitably, they will be used illegally by pirates, thus rendering the whole SCMS system utterly pointless.

Existing copyright laws do not address electronic piracy issues. Copyright specialists seem to be making it up as they go along because the territory is, as yet still largely uncharted. Significantly, the newest generation of audio CD recorders, as well as implementing SCMS, can also only use 'consumer' re-recordable blank disks. The purchase price of these blanks includes a licence fee component that allows the legal copying (for personal use only) of material from published CD's. This prompts three questions: How much of the fees raised in this way will be distributed to the artists? To whom will they be distributed, when no one knows whose music will be copied? And how do you reconcile the fact that a great many of these disks will be used by musicians (and others) to record their own original material, but they will still have to pay a licence fee for the privilege? It is interesting to note that many of the manufacturers of such equipment also have signif-icant interests in record companies and labels, and are therefore paranoid about piracy. The only way to combat serious piracy is to take the profit out of it by selling the original item at a fair and sensible price which then makes it uneconomic for the pirates to compete against it.

Capturing and displaying still and moving visual images is also changing. You don't need to send your photo snaps for processing with the latest digital cameras. Take the shot, look at it instantly, transfer it into a computer, enhance the image, import it into documents, publish it on the Internet or print it out and stick the picture on your fridge. (In the late 1970's and early 1980's, there was a generally held view at international photo-graphic equipment exhibitions such as Photokina that digital photography was really only 'science fiction' and it would be decades before it began to match the quality of film - and anyway, it would be unbelievably expensive. Correct - apart from the timescale and the cost! In June 1997, MacUser magazine reviewed no less than 12 digital cameras (11 of them in the sub-£1000 price bracket) and there are new and increasingly cheaper & more capable cameras entering the marketplace on a weekly basis. Yes, there is still some way to go before the output matches the quality of film, but the important point is that there are huge new areas of application that were unforeseen until recently. When you want to put images on a computer screen, there is no point in using a higher resolution than the screen can display. In addition, the quality of printed output from digital images is increasing as rapidly as the cost of the necessary equipment is falling. MacUser commented, *"Digital photography is moving gradually away from the preconceptions of conventional photography, and the further it moves, the greater the benefit."*

Conventional chemical film processing is under threat. Kodak is the world's largest purchaser of silver. What will happen to the price of silver when the market declines? It is however, worth mentioning that over half the world's population has never taken a photograph and there's an estimated world-wide market for 60 billion colour prints per year, so don't expect Boots the Chemist to stop taking in your processing in the foreseeable future.

These brief examples illustrate just one aspect of technology; whenever a new technology comes along, somebody will use it, and others will find new uses for it. It simply doesn't matter what we think. We ignore or ridicule such developments at our peril.

How is technology making it cheaper and more efficient to do business in your industry? No area of business is immune from the consequences of new technology. Old ideas may now be viable using the latest technology. How do customers currently find out about your products and services? How do they pay? How is it delivered? Who are your future competitors? What would an aggressive predator need to do in order to take away your customers or if you work in government, the people you are paid to deal with?

Hold on tight for the techno-ride of your life

Much of the technology we will be using in the next five to ten years has already been invented and discovered. According to Daniel Burrus in *Technotrends*, the time it takes for new technological developments to trickle down into our lives is shrinking. For example, fluorescent lighting was invented in 1852 and took 82 years to be implemented. Radar was invented in 1887 but took 46 years to be put into production. The ballpoint pen took 50 years since its invention in 1888. The helicopter took 32 years (far longer if you believe Leonardo da Vinci had the idea first). TV took 29 years since John Logie Baird developed it in 1907.

Most, if not all technological advances are now driven by purely commercial motives. Research and development has become hideously expensive and the results must be brought to market as quickly as possible, if its developers can ever expect to see a return on their investment. New technology therefore commands a high price. You can be sure that as the price for such technology falls, it is an indication that soon it will be replaced by something radically better. This technological merry-go-round is constantly speeding up as corporations try to keep ahead of their equally well-resourced competition. The race is on.

For the first time in history, each new discovery is recorded in the tiniest detail and stored on computer databases. Recorded knowledge is therefore growing exponentially. Research findings are often published electronically and shared amongst scientists throughout the world, further speeding up the development process of countless seemingly unrelated research projects. Another reason for the rapid acceleration in technology is how each new discovery is combined and applied to other technologies. These technology hybrids speed up developments even further.

Already we live among cyborgs, part-human and part-machine; Uncle Fred and Auntie Ethel are fitted with artificial hips, teeth, voice boxes and pacemakers, and held together with metal, plastic and synthetic fibre pins. Advanced research is underway to create artificial blood, hearts, lungs, kidneys, livers, pancreas', legs, eyes, ears and even brain cells. Artificial senses and sensors will be able to stimulate nerves directly. This could lead to all sorts of 'direct pleasure' products. And we all know which business sectors will embrace that technology!

Our brains work at speeds measured in thousandths of a second - not bad - but computers today already operate in billionths of a second. Parallel computers dramatically increase the calculation speed even further. The importance of computer speed cannot be over-emphasised. Each leap in processing speed makes it possible to perform even more complex functions and further helps eliminate humans from the process. This can mean less work for people in the future and the increased likelihood that computers will make many of the decisions affecting the lives of millions without people having a chance to intervene simply because nobody can ever think and respond quicker than the computers.

We are entering a new era in computer technology. In the future, computers will probably emulate biological principles instead of those from the world of physics. Extensive research is developing 'neural networks' which re-create the functions of the human brain. Our brains are constantly sending and receiving tiny electrical impulses via trillions of neurons. These advanced neural computers copy this process by connecting artificial neurons embedded in silicon chips.

Biotech tampering and its tasty future

For ten thousand years farmers have improved the quality and yield from the plants and animals they grow by selective breeding. For the latter half of the 20th century, science has been the main driving force in agriculture. It looks set to dominate it in the 21st century. Today, the largest farms are run by computers linked to sensors which monitor every aspect of the soil, its moisture and chemical balance, and the crops themselves. For millions, science and technology governs the food they eat; its growth, harvesting, storage, processing, distribution and cooking. Again, commercialisation is dictating future developments.

Modern biotechnology is defined by the Biotechnology and Biological Sciences Research Council as *"the application of our advancing understanding of living organisms and their components to create industrial products and processes."*

Biotechnology is not new and has been used in the manufacture of beer, wine, cheese and yoghurt for hundreds of years. But modern biotechnology and genetic engineering are set to revolutionise agriculture and industry. Selective breeding in the past was only used to improve our food and drink, but genetic engineering will also affect the drug and chemical industries with far-reaching ethical implications for life as we know it. Scientists understand better than they have ever done before how plants, animals and micro-organisms function. By studying them at their individual cell level, science has made massive leaps in advanced animal breeding, understanding how the body heals itself, how pesticides work against crop-eating insects and has provided the knowledge to create new animals and plants, as well as new pharmaceuticals and industrial raw materials.

It was only in 1953 when DNA (deoxyribonucleic acid) was discovered by James Watson & Francis Crick. DNA is the biological molecule which carries an organism's genetic information. Every organism carries its own genes. These genetic codes tell the plant or organism what chemicals it needs to grow and reproduce, and what type of cells are required. For the first time in the millions of years it has taken for living organisms to evolve on this planet, it is now possible to transplant the genes from one animal or plant into another, different species. For example, the anti-freeze gene in Arctic fish have been successfully transferred to tomato plants to protect them from harmful (and expensive) frost damage. Genetically modified branded "Flavr Savr", long lasting tomatoes were launched in the United States in 1994 and a tomato paste made from genetically modified tomatoes is already available in some British supermarkets. Other fragile fruits and vegetables will follow as the agrichemicals industry, farmers and food retailers look to technology to eliminate unnecessary wastage (or spoilage as its called in the trade). The lost profit represents too high a percentage of what they sell. It is in their interests to develop, grow and sell apples that stay crisp, strawberries which stay fresh for longer and bananas which don't bruise. Monsanto, one of the world's largest agrichemical conglomerates, insists its genetically modified foods are safe. But they and most other food producers say it is impossible to label foods which contain such ingredients. They probably mean it isn't commercially viable to do so, which is not the same thing.

We will be eating genetically modified foodstuffs whether we want to or not.

By understanding the genetic make up of plants, scientists have been able to produce plants resistant to herbicides, disease, salt poisoning and insect infestation. This means crops can be grown without the need for costly pesticides and herbicides and in areas of the world which traditionally have been too harsh to support them. This has profound implications for food production, especially in countries experiencing rapid population growth.

On a recent flight to Vancouver I sat next to a transgenicist who worked for the US Government in Washington DC. He told me how high value crops such as soya bean, maize, rapeseed, sugar beet, tobacco and cotton were being modified genetically by transferring particular genes from one plant into another, to make them resistant to a wide variety of insect pests, many of which have become immune to existing pesticides. Ecologists and many clinical geneticists fear that even the humble bumble bee will be wiped out. This means that honey producers could suffer and natural pollination in nature would decline. The consequences for this and the effects of cross pollination from genetically modified crops to surrounding weeds could be catastrophic.

Genetically modified corn has an added gene to protect it against the appetite of the corn budworm which eats about 5% of the world's corn crop, while bollworm resistant cotton was one of the first genetically modified crops. Up to 60% of processed foods use soya - it is included in chocolate, biscuits and cakes. The potential profit is staggering, although there are some major issues concerning its safety. No one knows what impact it will have on consumers in (say) 15 years. Think of all the profit the biotechnolgy companies would miss out on if they tested it for that period first!

Mr. Transgenicist was surprised when I asked "If these pests are now resistant to the pesticides, how long will it be before they mutate in order to combat the genetic modifications?" "That won't be for a while." "Then what?" said I. It was obvious, he believed it would then be an SEP (Someone Else's Problem).

Critics claim that biotechnology interferes with nature and poses real economic threats to farmers, many of whom live and work in under-developed countries and rely on the export of their valuable crops. But it's not just limited to peasant farmers. Using biotechnology it will be possible to grow large quantities of individual cells from many different plants. It will be possible to genetically grow millions of litres of orange juice in any country without the peel, pith and pips or the worry of crop failure, weather damage and insect infestation. This new biotechnology will certainly not be limited to orange juice. Entire economies could get wiped out. The US is one of the world's largest consumers of costly (and therefore high profit potential) vanilla pods. Madagascar's economy relies on its vanilla exports to countries all around the world. After all what would ice cream be without vanilla? Growing it genetically will remove those workers from the equation. But what will then happen to those workers who pick and process these crops? No one seems to care enough to avert their impending demise or the social and economic consequences within the affected countries.

Other applications for genetically modified plants include the creation of "accumulator plants" which 'eat' pollutants such as heavy metals and oil spillages, thus offering a biological solution to a chemical problem.

The successful cloning of adult sheep has already been achieved by embryologist Dr. Ian Wilmut and his team at the Roslin Institute in Edinburgh. The potential for human cloning poses serious ethical issues. International bans on such research and development may slow down its progress but ultimately, it is inevitable that scientists will satisfy their curiosity. If something becomes possible technologically, and a profit can be produced, it is always pursued. It could be argued that such research is merely a demonstration of the next stage in human evolution.

Open wide and swallow this robot, please

As discussed earlier, developments in genetically manufactured drugs will transform healthcare. So will nanotechnology. Progress in nanotechnology has been rapid in the past decade. Micromotors or 'midget machines' no larger than the size of a rice or pollen grain will be capable of roaming within our bodies under their own power, finding problems and relaying information or repairing the damage found. They will be able to treat blood clots, tumours, ulcers, clear cholesterol, 'search-and-destroy' viruses, repair torn muscles and ligaments and even deliver tiny amounts of drugs at highly specific sites within the patient's body. Invasive surgery will become less necessary.

Such devices will be powered by motors constructed at the atomic and molecular level from silicon, and be no larger than 1 millimetre square, its gears the diameter of a human hair and capable of over 195,000 revolutions per minute. Such a device already exists at the Sandia National Laboratories in Albuquerque, New Mexico. It is not science fiction.

Films such as *Fantastic Voyage* and *Inner Space* would become true. How long could it be before computer chips loaded with knowledge can be plugged into somebody's brain as described in William Gibson's novel *Neuromancer*?

All this and much more could lead to an extension of the average lifespan to over 100 years - that is, of course, if you can afford to pay for it. Don't expect it on the National Health Service.

The millennium timebomb

One final thought, on the 1st of January 2000, many of the world's computers will crash, breakdown or 'fall over'. Many will suffer this fate before that day. Why? They won't know what day it is, quite literally. The computer code used in some of the largest computer software applications were designed twenty or thirty years ago. To save computer memory at the time, dates were configured with 2 digits instead of all 4. In other words, 1987 would be recorded as 87. When it becomes 00 - it will create havoc. As this is written in October 97 (er, 1997) not many companies seem to be paying much attention to it. Few executives like the idea of 'wasting' millions of pounds on solving a technical problem which might not even exist. There have been numerous disaster scenarios including a complete failure of the National Grid (an estimated £4 million is being spent to ensure it doesn't), the entire telephone network breaking down and all records of the money in your bank account could disappear (or details of any overdraft!)

Expect concerns to intensify as we approach the new millennium. *The Economist* has described this issue as *"the single most expensive problem ever to have existed."* But sectors of the computer industry have already been warning businesses for the past few years, but to no avail. It doesn't seem to matter to them that the very survival of their organisations is at stake.

Is your employer taking this issue seriously enough?

Write to the chief executives of your bank and building societies requesting a confirmation in writing that your money will be safe from this potential problem and that their IT system has been audited and shown to be millennium proof. Write too to the chief executives of your pension providers and ask for a written statement on whether the companies they have invested your money in are millennium proof? Keep the letters safe - you may need them one day - possibly around 2nd January 2000!

Technological progress may have been rapid in the past 30 years, but it is nothing compared with what is in store for us in the future. By making the most of today's available technology, you will be better prepared to benefit from what is already being developed in research laboratories all over the world today.

Chapter 7
Your Health – a Future Diagnosis

"Many of us feel there is something missing in our lives today. Despite unprece-dented peace and prosperity, we are unhappier than we were. There is an epidemic of irritability and aggression, of depression and paranoia, of obsessions, panics, addic-tions, compulsions, relationships that are not working, careers that dissatisfy ... We feel like losers, even if our status would seem to make us winners... Despite greatly improved opportunities women are dissatisfied and men are confused. The result is an unprecedented rancour and divorce rate."
Oliver James, The Sunday Times 31st August 1997

Looking after yourself should be a personal priority, but in this fast paced world, many believe they simply don't have the time. We regularly go without sleep, fill ourselves with foods and drinks which clog our arteries, rot our teeth and bloat our bodies. In this chapter we will take a sideways look at the benefits of a healthier lifestyle, the consequences for those of us who fail to look after ourselves and a number of other topics related to preserving and enhancing our physical and emotional health in the 21st century.

Millions of us don't eat properly, we don't exercise, many of us don't sleep for as long as we should while others sleep too much. The combination of late nights and early mornings, coupled with the fact that at work we are constantly inundated with an increasing workload and worries about problems and deadlines. Indeed, will we keep our jobs? We worry about our kids and their futures.

On top of these pressures, we are surrounded by images of what is wrong with the world. We see pictures, often in graphic detail, of terrorist bombings, school massacres, motorway pile-ups, murders, rapes and other seemingly random acts of personal violence. All of these, and many more contribute to a general feeling of malaise in our so called civilised society. The personal impact of all this is difficult to pin down precisely - but we all know that life can be depressing - we seem to take it as part of modern day living. There is little we can do about it. Or is there?

How we feel about ourselves has a direct affect on so much of our behaviour. I believe each of us can do a lot to improve our personal wellbeing. We have choices which, much of the time, we either fail to realise, or fail to utilise and act upon.

"I hope I die before I get old." Lyric from Pete Townsend's *My Generation.* These words still strike a chord amongst today's youth - but for different reasons. Drink, smoke and inject - live life to the full - so what if it kills you - what is there to live for anyway? Townsend, added even more poignancy to those rebellious lyrics when, as a 50-something, he staged an impromptu performance of the song for guests at a backstage party when his rock opera *Tommy* was launched in London. By conveying the same words with anger and bitterness, they were as appropriate for those individuals now reaching the autumn and winter years of their lives, as those in their youth.

Getting Real!

The first rule of survival is to 'get real'. We must learn to become totally honest with ourselves. As I wrote in an earlier chapter, it is easier not to take full responsibility for our behaviour. We can then blame others. The treatment of addicts is rarely effective until they first learn to accept responsibility for their destructive behaviour and its consequences.

Survival for everyone of all ages, in the 21st century, requires a fundamental re-think about our desire and ability to look after ourselves better. If you expect anyone else to assume such a responsibility, you will be disappointed. When others, such as government let you down (as they will because of a lack of time, funding and resources) - you will be the one to suffer. Venting one's anger at those who fail us does not change anything.

Preparing for the future means looking at the consequences of our diet, smoking and drinking habits, and at our general level of fitness. What will your present behaviour create for you in say, 20 years time? Looking after yourself will be a growing trend in the decades to come. The benefits include increased happiness, lower stress, lower weight, more energy, a deep sense of feeling fit, and to crown it all you could almost certainly enjoy massive financial savings.

How prepared are you to accept the personal long term consequences for not looking after yourself? Perhaps you don't care. Aren't you worth it? Why is that?

- How could you improve the way you look after yourself today?
- How could you improve the way you feel about yourself?
- How could you move towards becoming healthier?
- What is stopping you? Be specific.
- What do you gain from behaviour which you already know is not in your long term best interests?

Two zookeepers were watching a large brown bear in its cage, making a great deal of noise and commotion. It was obvious that the bear was not in a particularly good mood. The trainee zookeeper turned to the older, more experienced zookeeper and asked, "Why is the bear so bad tempered today?"

"He's damaged his climbing frame and is sitting on a large, rusty nail which is sticking out of a piece of wood," the experienced zookeeper replied.

"Well, why doesn't he get up off his backside?"

"That's easy - it doesn't hurt enough yet!"

This way of dealing with pain is no different in humans. We tend to prefer 'the way things are'. We may not be happy with our present situation, but we rarely do anything about it until the pain becomes so intense that we are forced to get up off our own rusty nails. For example, many of us hate our jobs and endure relationships which do not make us happy, but we don't look elsewhere to find organisations and people who will enhance our lives - the nails don't hurt enough.

Many perceive sadness or disappointment and pain as unnatural or a sign of weakness. So we go through life 'happily discontented'. Things aren't necessarily good, but we will accept the unacceptable by rationalising our situation as one which could be worse. But our emotions are more powerful than our sense of logic. Emotions constantly push us towards pleasurable activities. It rarely seems to matter that some of these pleasures may be against our longer-term health interests. Professional marketers are highly skilled at finding those emotional 'justifiers' and so persuade us to buy their pleasure-satisfying products and services. If we are helped to believe that unhealthy behaviour is pleasurable, we will be more likely to buy into it.

What if your doctor conducted a series of detailed tests on you, evaluated the results, and told you that you will almost certainly die within the next 6 months if you did not change your eating, drinking or smoking habits? Would you change your behaviour? Probably. So for the purposes of this exercise, imagine the doctor has told you the bad news.

The benefits of pain and our 'pleasure sickness'

Our ability to experience pain is an alarm system from the brain - telling us that something needs our attention. Touch a red hot stove and your hand instantly and instinctively pulls back sharply from the heat. We respond when the affected nerve endings send these alarm signals back to the brain, which immediately tells our muscles to get our hand away from the source of the danger. Imagine what it would do to our hand if we had no feeling of pain - we could be severely burned; the fact that we cannot feel the pain wouldn't make any difference to the personal damage we would suffer. So, pain has some distinct advantages to us. But nagging, vaguely uncomfortable physical and emotional pains may be tolerated for quite some time before we seek treatment. This is particularly common among men, who may experience bodily pain, but convince themselves that it would be silly to see the doctor for such a minor complaint, (although it can be a wonderful opportunity to gain attention and sympathy from their partners as they soldier on regardless). In any case, men are usually 'far too busy' to see the doctor. Women tend to be more sensible. Is it just a coincidence that women live longer than men?

However, most normal people do not like pain and will go to extraordinary lengths to avoid it. Think for a moment about the ways we try to suppress pain; painkilling drugs are an obvious example, but what about how we try to deal with emotional pains such as stress, anxiety, unhappiness, depression, low self-esteem and poor self-confidence. We do whatever we can to block out the pain. We fill our lives with all manner of activities to 'take our minds off things'. I'm sure you've had an ache or pain and lost yourself in work, only to realise later that you forgot all about the pain.

We move away from pain and towards pleasure at every chance we get. The pursuit of pleasure and the avoidance of pain is a basic human condition. Everything we do has a 'positive intention' - in other words, we may believe at the time that eating a whole tub of Haagen Dazs ice-cream will make us feel better - it might in the short term. But later? So, even though all our behaviour has a positive intention, there are often negative consequences. Many of these negative consequences prompt further pleasure-seeking opportunities - which in turn create more, negative consequences.

We suppress pain by changing our moods, using a wide range of socially acceptable chemical substances - stimulants and depressants; including sugar, caffeine, nicotine, prozac and alcohol as well as illegal ones such as barbiturates and amphetamines (although some of these are regularly prescribed quite legally by doctors, too busy perhaps, to help remove the real causes of the pain.)

Many of these pain-avoiding substances are often sold as 'pleasure-inducing'. Take alcohol for example - is it a stimulant or a depressant? When I asked a group of individuals this question, the majority believed it was a stimulant. It is a depressant. To say we live in an 'addictive society' is not too far from the truth; for many, life is about 'drowning our sorrows' and trying to 'eat ourselves to happiness'. By combining these many strategies to cope with pain, we build up patterns of behaviour which take away the compelling need to 'get up off our nails'. How do you deal with the rusty nails in your life?

Sitting on a rusty nail may be uncomfortable, but sit there long enough and it is quite conceivable that the wound will become infected and lead to consequences far more severe than any initial discomfort.

In some ways - we would be so much better off if someone came along to push us down on our nails, just a little bit, to make us feel uncomfortable enough get up off our backsides.

Anyone who tried to do that could be seen as unkind. If we care about someone how could we possible justify deliberately inflicting pain?

This is a huge problem facing the families of many of society's alcoholics, drug users and others with personally destructive, obsessive or compulsive behaviours. It is quite common for a spouse or parent to cover up socially unacceptable behaviour by putting their family drunk to bed and clearing up pools of vomit and excretia. When the addict wakes up, life appears to have returned to normality. Where's the problem? The pain of this person's nail has been transferred to those around him. This is what is often described as a 'co-dependent relationship'. The supporting partner learns to feel needed by the addict, while the addict needs the partner in order to continue with the addictive behaviour. The addiction becomes an essential part of the relationship. Therapists know the pattern of co-dependent relationships extremely well. For more information on this self-destructive behaviour, read *Co-dependent No More* by Melody Beattie.

Self-confidence; the elusive component

Young people are fed so many images and conflicting messages that it is easy for them to become confused and unsure about what they think. They are constantly told what they should think and how to behave, and the so called 'style' rules can change very quickly. Young people routinely endure ridicule if they refuse to, or cannot afford to wear the best designer labels. The popular music scene is a perfect example of how marketing experts make the most of teenage insecurities. Young people are provided with a wide choice of carefully moulded singers and bands, each with a particular image, created specifically to appeal to a pre-determined section of the music market. In business terms it doesn't really matter which style teenagers choose - so long as they spend their pocket money. The same efficient attention to detail is employed in every other industry with a vested interest in the youth market: hi-fi equipment and electronic gadgets, magazines, clothing and soft drinks.

Advertisers and marketers sustain a youth culture teeming with individuals with varying self-confidence deficiencies. Many people feel inadequate about themselves because they do not compare favourably with those around them, the 'beautiful' and 'super-cool' people they see in magazines and newspapers and on television.   To blame business for all of society's problems would be neither fair nor true. Part of the responsibility for low self-confidence in our youth must rest with parents and teachers. Few realise what long-term harm they do, when in moments of annoyance or anger they call young people stupid, irresponsible, lazy, selfish, inconsiderate, athletically inadequate or generally worthless. Young people rarely receive the confidence-building encouragement they so desperately need. Consequently many teenagers enter young adulthood with a lot of low self worth 'baggage'. Low self-esteem is widely accepted as being largely responsible for the early dependence on alcohol and illegal drugs among many of today's youth.

Self-confidence is a fundamental ingredient for personal control, success and achievement. A lack of it has terrible, debilitating effects. A simple example comes immediately to mind: how many times have you seen someone at a party who you thought was physically or intellectually attractive, and yet were too shy to start a conversation because you convinced yourself that he or she would not be interested in talking to you?

Self-confidence provides a sense of inner calm and a feeling of overall control in life. Self-confident people accept themselves as they are and do not feel intimidated by others, nor do they let negativity get the better of them. However, it is worth pointing out that being self-confident does not mean ramming your personality down the throats of everyone you meet.   For anyone who suffers from low self-esteem, the good news is that confidence can be learned. Once the techniques involved are mastered, an individual will feel as though they are fully in charge of their life.

There are a number of external reasons why so many people suffer from low self-worth. However, by far the most common source is an inner willingness to accept a second or third class position in life. If told often enough, people come to believe the put-downs they receive from bosses, family and partners. They forget that no one, however 'important', has a right to make anyone else feel bad. At the same time, to a certain extent, anyone who suffers such treatment is partially to blame. They condone and perpetuate such behaviour by allowing it to happen. People tend to treat you the way you let them. Anyone who gets away with being rude, critical, overbearing, unreasonably demanding and insensitive to the feelings of others, is not going to change unless he or she is made to realise that this behaviour is unacceptable. However uncomfortable or frightening it may seem, anyone who is made to suffer in this way must do something about it. If you don't, you will never be in control of your life. Worse, you will spend your life being victimised by others. Whatever you derive from this book, it will amount to very little if you allow yourself to continue a life in which your self-confidence is undermined by others.

The first step towards being treated with respect is to learn to respect yourself, and part of this is knowing how to behave assertively. This does not mean screaming and shouting; assertiveness should not be confused with aggressiveness. Assertiveness means stating simply what you feel and think to those around you. It is about creating a 'win-win' situation - one where your rights and plans remain intact whilst you respect the rights and requests of others, so both parties are satisfied. Learning to be self-confident and assertive involves changing what could be deep-rooted and long-established patterns of thinking and behaviour. Making a distinct change in your behaviour will almost certainly feel uncomfortable.

Here's a very simple illustration; without thinking about it, fold your arms. Look at which arm is on top. This is the way that you naturally fold your arms and it feels comfortable. Now, deliberately introduce change by refolding your arms so that the other arm is now on top. This almost certainly will feel unnatural and uncomfortable. However, if over the next few weeks, you make a conscious effort to remember to fold your arms in this 'new' way, after two to three weeks, you will find that this 'new' habit becomes the normal, natural way you behave. The 'old' way may then feel awkward. You will have changed a habit.

Anyone who tries to achieve too much too quickly is likely to suffer from disappointment and frustration. Immediate changes to incorporate into your life should include eliminating these common non-assertive and self-destructive habits:

- Automatically saying 'sorry' when something is not necessarily our fault (this seems to happen in Britain more than anywhere else).
- Saying 'Yes' when you would prefer to say 'No'.
- Trying to please everyone all the time.
- Putting yourself down, even if you think it is a way of conveying modesty.
- Being afraid to ask for what you want/need.
- Agreeing with people 'just for a quiet life'.
- If complimented, dismissing or deflecting it. Never do this. Instead, thank the individual offering the compliment. It will make him or her feel good too.

- Asking for permission to express your thoughts and views.
- Expecting things to work out badly.
- Giving others permission to depress, upset, annoy, bully or frighten you.
- Sounding hesitant in the way you speak. Get rid of 'ums' and 'ers' in your conversation.
- Allowing others to dominate your time.
- Accepting poor standards of professional service.
- Blaming family and friends for your present position in life.
- Hating or envying others. This only harms you.
- Criticising others.
- Comparing yourself unfavourably to others. You are unique, therefore you cannot be compared with anyone else.
- Allowing things you cannot change to dominate your life.
- Being afraid to just be yourself.

There is also a lot to be said for developing a habit of acting self-confidently. After a while you will actually become more self-confident and more assertive. It is worth pointing out that there may be many occasions when you may feel lacking in confidence but that most of the time those around you will not know it. My old friend Richard is a case in point. He is highly successful at staging business conferences but for years suffered from a chronic lack of self-confidence. He would cringe inside at the merest hint of being made the centre of attention. This all changed on his birthday a few years ago. His colleagues had organised a visit from a 'kissagram' as a surprise. Unknown to Richard, someone videotaped everything. The young woman read an amusing poem and then gave him a big birthday kiss. He was dying inside with embarrassment. He desperately wanted to escape. Later, when all the fuss had died down, he was shown the video. Much to his astonishment he did not look the way he had felt. At the time he was not aware of what he had said and was very surprised to see that he appeared to be in control, which accentuated even further the gap between what he had felt and how he appeared to others. He told me later that the incident had changed his life. Now that he knows he does not look self-conscious, he no longer feels that way. He is far more relaxed and self-confident.

There are many assertiveness courses available these days. You will find them advertised in the personal classified sections of newspapers and magazines. If you want to learn to be more confident and assertive, why not take the first step by finding out more about these courses? Everyone who learns to be more self-confident invariably receives a special bonus: enthusiasm. Enthusiastic people are the ones who actually get things done in this world. Enthusiasm is what turns any idea into reality. And enthusiasm is linked closely with happiness.

Happy talk

Think back to your childhood for a moment - in particular the few weeks leading up to an especially memorable and enjoyable Christmas or other holiday celebration. Remember the excitement, the visits to the stores, the atmosphere and the general hustle and bustle. Maybe you wrote to Father Christmas asking for a bicycle, a dolls' house or a train set. Now think about that Christmas Eve, putting up your Christmas sock or stocking, possibly above the fireplace, or at the end of your bed. How much trouble did your parents have in getting you off to bed? Indeed, how much trouble did you think you would have going to sleep? Christmas Day would eventually arrive. The moment you were awake (sometime between 4 and 6am if it was like my house) you may have rushed to the pile of gifts under the Christmas tree and started ripping open your presents with total joy. You would try so hard not to make any noise because you knew that, for some reason, your parents were always particularly tired on Christmas morning.

When we grow up we tend to forget these intense feelings of joy and happiness. The closest we get may be while we make love passionately or, if we have children ourselves, watching their little faces when they open Christmas and birthday presents, re-living the moments we enjoyed so much at their age.

So what goes wrong? Why is it, that for millions of people, life is not as happy now as it was then? More responsibilities, stress and lack of time are certainly major contributing factors, but I believe the answer is far more basic than that. As adults we no longer have anyone to 'stage-manage' our happiness. When we were children, our parents would often build up our excitement in exactly the same way as professional actors and musicians build to a climax in their performances. This does not just happen by chance: it is totally stage-managed. When it is skilfully done, by the end of an outstanding show we are on our feet cheering and applauding. Many parents do something similar with their children to build their excitement in the lead-up to special events. I will always remember one specific birthday when I was a child. For weeks beforehand I was told by my father that my birthday present was going to be very special. Neither he nor my mother would tell me what it was, but they assured me I would absolutely love it. My mind did somersaults for weeks trying to guess what they had bought for me. It became something of a game - I would try to persuade them to tell me if my guesses were even 'warm' - they led me on, gently teasing me until, by my birthday, I could hardly contain myself. The present certainly lived up to my expectations. It was my first real fishing rod and reel. Up until then I'd had a toy one, no use at all in catching the 'whoppers' I was convinced I could catch. That fishing rod was used constantly for many years and I looked after it with all the love and care in the world. (This example came to mind because I was rooting through my parents' loft and there it was, a lot smaller than I remembered it, of course - but the moment I found it, my eyes glazed over as I replayed in my mind many of the fishing trips I went on in my childhood. And to think it was 'just' a fishing rod.) Obviously, happiness does not have to be related to receiving gifts, but my aim is to illustrate how feelings of happiness can last for a long time with a little careful 'stage management'. If my parents had not behaved in the way they did, without doubt I would still have appreciated the present but it would not have had anything like the same impact.

Even though our lives are rarely stage-managed as they were when we were children - they could be. The secret is to build into your own life an ongoing series of stage-managed events. Plan things to look forward to. For example, if you decide to take a holiday, make a point of reading all you can about your destination and places of interest before you go. Plan a year ahead if necessary.

Stage-managing your life need not concern only major events. Reward yourself for jobs well done. Tell yourself that once you have completed a particular chore you will spoil yourself by doing something special. Then make an effort to look forward to it - don't give it to yourself straight away, delay the enjoyment so that you can savour it. If you want to be happier in life, don't limit the stage-management to events in your own life - provide it as a service to your family and friends. Who knows, they might do the same for you? While on the subject of doing things for others, if you truly want to indulge yourself, try this: do something kind and generous for somebody else, but don't tell him or her - or any other living soul - what you have done. The warm feelings you experience when you help someone else are diluted when you try to take credit for your good deed by telling others. You know something others don't - it is a wicked pleasure. It is important to realise that it really is OK to feel good about yourself.

Striving for a permanent state of happiness is not only unrealistic but impossible. When we do this we are effectively chasing a 'happiness mirage': as we approach what we think is the key to complete happiness and success the 'mirage' moves off once again - far enough away to be seen, but still near enough for us to think that pursuing it is worthwhile. We have all said to ourselves, 'I'll be happy just as soon as I get that promotion' or 'I'll be happy just as soon as I have managed to save enough money for my dream house.'

Happiness is about now, this second, this minute, this hour. How do you really feel about your life right now? On a scale of 1 to10, what would you score? What would you expect to feel if you were to score 10? Is it realistic? If not, why not? Our expectations for happiness are often based on an idealised version of what we think others enjoy; we compare ourselves with something that does not really exist. Happiness and joy are always temporary. Your circumstances may seem dire. Perhaps you feel that you haven't much to be happy about. Try to imagine being happy at this precise moment, while you are reading this book. Tell yourself that there is nothing you would prefer to be doing with your time. Young children have the ability to become so engrossed in what they are doing that nothing else matters. We forget how to do this when we get older. We take everything far too seriously. We forget how to play. Our play becomes competitive - we need to perform well, we need to win. This means it stops being play. Happy people get totally involved in whatever they are doing. They concentrate on the process, not just the result. Because the process always takes longer than the result, they feel happier for longer.

Unhappy people want to be somewhere else while they are at work, and yet feel terribly guilty whilst relaxing because they feel they should be at work! They tend to feel the need to chop and change their activities constantly in much the same way as they would zap from TV channel to TV channel vainly trying to find something interesting to watch. It is highly likely that even if they find something, they will still keep zapping channels just in case something better crops up elsewhere. That is how they go through life - always on the look-out for something better. They don't know exactly what they want - just something 'better'. They insist on everything being perfect, all the time. This can only breed ulcer-inducing stress and dissatisfaction. Such individuals rarely feel happy or satisfied with anything. They lead unfulfilled lives, always feeling that there is something missing.

So many experiences that should be enjoyable are allowed to become an inconvenience or a nuisance. How many times have you arranged to go to the cinema, a concert, the theatre or a meal with friends, only to find that you are so busy with work that you have barely had time to look forward to it beforehand? On the night you have to rush madly to get there, by which time it has become more of a chore than a delight. This is what happens to the many people who fail to feel happy in spite of having all the ingredients and opportunities for a happier life. We make all sorts of excuses for not having fun: we are too young, too old, too fat, we are afraid of looking stupid in front of our children, our parents or our colleagues.

We favour what we already know; we like our 'comfort zones' - after all, stepping into the unknown is difficult. We insulate ourselves against possible discomfort, ridicule or unhappiness. The irony is that we can be made to feel unhappy simply by not stretching ourselves. I am not suggesting that you should go out of your way to experience pain or emotional turmoil, but the so-called 'Law of Reciprocity' states that you simply cannot enjoy real happiness or success if you have not experienced unhappiness or failure. It's only when we fail that we find out who and what we are. Are you one of those people who never gets around to trying new activities? Is it because you don't think you will be any good at them? You can have so much fun once you stop caring so much about the prospect of being laughed at. Those who are willing to 'have a go' find that the only ones who laugh are those who don't get involved themselves. Happy people accept what they cannot change and are happy with what and who they are. They like themselves and have learned that if they feel good about themselves, just about everything around them takes on a more pleasant appearance. Isn't it strange that it is OK to tell others that you feel fed up, tired, stressed and depressed? To conform in today's society it seems that you must look miserable and behave accordingly.

Happy people attract friends like a magnet. They know the true value of friendship and the importance of spreading happiness wherever they go. Happiness begins on the inside. Unhappy people believe (mistakenly) that happiness comes from outside. They are convinced that money, position or power equals happiness.

Tiredness is a serious problem in society. Fatigue leads to unnecessary stress and irritability, which makes us unhappy. Millions of people try to survive without enough sleep. Try to get into the habit of 'spoiling' yourself with a regular dose of the right amount of sleep.

According to the World Health Organization there are an estimated 100 million people suffering from depression at any one time. There is evidence to support the idea that depression in all its different forms has increased dramatically over the last fifty years. Common sense tells us that this increase in depression must be related in some way to the sheer pace and complexity of life in today's society. It is likely to increase unless we as individuals proactively pursue stress reducing strategies.

Strategies to stamp out stress

A successful life in the 21st century will require higher levels of physical and mental fitness to work under the relentlessly increasing pressure. Learning to deal with stress is a life skill for the future and deserves special attention. We need to accept stress as part of our modern lives, although admitting you suffer from stress is often seen as a sign of weakness and proof that you are unsuitable for promotion and added responsibility. Nearly everyone suffers from stress; it's how you cope with it that matters. More is now known about how the body stores and relieves itself of stress. Look at any top class sports figure, or business leader; they develop the ability to cope under intense pressure. Their level of physical fitness and mental training gives them their competitive edge. Anyone can copy and benefit from such an approach.

Stress can build up with the accumulation of a myriad of small seemingly insignificant pressures and commitments. According to stress expert Dr John Potter *"Stress is a response or a reaction to the demands we feel are being made on us. Our interpretation of whether or not we can cope with those demands causes both physical and mental effects."* It is now widely accepted that there is a direct link between stress, anxiety and depression and illnesses including diabetes, heart disease and cancers. These can be triggered by intense periods of stress. People in particularly high-stress jobs such as the police force and fire fighters, have been found to be more prone to illnesses such as cancer. Ambitious over-achievers who are highly competitive, aggressive, obsessive, ever aware of the shortness of available time, and 'driven', are characterised as Type A Personalities. They are heart attacks waiting to happen.

In this order, let's look at the causes, symptoms and coping mechanisms for stress. If you are in imminent, physical danger, your body will produce adrenaline to put you into the most resourceful state to help you cope with the situation. This will create a 'fight or flight' response in you.

Many causes of stress are often beyond our control; relationship problems, poor health, an insufficient living or work space, recent redundancy and unemployment, the lack of job security, working outside your comfort zones, too many demands leading to too much to do and too little time, being too demanding of yourself by insisting that everything in your life and work has to be perfect, too many demands from work superiors, constant interruptions, general unhappiness, too much unwanted noise, money worries, poor organisation, a new birth or death in the family, worry about members of your family, divorce, moving house, deadlines, changes, lots of responsibility, over-work and fatigue.

Each of these will induce stress; but many of the causes are interrelated and combine to turn up the pressure in our lives. Not all stress is bad for us. There are two basic types; EUSTRESS which is good and empowering, while DYSTRESS is harmful and debilitating. Trying to ignore or suppressing stress is not the answer - accumulated stress can lead to serious medical conditions

Stress - how would you like to pay?

The stress expert Dr. Malcolm Carruthers, says: *"Stress is like electricity - if there is an overload, the body blows a fuse."* How many of the following symptoms do you recognise?

- an inability to relax,
- sweaty hands,
- dry throat,
- aggressive and dangerous reactions,
- suffering 'road rage' while driving,
- generally exhibiting a short temper,
- a pounding heart,
- chest and recurring muscular pain,
- over-breathing when tense,
- finding it difficult to shake off colds or flu,
- suffering from migraines, rashes, stomach pains,
- highly critical of spouse, children or colleagues,
- drinking more alcohol than normal,
- eating poorly,
- stopped exercising,
- general apathy,
- you don't want to talk to anyone, especially about the way you feel,
- you've retreated inside yourself,
- you suffer panic attacks,
- cold hands and feet,
- intense butterflies in the stomach,
- diagnosed with an ulcer
- experience irregular palpitations,
- you want to go to the toilet more regularly,
- feeling nauseous,
- decision making feels more difficult,
- your attention span is shorter,
- a general feeling of listlessness or being 'run down',
- a loss of appetite,
- digestion problems and back pain, skin problems,

- chronic tiredness, insomnia or sleeping far more than normal,
- constant worry, suicidal thoughts,
- a sense of being overwhelmed by life, events and mood swings.

Do you regularly use the first 30 minutes when you get home to complain about what happened to you that day? If so, what longer term effect could this have on your partner? Why should you pass these feelings on to others?

Research has show that many couples in their 20's and 30's no longer have active sex lives; too little time and too much stress contribute to a dulling of the sexual appetite. A lack of sex is often cited as a major contributing factor to relationship breakdowns.

Do you work as part of a stressed out workforce? These are the telltale signs; a high turnover of staff, high absenteeism and illness, a widespread lack of co-operation, regular examples of conflict between co-workers, an apathetic attitude, workers indulging in abnormally high rates of smoking, drinking during and after work and illegal drug use.

If you suffer from any or some of the above - you're almost certainly suffering from stress. Stress rarely disappears without help. This can be in the form of self-help or from a counsellor or doctor.

Convincing yourself that you don't suffer from stress or that it will sort itself out if only you work through it, is probably the biggest mistake you can make. This is closely followed by 'relaxing' with alcohol, cigarettes, a few cups of strong coffee or 'comforting' chocolate. Nicotine and caffeine increase your metabolism and levels of anxiety, thus increasing, not decreasing, your feelings of irritability. Sugar produces a short energy boost, but the body then releases insulin to counteract the effect of the sugar which then leads to a massive drop in energy levels. You could of course resort to a wide variety of drugs to calm you down. Patients continue to depend on them to a lesser or greater extent, again and again and again. From 1980 -1989 British doctors wrote out an estimated 138 million prescriptions for Valium, Librium and Mogodon, all made by the Swiss owned pharmaceuticals giant, Roche. But none of these strategies is effective at addressing the root causes of the stress.

Try to identify the causes of your stress. Be as specific as you can. Come up with a possible solution for each cause. Who could help you? Would you benefit from learning to be better organised? Learn time management techniques (see chapter 8). To whom should you delegate some of your tasks? Do you need new skills to become more effective? If so, go on a course. Have a massage. Learn to relax through self-hypnosis. Take up yoga. Learn the Alexander technique. Autogenic training is highly effective for those in high-stress jobs. Listen to 'relaxation' tapes - those by Denise Linn are particularly effective. Or try the following visualisation exercise; breathing slowly and deeply, with your eyes closed, imagine a scene which you remember as relaxing and restful where you were happy and calm. Engage all your senses; with your eyes closed picture the scene, intensify the colours, hear the sounds - mentally turn up or tone down the volume of those sounds, feel the warmth of the sun perhaps, immerse yourself in the images, mentally rise above the scene and float in mid air. Recall your relaxed emotions. How can you intensify them? Use your imagination to add other relaxing memories to these images. Create others. Perhaps you could imagine your dream home in any part of the world. Design it in your head, walk through it, instantly decorating and furnishing it as you pass through each room. You can always return to this home sanctuary when ever you wish. You may want to try this exercise with your favourite relaxing music in the background or on headphones.

One of the most effective all round strategies involves physical exercise. Regardless of how little time you think you have available, doing something involving physical effort helps reduce stress whilst simultaneously giving you more enthusiasm and energy to cope with your stress. It also improves stamina, releases adrenaline and endorphins which produce a natural 'high' and relieves muscle tension - one of the prime physiological symptoms of stress. Exercise also provides a means to vent anger and frustration.

Other strategies to help reduce stress include acquiring a pet. Cat and dog owners report lower stress levels, and many people find that an aquarium provides them with a means of relaxation. Make it a personal priority to keep stress at bay by refusing to battle through it. Acknowledge its existence and invest in yourself by doing something to treat it.

Have a heart

With so many conflicting stories about what is good or bad for us, it is small wonder that so many people are confused. But health statistics are quite clear. Heart disease is the number one killer in Britain. According to the British Heart Foundation, heart disease was the cause of 45% of deaths in 1994. At the beginning of the 20th Century, heart disease caused only one death in six. Although a hereditary condition, many of these people would probably be still alive, if only they hadn't smoked, eaten and drunk themselves into ill health.

In the report, *Nutritional Aspects of the Development of Cancer*, it was found that up to 2/3rds of cancer cases were linked to the types of food people ate. Cancer is the second biggest killer in Britain affecting one in three people, and represents one of the highest cancer rates in Europe. Men suffer most from lung cancer, while breast cancer kills most women. The deathrate in Britain from heart disease in men aged 35 to 75 may have fallen between 1980 and 1990 by 23 per cent, but it fell in Sweden by 33 per cent and in the United States by 35 per cent during the same period. Diabetes affects 1.4 million people in Britain and according to a MORI poll up to 75% of those surveyed did not realise diabetes can cause heart disease.

Cancer, cash and cigarettes

28% of men and 26% of women smoke, a significant drop in the last 20 years. But smoking is still a major contributor to heart disease. Statistically, better-off people have given up smoking, but poor people haven't. Middle class men and women smoke the least. In the Policy Studies Institute *Poor Smokers* by Alan Marsh and Stephen McKay, smoking is highest amongst the least well-off families. 75% of people on income support also smoke. The authors claim that smoking amongst these groups contributes to increased hardship for women as well as their children. For many poor and unemployed individuals, smoking is cited as one of their only pleasures but represents 15% of their weekly income. The authors also point out that the ever increasing tobacco tax is a device for reclaiming social security benefits. *"...tobacco tax recovers for the Treasury nearly 17% of all income support paid for the support of claimants who are parents of dependent children and who smoke...and amounted in 1991 to £530 million a year."*

Smoking trends indicate a reduction in smoking in The United States and Western Europe, although teenage smoking rose from 8% to 12% in the two years to 1994, despite the growing evidence that it is a leading cause of death. Up to 30% of teenage girls now smoke. Interestingly, in 1993 Professor Sir Richard Doll, who pioneered research into how smoking leads to lung cancer, published the findings of a 40 year study of smoking by doctors which found that smokers are three times more likely to die in middle age than non-smokers. The findings confirmed a significant increase in lung cancer amongst the smokers as well as heart disease, bronchitis and emphysema. Of the 35,000 doctors who took part, 20,000 were dead at the end of the study.

In the United States, cigarette companies have agreed a $368 billion settlement over the next 25 years to pay for anti-smoking campaigns and other public health initiatives. However, tobacco firms are probably not that concerned. While smoking has been cut to 25% of the US population (perhaps the 150,000 people who die each year from heart disease contributed to this drop!) and to 40% in Western Europe, hundreds of millions of Eastern Europeans and Asians are starting to smoke, seeing it as a sign of their

Western style affluence. Western tobacco companies are busily building factories to satisfy this new found hunger for nicotine. Most of these countries have few if any regulatory restrictions prohibiting the sale of cigarettes. Tax revenues will be a welcome addition to government coffers - or should that be 'coughers'! Expect the incidence of lung cancer and heart disease to increase even further in these regions. Dr Paul Kleihaus, a director of the World Health Organisation, said when he presented the 1997 annual global health report, *"We [the West] are truly messengers of death worldwide"* as he announced details of how Western life and foodstyles would result in the expected number of cancer cases to double in developing countries over the next 25 years.

Bulging Britain

The biggest factor linked to heart disease is obesity. Britain has one of the highest incidents of obesity in the world - our foodstyles not only include high percentages of processed food, a high saturated fat content but it's so easily available. In the past 30 years or so, as food has become more widely distributed, there is now more widespread obesity than ever before. It seems to be more of a problem in one of the world's most affluent countries, the US where there are an estimated 58 million obese people. And they seem to be getting 8% fatter every decade. In *The Sunday Times* (14th June 1997) Dr John Foreyt of the Baylor College of Medicine in Houston, stated that he had found that in Starr County, Texas (the second poorest county in the US), up to 50% of the Mexican-American population had diabetes, and that the number one source of calories was Coca-Cola. Poor people from ethnic minorities are three times more likely to be obese than white middle class Americans.

In Britain, according to the National Audit Office, in the last 10 years, obesity has increased from 7% to 13% in men and from 12% to 16% in women. This is largely due to the fact that humans have been used to physical work, which has now become less common in society as a result of the increased introduction of machinery and technology.

Medical cures for obesity represent huge profit potential. In the US up to $30 billion a year is spent on diet pills and weight-loss programmes. Just like everyone else in society, obese people want life's short cuts too. For those who cannot, or refuse to limit their food intake and lead a healthier lifestyle, Professor Stanley McKnight and his colleagues at the University of Washington in Seattle may have an answer. They have bred 'skinny mice' by deleting a gene and feeding them a high fat diet. They stayed thin. It opens up possibilities for controlling obesity in humans. Meanwhile, the pharmaceutical company

Hoffman-La Roche, has developed Xenical, a drug which blocks the body's absorption of fat in the food they eat and which, the manufacturers claim, can cut about 600 calories a day.

Forget the crash diet - here's a crash course in body maintenance

By understanding the basics of how our bodies operate, we can minimise the risks of ill-health. We are designed for excellence. If we look after ourselves we can expect to gain many decades of good use. What we eat and drink determines how we function. In exactly the same way as a motor car; if you feed it with rubbish we will not get the best performance out of it. How much physical exercise you 'find the time for' will also influence your level of fitness and your degree of muscle tone.

Everything we eat and drink is converted into energy. These energy units are measured in calories. Our bodies need a certain number of daily calories in order to function; growing our hair, finger and toe nails, processing and digesting food, pumping blood, eliminating waste matter etc. If, on a daily basis, our energy intake is greater than the energy we use, this energy is put into storage - namely deposited as fat on our thighs, stomach, arms and under our chins.

When this happens consistently over a long period, we become overweight or obese. However, by ensuring that we control the initial intake of calories and that excess calories are burned up regularly through a variety of physical activities; walking, climbing stairs, sex and sport we can maintain a healthy body. What follows is the simplistic description of how we function.

Imagine someone has started a new job shredding paper. Each day this woman has to shred say, twenty large boxes of paper. If by the end of the first day she had shredded only about, eighteen boxes of paper - that was OK, but next morning another delivery of 20 boxes of paper would arrive. If by the end of the second day only 18 boxes were shredded, the other two boxes would also be put into storage. This would go on day after day. After just the first week she would have 10 boxes of paper in storage. After a month it would be forty boxes. The boxes would keep accumulating. Her small warehouse would rapidly fill up with un-shredded boxes piled high in the corridors surrounding her work area. Eventually she realises that she has to get this problem under control. She decides to speed up the box shredding process. By increasing her daily schedule to 22 boxes she would slowly get rid of those stored boxes. Interestingly, she discovers that the more boxes she shreds, the more capable she becomes of shredding even more.

Improvements in her personal planning, and her shredding technique all combine to make a positive contribution to the speed of the shredding process.

Our bodies work in a similar way.

The rate at which we burn calories (or shred our own boxes of paper) is what is known as our metabolic rate. The higher the metabolic rate, the more energy we burn. When we are young, our metabolism is at an all time high - that's why so many kids can eat such a lot and not put on any weight, while older individuals merely look at a fattening food and instantly pile on the flab!

As we grow older our metabolisms slow down. This is a natural process and is irreversible (although we can influence the process - there's more about this in a moment). Therefore, if when we were younger we ate a lot, our metabolisms would burn it up. However, by continuing to eat the same quantities of food as we grow older, we put more of that food energy into storage because our bodies use less energy to carry out its bodily functions.

This is where regular exercise can help. Exercise not only burns up the excess calories but it provides an additional benefit. The process of exercising actually increases the metabolic rate; meaning that our bodies will not only use up the excess, but calories will be burned more quickly in the future. It's a bit like moving our bodies up a gear - from 2nd gear to third or top gear- or even into turbo! People who exercise win both ways.

The other, lesser known part of the equation involves dieting. "Dieting doesn't work" is a common enough saying, but it is worth a closer look at the reasons 'why' it doesn't work.

Historically, most human beings have had to deal with the possibilities of food scarcity and even famine. In the past, if you were wealthy, food was always available. If you were poor, some of the time food would be in short supply.

For the first time in history, most people in the developed world no longer have to worry about the prospect of going without food. But our bodies have evolved in such a way as to defend itself against food shortages. When we go on a diet; limiting our intake of food, our bodies 'protect' us by going into a survival mode by actually slowing down our metabolisms. This means that our bodies try to hold on to those precious and potentially life saving mounds of fat we are so desperately trying to get rid of. The more we limit our food intake, by trying to starve ourselves, the slower our metabolism gets. Various bodily functions will shut down. An easily recognisable, but not infallible telltale symptom of someone with an eating disorder is the poor quality of their hair; the body has decided that it is a non-essential function. The more serious and long-standing the eating disorder, the more bodily functions will be affected, some of which can cause lasting and permanent damage.

The body's self-protection ability can make it intensely difficult and frustrating for anyone who tries to lose weight simply by cutting down on the volume of food they eat.

When you 'fail' at your diet, the food intake goes back up to the previous pre-diet days, but now that your metabolism has slowed down you will burn less energy than before the diet - so the cruellest blow of all - you will pile on even more weight!! Life is no longer just 'a bitch' - it's 'a fat bitch!'

This is why exercise plays such a crucial part in any weight loss programme. As we discussed earlier, exercise increases the metabolism, so when the food intake is controlled, the exercise increases the amount of energy burned up.

Admittedly, the above is a very simplistic view of how our bodies function. But without such an understanding it is easy to see why so many people beat themselves up over their weight - believing they are doing the right thing by going on a diet, but failing to achieve the desired results. This, in turn, makes them feel even more depressed and convinced that they simply do not have the willpower to make healthy changes and improvements to their lifestyle.

Are you a slave to your tongue or a reconstituted hamburger?

Looking after yourself is all about getting the balance right for you. Your doctor should be consulted to advise you on a healthy combination of diet and a safe exercise programme. If your doctor is overweight and unfit - find one who isn't!

Being unfit and overweight leads to an increased possibility of disease and illness. It makes you lethargic and apathetic, more prone to stress, depression and other performance limiting emotions and physical afflictions.

Whoever coined the phrase 'living in the fast lane' could not have foreseen just how fast life would become in the latter part of the 20th century and into the 21st century, although increased stress amongst many workforces gives some indication of what we must learn to contend with. In some ways, we have all been entered into a 'Global Olympics' or 'Grand Prix '; we may not like the idea of racing against other countries and business competitors, but we simply don't have much choice. Our financial, emotional and physical survival depends on it. The race has already begun - though many haven't even realised they are part of it.

Personal health is a pre-requisite for peak performance. Over the last ten years or so I have interviewed countless successful individuals for radio, television and magazines. Without doubt, a significant factor common to most of them is the fact that they manage to find the time in their busy schedules to exercise regularly. One would be tempted to think that the most successful people simply wouldn't have the time; they must have more important things to do. But no - exercise is an integral part of their lives.

Those people who are trying to emulate the most successful often eliminate this trait from the equation - mistakenly believing that if they simply work harder they will achieve success sooner. It's a fallacy. Those people who don't exercise seem to believe (perhaps conveniently) that by exercising they will use up what little surplus energy they have. The reality is different - those who look after themselves by including regular exercise as part of their lifestyle, know that exercise gives additional energy - it does not take it away. A half-hour workout can be more relaxing than 30 minutes 'vegging out' in front of the TV. It's strange but true.

Exercise also improves your ability to think more clearly, it increases muscle tone, which improves your breathing and posture. It increases your enthusiasm and zest for life. All of these improvements help to make you more effective and productive at work and at play.

The benefits of looking after yourself include less chance of needing medical treatment. If you choose to believe Dr. Vernon Coleman, this is a safer option. In *Betrayal of Trust* he states that four out of ten patients given drugs by doctors suffer side effects. One in six hospital patients in Britain have been made ill by doctors - that's 982,485 patients a year. 85% of medical procedures are a 'gamble', while the drugs industry is deceitful, corrupt and ruthless. According to Dr. Coleman, iatrogenesis, or doctor-induced disease, *'is now the commonest cause of serious illness in the developed world."* He even goes so far as to state that prescribed drugs continue to kill more patients than illegal drugs such as cocaine and heroin.

The pharmaceuticals industry is awash with cash and has become the world's most profitable industry. Glaxo Wellcome is capitalised at almost £37 billion, while Zeneca is worth about half that at approximately £17.2 billion. They can confidently predict that spending on healthcare will continue to rise well in to the 21st century. In *Power and Dependence*, author Charles Medawar accepts that the benefits of many drug treatments have been great, but pharmaceutical companies exert enormous power over government and the medical profession. *"The providers have made a secret of drug safety and methods of drug control to an extent which seems unrivalled in any other area of public life. The secrecy for the most part, has nothing to do with protecting legitimate trade secrets or personal privacy - nor is it compatible with what science should be. It seems to have much more to do with protecting professional, commercial and political reputations; we link it with the pursuit of unfair advantage and unjustified power."*

Pharmaceutical companies rely on a diseased population, so why should they want everyone to get well? It is therefore not in their interests or cash starved governments to pay any more than lip service to widespread and on-going health education initiatives which improve the health of the population. Government healthcare costs and pensions are significantly less for dead people!

What should you do if you look after yourself well, but become ill? Ask your doctor lots of specific questions. With health service cutbacks, options are rarely offered freely any more. It's an effective way to save cash. So ask as many questions as you can. On what grounds has he/she diagnosed your condition? What symptoms have led to the diagnosis? How sure is the doctor that a correct diagnosis has been made? Beware of the stock answer, "In my clinical judgement." This means little or nothing. What is it based on? What drugs are being prescribed? Why? Are less costly generic drugs as effective? What are the possible risks and side effects? If antibiotics are being prescribed? Are they really necessary? Or are they just a convenient way of providing you with a 'solution'? What are the likely consequences if medication was not accepted? What other non-pharmaceutical alternatives are there? If gouging a hole in your body is recommended, what are the risks? What are the advantages? Are non-surgical alternatives feasible?

With an estimated 18,000 known diseases that have no effective treatments or cures, the medical profession has a long way to go before it can deliver comprehensive healthcare - if indeed doctors will ever be able to. Taking responsibility for maintaining your own health will be the preferred option for millions in the future. Or perhaps you would be happier spending money on health insurance to give yourself permission to lead an unhealthy lifestyle, confident in the knowledge that if or when you become ill, someone else will have to pick up the tab? The choice is yours.

Chapter 8
The Time Factor:
Deadlines and Detail

"Time is what stops everything from happening at once."
Terry Pratchett

Slavery is alive and kicking. Our master is that b*****d "Father Time". We are drowning in demands on our time. The busier we become, the more we are forced to endure.

Your time is a much sought-after prize. Far more so than you might imagine. More and more of our lives are being taken over by 'time robbers'. Many have developed highly sophisticated methods to gain and hold your precious attention. The more they can disguise it to appear beneficial to you, the better. Why? No one can persuade you to part with your money (or the time you have traded to acquire it) unless they first attract and hold your attention.

Can you imagine being surrounded by school mates in your school playground? Some are your closest friends, while others only pretend to be. Everyone has gathered around you because they want a share of the money burning a hole in your pocket. All are jostling for position, pushing and pulling you in all directions. You'd like to have some quiet time to work out what you want to do with your cash, but you can't - a little goes to one person, more to another, until eventually there's little if any left. The crowd has moved on to surround someone else in the playground to divest them of their pocket money.

This might sound a bit implausible or somewhat passive; an individual simply handing over money without much resistance. In reality there is often a great deal of resistance, but millions of people succumb to the pressures. 21st century survivors need to strengthen their defences. How we already spend our time is worthy of some attention.

Future tense?

As we explored in the previous chapter, burn-out and stress have become commonplace within business and is almost entirely down to 'time'. We simply don't have enough of it. And there will be no let up. So much for the promise that technology would free us up to enjoy more leisure time. 'Time famine' has become an international issue.

Every so-called advanced society comprises millions of frenetic and stressed-out individuals, shackled to the corporate treadmill as it spins at an ever increasing speed. There is no time (or so it seems) for the deeply satis-fying and fulfilling moments in our lives. The more sophisticated the society, it seems, the less time there is for quiet reflection, religion or the spiritual elements of our lives. How many people do you know who live life in the fast lane, earn a good salary, enjoy many job perks but still feel there is something important missing from their lives; a nagging sense that "something isn't quite right"? How many parents are missing their children growing up because they leave early in the morning before their children get up, and arrive home after they have gone to bed? No wonder more and more people are deciding, "enough is enough".

'Downshifting' is in. A recent MORI survey stated that 1 in 4 workers would be willing to take a pay cut in return for more time to spend with their families and to develop interests outside their work, such as hobbies, sport and voluntary work within the local community.

For global businesses, as one set of workers finishes for the day, others within the same organisation, in another part of the world, are arriving at their work stations to pick up where they left off. But as more businesses become global operations, the time pressures become even more intense. Tasks must be completed even faster and with less room for error. Everyone wants to improve the quality of their own lives, but the increasing pressure to do things more quickly is at odds with an 'improved quality of life'. Invariably, the most fulfilling and satisfying activities take time. Those activities which demon-strate 'quality time' inevitably involve doing things more slowly.

Finishing later and starting earlier has become, and will remain the norm. Those in full time employment are working longer hours and have little free time. While those who are out of work have far too much free time, and zero earning time. This imbalance is becoming more common and will almost certainly create massive problems in society in the decades to come. Job insecurity makes us too afraid to refuse the extra (and often unpaid) hours in our jobs. Meanwhile, those without work are becoming more and more restless and dissatisfied with being cast aside and ignored.

How can we possibly slow down when so much of our lives are careering out of control?

Here are a few points to remember about time:

- You will never be able to do enough, quickly enough. It is unrealistic and it does not work. Anyone who tries to do so will fail. The consequences are increased stress, fatigue and burn out.

- Most people do not know how their time is used.
- Misusing time is merely a poor habit. It can be changed.

Learn to think about your time. How do you spend it? How do you invest it? Accept that you will always be able to find the time to do those things that mean the most to you. Many of the tasks you don't seem to get around to are probably not that important.

The position you are in today is the result during your entire life to date of how you have spent and invested your time and money. Likewise, the ways you invest your time from now on will determine your future.

Saving time has become a national obsession. Time saving gadgets and fast-food restaurants help perpetuate the myth that we can 'get everything done' if only we could save just a few minutes here and there. We cram activities, meetings and tasks into our carefully logged diaries and time planners. We are deluding ourselves.

Time is our greatest potential asset. Used wisely over a long period it will provide huge returns; financially, emotionally and spiritually. The less time we have, the higher its perceived value, and therefore its price. If you want to make money - find a way (or many ways) to help others save time or gain more enjoyment from what little time they have. A perceived lack of time has led to a growth in paying others to do our washing, ironing, cooking and cleaning. Cooking a meal involves buying the food, preparation, cooking, serving, cleaning and washing up afterwards. Is the price of a prepared meal worth the time saving? For many it is. Takeaways and inexpensive fast-food outlets not only satisfy our palates, but also our relationship with time. Its worth remembering that each time we pay for 'fast food', we also hand over of the responsibility for our health to others.

Businesses and individuals buy into the belief that time saving equals cost saving. And cost saving increases profit. Therefore it must be worthwhile. We are constantly trying to ensure that each task and activity delivers the maximum benefit for the least time investment. For any activity, the ratio between the 'time cost' and the 'happies' it produces are constantly being assessed and re-evaluated. This is not confined to 'products', but increasingly includes our relationships too; new friends can only be fitted into 'time windows' by eliminating acquaintances. Intimacy requires time. So, if you don't get involved, you'll save some time.

Lee Burns, in his book *Busy Bodies*, expresses the dilemma we face; *"We want to spend less time working so that we have more time to enjoy the leisure-time goods bought with the fruits of our hard work, yet we also want to spend more time working in order to earn more....as wages fall, workers strengthen their work commitment; and as wages rise, workers 'buy' leisure time by working fewer hours."*

Earlier, in the chapter about money, we looked at how time is routinely traded for money. Your money is a representation of your time. How much are you paid per hour? Work it out. If, for example, you are paid the equivalent of £5 per hour, every time you pay £5 for something, you are effectively exchanging it for an hour of your life. Is the product or service you are buying really worth it? What if the cost was £300. Is the item really worth 60 hours of your life?

Most of us don't think about our time in this way. Perhaps we should.

Everything can be quantified by time. Indeed, the fast-food giant McDonalds has devised its own 'international time currency': prices for their products are gauged according to the number of minutes an average consumer would have to work to earn enough to pay for a Big Mac!

Bill Gates, head of Microsoft in his book *The Road Ahead*, suggests that once the information superhighway becomes a reality, we will be deluged by messages. This will result in more time pressure. Therefore to attract our attention, advertisers may offer a small electronic cash payment in return for the time we spend reading an advertising message. Depending on how much an advertiser wanted you to devote some time to their product, the price would go up. This prompts the thought that the unemployed, especially in countries where Internet connection calls are free, could become full-time 'advertising consumers' - browsing the Internet and harvesting the 'reading' payments with little or no intention of buying anything.

Who is trying to steal your time? Before looking at numerous ways you can improve your future effectiveness, let's look at how your time is taken from you and what consequences you may suffer as a result.

The truth about time management

We are fed the idea that if we work harder, do more and learn to become faster and more efficient by using the latest gadget or electronically designed organisational tool, we will somehow manage to achieve the results which we are looking for? When we fail, as we invariably do, this adds guilt, frustration and additional stress and pressure to our lives.

Conventional time management does not solve the 'time famine' problems which so many people suffer from today. No one can constantly increase their productivity - there comes a point when no further improvements can be made. That is, unless you take a different approach to time.

Time is finite: no matter how young, old, rich, poor, intelligent or otherwise, everyone gets the same 24 hours in a day and 168 hours in a week. You can't stop time, save it or accrue interest on it. So much has been written about time-management that it would take weeks to read it all. Companies have sprung up all over the world offering seminars on their own unique time-management techniques. Their systems usually involve purchasing 'luxurious' and often expensive time planning diaries and so forth. No doubt some of these services are valuable, but it seems to me that many are a waste of money and the time they are meant to save.

Mark McCormack, Chief Executive of the sports-management company IMG is well known for his devotion to time-management. He says, *"Mastering time is to do the things you planned on doing, when you planned on doing them, and for no longer than you planned."* A simple and effective philosophy, but how to put it into practice? There is one essential element needed before it can work: planning. You cannot use your time effectively if you do not consistently plan the way you are going to spend and invest it. (This does not have to mean pre-determining everything you do, at all times. Let's be realistic here.) So often we stumble from one deadline to another, merely trying to cope with the demands that others make on our time. We can easily find ourselves bogged down by relatively insignificant matters, or comforting ourselves by over-concentrating on the elements we most enjoy.

As discussed previously, businesses spend large sums to attract and if possible, hold your attention. The effect of these and all other unsolicited intrusions into your life, is less time to spend on yourself and your future well-being. We may be luckier than many of our ancestors in that we now have a multitude of ways to spend time. We may be suffering from stress and ever-increasing work hours, but compared with those of our grandparents, today's working hours and conditions are far less harsh. Working hours are shorter, holidays are longer and we get them more often. So why is it then, that so many of us suffer from a 'time famine'?

We say, "I haven't got time - I'm too busy." What we actually mean is we are too involved in doing things for others, unable to see the importance of dedicating a little time every day towards pursuing some of our own goals in life.

You have a choice: you can react to what's going on around you, or you can influence it. You can take control for yourself, or you can submissively allow others (family, friends, work colleagues or business clients) to dictate what you do and when. Obviously some of your time will have to be spent responding to the demands of others; but if you are doing this for most of your time, you will never reach any of the goals you have set for yourself.

It's not what you've got - it's what you do with it

The most successful people in the world don't get any more time in a day than you or I, so it must be a case of 'It's not what they've got, but what they do with it.' People who use time effectively have made a fundamental decision: they dictate the terms of how they spend it.

Organised people know how to set priorities, plan ahead and follow through on everything they decide is important. Being disorganised is a massive and needless waste of time. Indeed, organised people will tell you that it makes their lives far easier.

'Catching up' versus 'Getting ahead' time

For the purposes of gaining control of your life there are basically two types of activity that use up your time 'Catching-up jobs' and 'Getting-ahead jobs'. Catching-up time represents many of the non-essential meetings, 'phone calls, letter/memo and e-mail writing, and other activities we tend to spend our time on. Getting-ahead time is the time we invest in ourselves and our businesses, developing the projects and activities which take us towards where we want to go in life. These include building and enhancing relationships (either at work or at home,) planning and implementing a personal learning programme and choosing to take regular exercise. Simply by increasing the number of your Getting-ahead tasks, you will increase dramatically your future chances of success. Add to this a reappraisal of your Catching-up tasks, by eliminating as many of them as you can and you will see immediate improvements in your use of time - guaranteed!

The only problem for many people is that they become locked into constant catching-up. Are you? When an individual's schedule becomes 'too full', personal goals and priorities are often the first to be put off to some undefined time in the future. Do you only start on your 'Getting-ahead' tasks and projects once you've finished your 'Catching-up' ones? With so many distractions in our working lives, there is usually very little time left over to work on these Getting-ahead tasks - but they represent the most fundamentally important aspects of our lives. So, what happens? Our lives are filled with unsatisfying, unfulfilling and life-consuming 'busy work'. It is a sad fact of human nature that, although Getting-ahead goals should never be relegated in favour of Catching-up tasks, they often are.

All effective people write daily 'To do' lists. But 'To do' lists have one shortcoming; they are mainly for Catching-up time. They usually include the mundane - calls to be made, letters to be written etc. Without doubt, writing these lists are an invaluable help in making sure you become more productive on a day to day basis. But in doing so, Getting-ahead tasks can be relegated in favour of more immediate, pressing and urgent tasks.

The clock governs our lives. But it is unrealistic to continue trying to cram more and more into your day - something will eventually 'give' - and it will probably be your health. More and more people are turning to another tool to help them use their time more effectively; a compass.

Dr. Stephen Covey defines the clock as representing our commitments, appointments, schedules, and our goals (which should be what drive our activities). While the compass represents our vision, values, principles, mission, and our conscience (which should be what drives our direction).

The most effective people always have a separate list of this second set of priorities representing their life's compass. Once you have invested the time in thinking about and deciding your own priorities, life becomes more straight forward, less stressed and more focused. His books, *The seven Habits of Highly Effective People* and *First Things First*, are strongly recommended.

How would you benefit from using a personal compass in your quest to invent your own future?

Quite rightly, Covey dismisses the faster, harder, smarter and more, approach to time management. Why? Because it doesn't work. You simply cannot manage time in the sense of creating more of it but you can manage time in terms of how you choose to spend or invest it. "Getting more done in less time" is not necessarily the answer.

Many people go through life being forced into doing what is urgent rather than what is important.

How much of your time involves reacting to the urgent, rather than investing your time in what is important - important to both you and your employer?

Covey has developed a simple concept which shows how we spend time in 4 different ways. Everything we do in our lives can be sorted under two simple headings: Urgency and Importance.

Any task is either urgent or it is not urgent. Similarly, everything we do is either important or it is not important.

Covey has developed a simple matrix which consists of just four boxes:

1. Urgent & Important	2. Not Urgent & Important
3. Not Urgent & Not Important	4. Urgent & Not Important

At the same time, this simple little matrix is also tremendously powerful, because the entire life of every individual is contained within it. Try this experiment:

Think of any activity that you might undertake - it could be answering the 'phone, taking the dog for a walk, having a bath, writing a business plan - anything at all. Now decide, within your own terms of reference, which of the four boxes each activity belongs in. Think of other activities and decide which boxes they belong in.

Compound interest has been described as the 8th Wonder of the Modern World - and time spent in what Covey describes as 'Quadrant 2' is the direct equivalent to compound interest in terms of how you invest your time. The more time you invest in Quadrant 2, the more interest compounds - and this shows up very rapidly in your monthly "statement of account in Quadrant 1"- the more you work in Quadrant II the less you find building up in Quadrant 1 (Urgent and Important) you do things before the deadline forces you into doing it, because you are not frittering your assets away in Quadrants 3 & 4 which leads to a lot less stress in your life.

Getting organised

Learning to become better organised will save you countless hours. It will also reduce stress and anxiety in your life and start to move you towards your future goals. A disorganised person is forced to spend their life rushing around trying to cope. Organisation boils down to basically just one concept: learning to think ahead to anticipate problems and delays. Being aware of the areas of chaos in your life can be rather depressing, but by taking small steps towards becoming organised you will quickly find that life becomes far easier. This in turn will motivate you to organise more areas of your life. A word of warning: you can fall into the trap of being too well organised. Being organised is supposed to make your life easier, not take it over.

Whatever you decide to do to improve your organisational ability, you will have to implement a number of systems - the simpler they are the more likely you are to stick to them.

Writing it down

The first step towards getting more done in less time and focusing on the non-urgent and important, is to get into the habit of writing down everything you ever want or need to do. If you do not already keep a daily 'to do' list, this is the time to start. You cannot hope to be in control without being able to see at a glance what needs to be done. Trying to keep such information in your head is a waste of mental ability. Once something is committed to paper it is far more likely to be completed. What is more, you get a wonderful sense of satisfaction and accomplishment when you can cross tasks off your list when they have been completed. To make the most of your time and to be organised involves developing some form of personal system. No individual system is better than any other, it is simply a matter of personal choice. You must find something that works for you.

As someone who hates paperwork with a vengeance, I have developed a system which is as simple as possible. Maybe it will be of help to you. I use a fairly thick, ruled hard-backed notebook (as opposed to a note pad), about twice the size of this paperback book. My whole life revolves around this book - everything (except diary information) goes into it. I scribble in it, jot down phone numbers, write notes when I am attending meetings and list everything I need to do. This book has become well worn and well travelled - but I know that everything I have done is in that book. As no one else needs to see it, the notes can be (and often are) messy. Needless to say, as something so important in my life, it is never out of my sight. I have given myself a number of rules relating to this book. For instance, I have banned writing notes on isolated scraps of paper. If unavoidable, I will stick the note inside my notebook as it is, rather than waste time rewriting it in the book itself. On the left side of each double-page spread I write my 'to do' lists, which I usually date at the top. All items on these pages are given a small left-hand margin so that as each item has been completed I can tick it off. It is then easy to see at a glance which items are still outstanding. I try to make a point of dating my weekly priorities and my daily 'to do' lists as this helps me find any notes that relate to particular projects I am involved in. I make no attempt to write tidily or to ensure that every page is written on - some look like battlegrounds littered with dead doodles.

At the back of the notebook are listed my short-, medium- and long-term goals, personal priorities and any other promises to myself. This way I can keep them in my mind by looking at them on a regular basis. It goes everywhere with me and is in constant use. Whenever I have a few spare moments I flick through the 'to do' pages, reminding myself of what needs to be done and ticking off those tasks I have completed, crossing out tasks I have decided not to do and adding anything new. I find myself continually wanting to do something - anything, to get an item or two 'ticked off'. By ensuring that everything goes into the book, I know immediately where everything is. Every couple of months or so, I go through the book and use a coloured marker to highlight every name, address and telephone number. I then transfer these en masse into my computer database. This way, I rarely lose phone numbers or addresses.

Give this simple system a try, it might work for you. If you are not yet in the habit of writing 'to do lists - please start. It quickly becomes a good habit and once something is written down it takes on a tangible quality. By looking through my older notebooks I can see how productive I have been, which has the effect of encouraging me to get even more done.   Write down every task that needs doing: social, family and professional obligations. Once you have written everything down, go back over your list item by item. Learn to notice which tasks are Catching-up and which ones are Getting-ahead. For every item, ask yourself what would be the worst thing that could happen if you decided not to do it. It may be that by ignoring a few of the tasks you can save yourself a great deal of time.

Next, ask yourself which of the remaining tasks you could delegate to someone else. The aim is to free up as much of your time as possible for your Getting-ahead projects. With a little careful planning, you should find you are able to start on personal projects which up until now you have never felt capable of beginning. Remember: the more Getting-ahead tasks you complete, the more productive you will become.

Activity versus achievement

Those who work 16 hours a day, every day, thinking it's the way to get on, are deluding themselves by confusing activity with achievement. Remaining busy generates nothing except stress and/or chronic fatigue. There is a huge difference between working hard and working smart. Everyone needs to be able to sit back from his or her situation and evaluate whether time is being spent in the most efficient and productive way.   Procrastination is also a serious form of 'achievement constipation'. Filling time with low-priority work is easily done and is often a form of procrastination - delaying the start or completion of an unpleasant or daunting task.

There are a number of remedies: you can identify the unpleasant task and then try to decide on its smallest and least daunting aspect. Give yourself a maximum of five minutes to work on this aspect of the task. You might find that, once you have got started, it will be much easier to continue.   When you survey your list of tasks, notice which ones are the most difficult. Start with them first. Once they are completed you will experience the enormous satisfaction of knowing that the rest of your tasks will be easy by comparison. Given the chance, most people will readily try to off-load jobs on the first available person who'll agree to do them. They take advantage of the fact that most of us have difficulty saying 'No.' It's so easy,   whether at work or socially to find yourself snowed under with projects, jobs and chores you'd never choose to do. If you feel that a task will impinge too much on your precious time, don't be afraid to say 'No' firmly and politely.

The top ten time wasters

1. Perfectionism - trying to get things absolutely right when it is not really that important or necessary.
2. Letting work expand because it is enjoyed too much.
3. Commuting to and from work at the same time as everyone else.Travel earlier or later to save time.
4. Failing to delegate.
5. People who consistently waste your time. Weed them out of your life if possible. Politely re-educate those who cannot be ignored.
6. Watching television just because it is 'on'.
7. Concerning yourself with 'busy' work rather than 'productive' work.
8. Allowing interruptions to wreak havoc with your plans.
9. Worrying. It never improves a situation and often only makes things worse.
10. The telephone. A wonderful invention but all too often it is allowed to dominate our lives both at work and at home.

From this list, two items deserve special attention.

"I hope I'm not interrupting but...

Three factors create the optimum environment to feel good about yourself at work; feeling intellectually stretched, being appreciated and recognised for your efforts and being left to get on with a task with no interruptions. Being constantly interrupted is a motivational killer.

How many times have you been in the middle of something that demanded your undivided attention only to be interrupted? Interruptions are part of everyone's life, especially for parents of young children, but anyone who allows interruptions to govern his or her life is asking for trouble. If you have Getting-ahead projects, it is absolutely essential to build at least half an hour of uninterrupted time into every day of your life. If this means getting up before the rest of your household, or going to bed after everyone else, then this is what you must do.   By the very nature of many of our jobs, dealing with interruptions is what we are paid for. However, by exerting some gentle control over your working environment, it is often possible to build into your working day at least half an hour in

which to get on with important projects. If you fail to set aside this time deliberately, projects have a habit of not getting completed - or worse, of not being
started. There are obviously many exceptions to this, but most interruptions
occur because one person believes his or her time is more important than
anyone else's.

The telephone; tool or tormentor?

For many of us, the telephone plays a major part in our working lives.
However, we are often slaves to its demands: everything stops when it rings.
At other times, no matter how hard we try, we cannot get off the 'phone. It is
so easy to chat aimlessly, wasting valuable time. To gain control over the use
of the telephone in your life, here are a few suggestions. (This is assuming, of
course, that you are not a professional telephonist.)

- If possible, try to arrange your day so that there is a period which is
  'phone-free' - those you speak with on a regular basis will get to know not
  to call at that time.
- If you haven't someone to answer the 'phone for you, install an
  answering machine. Your message should assure the caller that you will
  call him or her back as soon as possible.

Many answer machines allow you to hear incoming messages as they are
being recorded. If a call sounds particularly important you can pick it up
immediately and deal with it (or ring the person straight back if you don't
want to give away that fact that you are screening calls). The sooner you
realise that it is quite acceptable not to answer the phone just because
someone wants to talk to you, the sooner you will gain more control in your
life. By learning to use the phone for your convenience, you will fundamentally improve the way you work. So many people fail to realise how the
'phone dominates their lives, so it is quite easy to subtly ensure that you 'call
the shots'.

- Before each call, write down one-word reminders of points you want to
  discuss during the conversation. This will focus your mind and avoid
  wasted time.
- If possible, go through your entire list of 'calls to be made' at a pre-determined time. Each day save all your non-urgent calls for this time and
  make each one straight after the next. When you know there are more
  calls to make, each one has to be shorter and to the point. It can become
  a bit of fun trying to get through as many calls as possible in the shortest
  time. If someone starts to ramble, you can honestly say that you have to

make another call, adding that you will have to carry on your conversation at a later stage.

- If you anticipate beforehand that some calls will have to be long, schedule them near the end of the time period you have set aside. This way you ensure that all your other calls are not left outstanding if the longer calls take even more time than you envisaged.

- If you cannot get hold of someone, don't leave a message asking for that person to call you back. Give a precise time when you will call again - 3.25 p.m. rather than 'around 3.30-ish'. Be precise. Then make sure you call at the exact time you have promised.

By organising your telephone use, you will increase your productivity and efficiency - and free up more of your time for Getting-ahead tasks.

How often have you set unrealistic deadlines for tasks and activities? For many this is the main source of unnecessary stress in their lives. Afraid they will be perceived as 'slow', they keep over-promising. When you tell a superior how long it will take you to perform a task, log the actually time it takes. If you consistently under-estimate such time, learn to be more realistic. Trying to beat or meet deadlines is admirable, but not if it produces exhaustion. This makes you less likely to meet future targets.

Being better organised will reduce wasted time, and some of the time reclaimed can be devoted towards planning for your future.

Television: the time bandit of the century

The 19th century was characterised by families sitting around the fireplace, entertaining themselves with parlour games and impromptu concerts and singalongs around the piano. For much of the 20th century we have sat silently in front of the TV screen - or the 'plug-in drug' as it has been described by author Marie Winn. In the 21st century we will sit in front of sophisticated interactive TVs and multimedia computers, far more powerful than those in use today. They will be more stimulating than broadcast TV.

Are you one of the hundred of millions who, on a daily basis, switch off as you switch on? Television must be at least partially responsible for the widespread apathy, docility and boredom in our society. Entertainment programmes for teenagers and other young people in particular tend to concentrate on fast action, quick-fire editing and visual effects, cramming as much stimulation as possible into the shortest amount of time. Our stimulation must be instant, just like our coffee. No wonder reality seems so slow and dull, by comparison.

Most people fail to understand exactly how they are manipulated into spending their lives in front of the screen. To be one of life's players requires effort, but as watching TV is carefully engineered to require so little, it is the easy option. It's no wonder TV has become such a widespread, daily, international addiction.

According to the British Audience Research Bureau (BARB), the average person in Britain watches TV for 3 1/2 hours per day. This means, based on present statistics, by the time a person reaches 80 years of age they will have spent a total of nearly 11 solid years watching TV. In the States it's a staggering 15 years! According to Marie Winn, pre-school children in the US spend more than one third of their waking hours in front of the TV screen. Remember these figures are averages - many people watch far more television. The television set is switched on first thing in the morning and is watched constantly throughout the day and late into the evening. This happens every day in a significant number of households. Not even John Logie Baird could have predicted how his invention would take over the lives of so many people.

Not all television is a waste of our time. But millions are largely unaware of the time they sit in front of the screen, swallowing whatever they are fed. It is outside the scope of this chapter to explore all the issues surrounding the quantity and quality of television programming, its positive and negative impact on society, and how it affects the behaviour and self-esteem of individuals. But based on the fact that television consumes so much of our time and millions experience a chronic lack of time, it's worth taking a moment to think about any personal costs associated with television viewing.

Time famines produce additional stress in our lives. To counter the effects of such stress, millions spend most evenings 'relaxing' in front of the TV. We have been conditioned to believe that TV watching equals relaxation. But does it?

One of the biggest criticisms of the Internet is that high quality information is buried amongst so much dross. It takes time to wade through the rubbish to find useful nuggets. The value of information rises when experienced and professional editors are paid to sift and condense it for us. The Internet is already improving in this respect, as ways for viewers to pay for it become more commonplace.

High quality television production involves condensing information into shorter time segments. But inexperienced staff and very low programme budgets make all but the most basic editing too expensive. So we, the audience, spend more time receiving less information. In the past, high quality TV used to do this for the audience - but this will happen less and less in the future, as programme production budgets and quality reduce even further.

With so much at stake and growing commercial pressures, TV companies must devote more effort into convincing us to become couch potatoes.

Fully understanding the basic human needs for stimulation, TV companies and programme makers use whatever devices they can to attract and retain audiences. If this involves packing programmes with 'exciting' violence, sensationalism, or titillating sex, they will do so until someone tries to stop them. The media pays lip service to what it sees as regulatory interference. Such individuals or organisations are routinely mocked, ridiculed and criticised for imposing so called censorship on the media. The media constantly refute the arguments voiced against sex and violence on TV by claiming that there's no proof that it does any harm. They conveniently argue that when something cannot be measured, there are no consequences.

It has been estimated that the average 18-year-old has seen over 500,000 TV commercials. Further estimations indicate they will also see up to 15,000 fake deaths and mutilations, plus a wide array of sexually-based violence - almost exclusively against women , countless 'exciting' scenes of violence to property, and car-chase wrecks. This does not include the real violence shown in news and documentary programmes. All this stimulation is absorbed by passive, uninvolved viewers of all ages. As there is no 'proof' to the contrary you and your kids are safe. Somehow I doubt it.

Media employees MUST attract audiences and will do what ever they can to do so. Television (and every other type of print and electronic media) is keen to promote the idea that they are entertainment or important information services. We are deliberately misled by the media into believing that television is an inexpensive, value-for-money entertainment and information service. The reality is that television is the most powerful sales medium ever developed. Non-commercial organisations such as the BBC may not compete for advertising revenue (yet), but consistently large viewing figures are crucial for their continuing survival. Why should viewers pay a TV licence if the programmes are not worth watching? TV companies cannot sell advertising space unless sufficient people watch.

As someone who worked on TV for nearly 10 years far more effort goes into persuading you to sit in front of 'the one eyed monster' than most people think.

During four years as a BBC continuity announcer, my job involved writing scripts to persuade the highest number of people to watch the BBC's programmes. My colleagues (and counterparts on competing stations) assembled the most eye-catching promotional trailers to make the upcoming programmes appear as enticing as possible. Study the trailers yourself when you next watch television. Ask yourself: who benefits most if you decide to watch those programmes?

The more we watch, the more our lives are controlled by it.

News; the 'feel bad' factor

News is often obsessed with murder, terrorism, rape, war, famine, scandal, political corruption, disease and poverty. We have been conditioned in this 'fast forward' society of ours to expect pace and excitement in everything we see on TV, including the news. The news must be punchy. It often conveys forced urgency. Many of the subjects treated with a 'hard' news approach are often, on closer inspection, far more mundane than we are led to believe. I should know; for seven years I read the news on television, most of that time anchoring the early evening TV news in London.

We are led to believe that knowing what is going on in the world is important. But is it so important that we listen or watch the news at breakfast, read a morning paper on the train going to work, listen to the radio news at lunchtime, read an evening paper on the way home, and then tune into the TV news before we go to bed? And on Sundays we wade through mountains of newsprint. We have become news junkies, rarely missing opportunities to watch, listen to or read about what is happening at home and in the lives of other people throughout the world. Surely, such mass consumption of news is taking 'watching others living their lives' to extremes? Countless men and women spend at least an hour and a half every day being told what others are doing. Make a decision about how important the news is for you; deliberately ration your intake if necessary.

I am not trying to suggest that you should stop watching television. But if you are serious about taking control of your future life, it is in your best interests to consider carefully the effect that television has on you and your family. We have come to believe that if we are offered something, then, by definition, it must be worth having. We accept it without taking a moment to question its true value and relevance to our lives.

Television steals the lives of millions, creating many unattainable 'wants' and 'desires' to which viewers would remain immune if they did not watch so much. There are many top quality programmes and there is nothing wrong with wanting to spend the occasional few hours in front of the TV. The biggest problem is when watching becomes a substitute for living.

"If you aren't in control of your life, somebody else is." Anon

Scoring goals

What would you need to do to take a more proactive role in your future? Taking responsibility for your own future is the only answer. But managing yourself effectively can only be achieved by clearly defining who you are, deciding what you want to accomplish, and developing a plan to help you get there.

Much has been written on the subject of goal setting. Countless experts urge their readers to write down specific and achievable goal plans. But it's a fact that most people accept the rationale for such an approach, but they just don't seem to get around to it. I constantly meet people who claim to be too busy trying to achieve what they want 'in their mind'. By convincing themselves that writing down goals will take time they cannot afford to lose, they miss the point. Written goals are not only more tangible and therefore more achievable, but when you see them in writing, you can question them more effectively.

But why would you want to question your goals? Simply because some goals are almost certainly not yours, they've been planted by well meaning partners, family members, friends and colleagues. Other goals which need to be questioned are those which are unattainable, unrealistic, and based more on fantasy than reality. It's worth knowing the difference between a goal and a fantasy.

"A goal is a dream with a deadline." Anon

It's a bit of a cliche to say that life is all about the journey, not the destination but this is illustrated very well by my friend Richard Rees, a former BBC TV producer. Richard decided to walk the entire length of the Pembrokeshire coastal path in west Wales. It is an 80-mile trip through some stunningly beautiful cliff-top scenery. I was brought up in Pembrokeshire and know the route extremely well, having walked much of it myself. He told me that it had taken him a week, he'd been exhausted and had blisters all over his feet. I tried to console him by saying that all that beautiful scenery must have made it worth it. I wouldn't know,' he said. 'All I saw were my feet!'

Isn't that exactly how so many of us live our lives - too busy, with our heads down, to appreciate what's all around us? Your journey into the future need not be one where you only see your feet.

Why we should all copy best business practice

The most successful businesses have clear objectives, strategies and visions for the future. The most effective senior executives devote most of their working time (or they should) looking far ahead at future opportunities and threats to the enterprise. No business can expect to succeed in the 21st century without detailed plans for each aspect of the company; marketing, sales, financial, environmental and human resources. Planning in business has never been so important as a survival tool for the future. It isn't an easy option. It requires effort and thought, and often leads to initial confusion as each new question throws up unexpected answers and even more difficult questions. It's certainly easier not to bother. Any business that doesn't regard planning as a priority is headed for potential disaster.

Small business guru, Michael Gerber in his book *The E Myth*, identifies one of the key mistakes made by most small business owners; they are too busy *"doing it, doing it, doing it"* to be a real business owner. They have merely started a business to create a job for themselves. If you run a small business, how much time do you devote to planning for the future growth of the business (working on it) and how much do you work in it? Even if you don't own a business, constantly *"doing it, doing it, doing it"* will never permit you to plan for your future.

People also justify a lack of planning (apart from blaming the shortage of time) by their belief that situations change too much. Effective planners know this to be true, but adjust their plans accordingly. Constant 'course corrections' are made to keep them on track.

Anthony Robbins, the American personal development trainer, tells the story about the time when he was taught how to drive a racing car. Shown how to take corners at high speed, when he did as he was instructed, everything was fine. But on one occasion he got into a skid and could see that he was headed towards a wall, seemingly out of control. **BAM** - he hit the wall. Shaken but not hurt, his instructor then took him through what happened. Robbins had made a fundamental mistake; during the skid, his eyes were transfixed on the wall he was headed towards. His instructor said he should have turned his attention towards where he wanted to end up. By doing so, all his energies and effort would then have combined to maximise the likelihood of being able to manoeuvre the racing car out of the skid and away from the rapidly approaching wall. In your life, how much do you focus on the 'walls' and how much on where you want to go?

In some ways, a lack of focus and a clear set of goals and strategies is easy to understand. Many of us simply have too many choices. Or our lives are filled with time consuming distractions. What are the biggest time bandits in your life? How many of them can be avoided?

Try to assess how much control you believe you have in your life. The way we perceive this degree of control directly affects our behaviour. If we convince ourselves that we have little or no control over a significant proportion of our lives, then it is easy to dismiss any attempts to create a better future for ourselves.

Frankie is a trustee and the former Managing Director of the charity Business Wise. It teaches a growing number of British 14 to18 year olds who have been expelled from school for truancy and trouble making, how they can look after themselves by learning how to run their own businesses, rather than being 'forced' into a life of crime, or drugs, or both. Self-reliance is the aim - and their results are impressive. She describes how the tutors' first priority is to overcome what she calls their 'locus of control' and their 'locus of influence'. It is common for these 'problem' students to exhibit initial resistance to the course they have chosen to attend voluntarily. Many of these tough and streetwise kids have grown up being told by teachers and parents that they have no control over their future. Their inner belief of low self-worth is reinforced. This goes some way towards explaining their overriding apathetic attitude and a self-destructive nature. Once they are set tasks which demonstrate how they can have a direct impact on their own lives, many go through a rapid life-changing experience.

The first step towards creating a more fulfilling and rewarding life is to devote some time to thinking about what you actually want from life. If you could determine your future, what would you choose? It's too easy to say, "Earn more money." It is rarely the only answer. It is common for people to shy away from thinking too deeply about who they are, what they want, and where they would want their lives to lead, because they are worried they may discover something frightening about themselves which could mean scrapping what they do, or even ending a marriage or relationship. When you look deep inside yourself, you may find some demons. I would not want to recommend that anyone end a relationship, but nor would I encourage people to stay in an unhappy one. Only you can decide if goal-planning benefits outweigh any potential down side.

If you haven't already done so, make a list of things you want to achieve in say, the next six months - in your work and personal life. Then go through each of those items and quiz yourself about what are the deepest motivations for each item on your list. Why do you want to achieve it? What will it prove? What are the personal benefits? What could be the negative consequences to yourself, your spouse or your colleagues? By questioning your goals in this way you will ensure that you do not end up in Stephen Covey's words, with 'your ladder leaning up against the wrong wall'. It is easy to get swept away with the idea that all of your 'mind' goals are worth pursuing - when they are written down you can often see them in a more pragmatic light. This will save you a great deal of time and possibly a lot of angst, stress and heartache!

In *The Fifth Discipline Fieldbook* by Peter Senge, Richard Ross, Bryan Smith, Charlotte Roberts and Art Kleiner, there is a powerful exercise on creating a personal vision which involves creating a relaxing and comfortable environment and then recalling an important image or memory; something significant and thought provoking when you felt that something profound had happened. They go on to ask you to imagine the best relationship you could ever hope for, the best home you could live in and write in detail in the present tense (this is important) what it looks like, feels like, and which individual words you would choose to describe it accurately. It is important to concentrate on what you want rather than on what you have been told you want by teachers, parents, colleagues, or your partner.

Better questions for better answers

The questions below are intended as a start in helping you to formulate your own goals. Please re-visit those questions listed in the first chapter too.

- What are your worst fears about the future?
- People respond well under the imminent threat of a crisis. What personal crisis can you create to motivate yourself into doing something about your future?
- What have you ever won or been particularly proud of?
- What specific tasks and activities do you most enjoy?
- How much more time would you choose to spend with your family and friends?
- What is really stopping you?
- If you were made redundant this week, how would you feel about it and what would you do?
- If you did not need any money at all, what would you choose to do with your life? Why?
- How much of your time do you think you 'spend', and how much do you 'invest' in yourself?
- What new set of skills could you master to maximise the chances of future success and security?
- Which decisions could you make to improve your health, career and relationships?
- What can you do to improve the quality of your partner's life?
- How could you contribute something to the lives of others less fortunate than yourself?

- What excites you the most?
- It is exactly one year's time. Describe in detail how your life has improved.
- Who do you most admire? What qualities about them are the most impressive?
- Which decisions are you afraid of making?
- Which decisions have you failed to make? What can you learn from this?
- Which new decisions could you make to improve your health, relationships and your career?
- If you knew you could not fail, what would you want to achieve in your life?
- How could you produce better results in each area of your life?
- What are your personal values and ethics?
- What are your prevailing attitudes about yourself?
- How prepared would you be to give up a day's work to have more free time?
- What is the best thing that has happened to you in the last five years? Why?
- How are your customers changing? What do they need which they may not even realise they need?
- What do others really think about you? How do you know?
- How can you create more alliances and partnerships, not only in your working life but socially?

Now read through your answers and remind yourself that you have not given any right or wrong answers - they are simply a tangible description of what you think and believe about yourself, your life and your future. The answers represent you - so say 'hello' to yourself. When you have finished these questions, try to think of your own and don't keep them to yourself. Why not photocopy the pages of this chapter which list these questions and distribute them amongst your family, friends and colleagues? You have my permission to do so. It could provide them with some interesting thoughts about their own present situation and future prospects.

Our relationship with time is often clearly defined by our employers. Increased time pressure within the workplace is intensifying for millions of workers but with less supervision becoming the norm, our ability to organise our own time and work priorities is a key work skill. The remaining chapters of this book explore in detail how our working lives are about to be transformed.

Chapter 9
I Work Therefore I Am

"...where men are subjected to over-guidance and over-government, the inevitable tendency is to render them comparatively helpless."
Samuel Smiles, 1866.

Losing your job ranks as the biggest fear amongst today's workforce. Job security has gone. The future holds many changes in the world of work as we shall explore in the next three chapters. As you will read, there are many serious challenges ahead in the workplace, but there are also lucrative opportunities for the most flexible and knowledgeable workers. This chapter focuses on how work and the workplace is changing so radically in Britain and the rest of the world. The next looks at the options available to improve your job security and income generating potential. Finally, the third chapter in this section outlines proven steps that you can take to increase your influence and market yourself more effectively within your organisation, or your industry sector.

Anyone who naively believes that loyalty, hard work and competence will be enough to guarantee their job in the future could receive a nasty and costly shock. For many people this is a hard idea to accept. A few decades ago, only self-employed people were thought to lead insecure lives. Today and in the future, experienced self-employed individuals are far more secure than their employed counterparts. The self-employed seldom allow themselves to become reliant on just one customer or client. It's too risky - but that's exactly the situation most employees are in. Even the most competent employees are at the whim of their employer and their ever demanding customers.

You, and you alone, are responsible for your future employability.

It is sad to see so many workers laid off in their late forties and early fifties who face the prospect of long-term unemployment, possibly for the rest of their lives. Their feelings of anger, frustration and bitterness are understandable. They often feel badly let down by their employer. However, their thinking is based on the belief that somebody else is responsible for their lives. In the past, an employer may have taken on the role of paternal benefactor, but times have changed. Any employer who promises security is either foolish or dishonest.

The charity TV show *Comic Relief* included a report on young orphans in Ethiopia. It told the story of how a seven year old looked after his five year old brother. The film included a drop-in centre where these children could purchase inexpensive food. No one was given anything for free. Those who ran the centre realised that free handouts are not the answer because it creates a dependence culture. If a child did not earn enough money from collecting and selling coffee beans or useful rubbish from the local tip, they did not eat that day. Yes, it is harsh. It could even be described as cruel. But it works. It is more cruel and potentially more harmful to give help when you suspect that you will not be able to sustain it. These children learn a valuable lesson which stays with them; they have the power to influence their own lives.

Similarly, in the global economy, no employer, however paternalistic they may be, can guarantee employment to their workers. Ultimately, employers are responsible only for their company's survival and growth. That's their job. Many corporations certainly take their roles as employers very seriously, doing everything in their power to look after and nurture their employees as their way of saying 'thank you' for years of loyalty and hard work. In the 19th century there were a number of family owned companies, such as Lever Brothers and Kelloggs, whose owners took it upon themselves to instigate welfare programmes for their staff. In the case of Lever Brothers, the company went to the expense of building Port Sunlight, a small town in Cheshire, for its workers to live near its factory. In its day, this was seen by other industrialists as nonsensical, even a waste of money. But at Lever Brothers, the business owners cared about their employees and realised that if they looked after them, they would develop a happier and therefore more efficient and productive workforce.

Today there are still many corporations with similar ideals; Motorola and Hewlett-Packard come easily to mind as organisations which treat their staff with supreme respect and consideration. So too did 'Big Blue'. IBM staff always believed that they had a 'job for life'- the company certainly thought so too. But when IBM lost millions in the early 1990's, the new management at the time realised they had no choice but to sack tens of thousands of employees. This was particularly painful for both executives and staff, many of whom had devoted their lives to IBM.

Even in Japan, where corporations have become renowned for their loyalty towards staff, employers have been forced into re-appraising their implicit life-time employment contract. For the first time in Japan, companies are bringing in outplacement consultants to help ease former employees back into the job market. Being made redundant is an earth shattering experience for most, but in the Japanese culture where saving face is so important, redundancies have led to suicide amongst many employees; to them, their work is who they are. Take that away and they have nothing. The identity of some people is so inextricably linked with their job, not just in terms of meeting their needs but also their status, relationships and other key sources of personal fulfilment. It is difficult not to take redundancy personally. No matter how convincingly anyone says that it is the 'job' which is no longer necessary, rather than the person doing that job, redundancy still carries a great stigma. Redundancy is becoming more widespread and will continue to do so in the decades to come. We must regain the concept of ourselves as individuals with talents and skills which we hire out to others.

Alvin and Heidi Toffler are regarded by many as the most accomplished futurists. Their trilogy *Future Shock*, *The Third Wave* and more recently *Powershift* are detailed sociological and technological studies of the future. In *Future Shock* (written in 1970), the Toffler's explain that humankind has existed for approximately 50,000 years, or the equivalent of 800 lifetimes. 650 of those lifetimes were spent in caves. Most of the consumer products we use today have been developed in the 800th lifetime.

The industrial revolution took place only about 200 years ago, a mere blink of an eye if taken in the wider context of life on this planet. At that time, society as we know it today was created for the first time, a massive migration of people from the countryside into what have become today's cities. Imagine how difficult it must have been for so many people, used to working in conjunction with nature's seasons, to suffer the culture shock of turning up for work at precisely pre-determined times, day in, day out for 50 or 51 weeks every year (perhaps you have inherited the same symptoms!).

But before the Industrial Revolution, for generation after generation, our ancestors lives changed very little from year to year, decade to decade from century to century. That's all changed. There has been more change in the 20th Century than in any other period in the past. It is continuing and accelerating. Just as society has grown accustomed to such unnatural ways of spending our time, everything is changing again and in some profound ways. Just because we cannot always see the changes, it doesn't mean that nothing is happening. It is often very difficult to decipher the changes clearly, amongst the constant fast-moving advances around us.

Trends in the workplace

Tens of thousands of redundancies are routinely announced in the media. British Telecom, employed 240,000 staff when the company was privatised in 1984. Today, one of the largest and most successful companies in the World, it made over 110,000 people redundant between 1990 and 1995 alone. In July 1995, Sir Brian Pitman, the chief executive of Lloyds Bank said, *"One in five banking jobs will be lost as a result of new technology"*. He predicted a loss of 75,000 at that time, in addition to the 90,000 jobs which had already gone. How many more will go? BIFU, the Banking Insurance and Finance Union predicts another 150,000 jobs going by 2002. About 5,000 bank and building society branches have closed since 1990. Careers Advice teachers in our schools and colleges spent decades promoting the so-called 'security' of banking as a profession. How times have changed in just a few years.

At the moment (late 1997), the motor manufacturing industry employs 1.5 million people in Europe. There is manufacturing capacity for 20 million cars, but demand for only 13 million. Worldwide production capacity is nearer 68 million vehicles but demand for only 48 million. Opportunities for overseas sales are shrinking as developing countries in Asia and South America are keen to build their own manufacturing plants. Indeed, Korea's Daewoo plan to increase the sales for its budget priced vehicles in Europe to 680,000 cars by 2000. When Renault announced 4,100 redundancies at its plant at Vilvoorde in Belgium, and another 2,760 of its 100,000 French workers were also axed, politicians became highly agitated. Angry workers held demonstrations and sits-ins in an effort to protect their jobs, even though there was little or no possibility that any action would make any difference. More drastic staff cuts in Europe are inevitable. It has already begun. Estimates indicate that the motor industry will lay off up to 10% or 150,000 of its workforce in the next 5 years. This highly automated, technology-driven industry enjoys massive financial incentives from national governments in a bid to create or save jobs. Not even this industry is immune to the radical changes taking place in business. The European chemicals industry, which contributes a significant proportion of European exports, will also decline as more state-of-the-art processing plants are built in Asia (a traditional market for the European producers).

Global manufacturing output is rising, but employment in that sector continues to decline. The so-called 'industries of the future', employ up to just 3% of the workforce.

At the beginning of the 20th century, jobs in agriculture accounted for about 60% of Britain's jobs. Today it is less than 5% and is still falling. Central

Statistical Office (CSO) figures confirm that the numbers employed in the manufacturing and construction industries in Britain continue to decline. Manufacturing has seen a drop of about 790,000 since 1990 (from 4.6 million to 3.8million). The Building Employers' Federation, believes 460,000 jobs have been lost in their sector since 1989. These jobs are unlikely to return - ever. Despite a 10% growth in this same period, the computer industry and related businesses cannot take up the numbers. In any case, many of these jobs require highly educated individuals, rather than the relatively uneducated manual workers whose jobs are being shed.

Many of these jobs have been replaced by a burgeoning service sector. A significant proportion of these jobs are low paid, with little or no job security - often dismissively described as the 'McJob'. Growth is seen amongst 'knowledge workers', where fees and demand for their services can be high. But the numbers of these workers will remain relatively low, and will certainly not offer opportunities for the unskilled masses. In the report *Towards Employability* by the independent research group Industry In Education found the lack of "employability qualities" among school and college leavers may be costing Britain £8 billion, or more, each year. This report also concluded that few young people had considered how their personal qualities and character might influence their career. They believed, mistakenly, that employers were only interested in their academic and vocational qualifications. Few felt that respect, politeness and "customer care" qualities should be prerequisites of employment.

Technology is becoming capable of performing ever-more complex tasks and is eradicating jobs higher and higher up the organisational tree. The tide is rising and will envelop more and more workers who have traditionally felt safe on higher ground. It is estimated that most European corporations are still over-staffed by up to 20%. A high proportion of these are in administrative and management positions. As competition intensifies, anyone who does not 'add value' by increasing sales revenues, or cutting costs for their organisation, will have to be shed. What will happen to them all? Will you be one? Conversely, owners and employees at micro and small firms who already rely on technology, will have less fat to trim and are more likely to thrive.

More and more medium and large companies will join those corporations which have already flattened their management structures. If you are currently working in middle management, or are dependent on the income of someone who is a middle manager - you are almost certainly an endangered species.

Sunset or Sunrise? Take your pick

Clinging on to a 'sunset' job is often very painful and misguided. One such job category is the milk delivery man. A part of British life for the last two centuries, they are dying out as more of the population buys its milk from supermarkets. Adding other product lines such as orange juice, mineral water, potatoes and eggs to their slow-moving battery-powered floats, has prolonged the agony as their market continues to decline. A series of TV commercials were created to persuade more people to use their local Unigate milkman. Featuring a cute little boy who really loved his milkman, it was filmed in a warm, emotional style. The viewer discovered the milkman was also his dad. You can imagine the rationale behind such a commercial: 'If you don't get your milk delivered to the door, lots of cute kids like this one will suffer when their dads lose their jobs!' You can't blame anyone for trying to protect an industry, but sometimes such attempts are as futile as King Canute trying to hold back the tide.

In the decades to come, more and more industries and jobs will be eliminated. The temptation is to do something, anything, to hold on to the past. Many individuals understandably feel powerless and insecure about how to reposition themselves. Conversely, the mistaken belief held by so many individuals and organisations, is that they have the power and ability to stop the un-stoppable. It's almost as if some businessmen (and they are predominantly men) feel they are invincible, and capable of dealing with the problem.

How sure are you that you are not part of a sunset industry? Knowing when to accept the inevitable is a key survival skill in the workplace. If you suspect your medium or long-term position could be in jeopardy, do something about it NOW. Don't wait until it's too late. Acquire the new skills you need to move into a sunrise industry, if that is appropriate. The secret is to do it before you get caught in the rush.

Governments all over the Western world are throwing millions of dollars at industries which are dying. They will die. Prolonging the agony will probably not help, but, for government, being seen to help is sometimes more important. More important than accepting the reality and futility of the situation, and offering those affected the real help they need, such as opportunities to acquire valuable training in skills that are in demand. This should not be provided by government whose skills-based courses have been shown to be ineffective, but it would take a brave politician to stand up against the ever-critical media to say what needs to be said, and do what needs to be done.

Let's take a look at other industries and job functions which could be on the 'endangered species' lists;

- Royal Mail postal workers
- Government bureaucrats
- Business administrators and secretaries
- Jobs in UK manufacturing
- Commercial property developers and agents
- Telecommunications and broadcasting staff
- Manual and agricultural labourers
- Middle managers everywhere
- Travelling sales people
- White, middle-class men
- Most working-class men of all races
- Service-industry functions that depend on any of the above

This list is not comprehensive, nor is it in any particular order. What if you are part of this list? You have a number of choices. Firstly, you can do nothing (there's nothing like a bit of 'denial' to make you feel better!) or you can give some serious thought to creating an 'exit' strategy.

Top of the 'endangered' list must be Britain's largest employer, Royal Mail, with its 190,000 staff. Under increasing commercial and political pressure to make radical improvements to productivity and efficiency, the Royal Mail will almost certainly go through major upheaval in the next few decades. Its management and staff can expect an uncomfortable ride. Highly automated, more commercially astute competitors are waiting in the wings to take over potentially lucrative contracts. Royal Mail can expect intense competition from the four largest international courier companies (TNT, UPS, DHL and Federal Express) and offshoots of the £20billion direct mail industry that has to safeguard its own parcel deliveries. Technology is also a major threat. Sophisticated high speed post-code readers and sorting equipment is being introduced to increase efficiency and cut running costs in what is an historically labour intensive business.

But the biggest threat is electronic mail. More and more data and documents are being sent and received electronically. This will increase exponentially in the decades to come. A piece of E-mail can be sent for a fraction of the cost and at a speed with which 'snail mail' cannot even begin to compete. As Nicholas Negroponte, in his seminal book *Being Digital*, points out - the world is moving away from the sending and receiving of atoms to one where we transfer 'bits'. What does this mean? Simply, you no longer have to send information on a piece of paper (comprising atoms) instead you can send it in electronic form (computer 'bits' and 'bytes') to be decoded on arrival, and printed out on ever-improving home and office-based colour printers.

In the future, over-stretched Royal Mail staff may feel tempted to call for industrial action to preserve jobs, working conditions and pay. But, ultimately will they exercise the same degree of caution as other workers in British business today? Probably. These days, few workers can afford to risk the loss of their jobs. In 1994 only 278,000 working days were lost through industrial action - a far cry from a peak of 29.5 million days lost in 1979. They are no longer fighting individual redundancies, but redundant industries.

Unemployment: 'It's only just begun'

Jeremy Rifkin, in *The End of Work*, claims there are more than 800 million people who are currently unemployed or under-employed in the world today. He believes, with good reason, that this figure will rise sharply within the next ten years, as technology eliminates more and more job functions. Rifkin feels *"We are entering a new phase in world history"* and *"moving us to the edge of a near workerless world'"*.

Whenever you hear political parties carping on about the opposition's inability to lower the unemployment figures, they are being conveniently unrealistic for party political purposes. Unemployment is a global issue. It is rising all over the world, and will continue to do so whether the country is run by socialists, communists, or a right wing dictatorship. The reasons may differ slightly but it is one of the symptoms of our times.

The idea that unemployment is an internal, political issue, helps further perpetuate the myth that a single government has the power to control the employment or unemployment of a nation. This is no longer the case. It also implies that government is actually responsible for the population's employment. But can it be? Society may be structured around work, but no responsible government can assume this role any longer. Government MUST catalyse society into recognising the situation for what it is and find ways to deal with the inevitable. Simply shedding existing responsibilities and allowing the status quo to appear to continue, because it is politically expedient, is guilt through inaction of the worst kind.

By tracking a 5% sample of National Insurance numbers since 1982, a CSO survey shows that 1 in 3 men and 1 in 5 women have been unemployed at least once since 1992. This represents 8.7 million workers. Up to 25% of unemployed men have experienced up to 5 periods of unemployment in the last 10 years. A growing proportion of these workers are from the white collar sector. A 1996 NOP survey showed that nearly three fifths of voters believed their jobs to be less secure than two years previously, and that 55% believed their jobs would become even less secure in the next two years. Many of these sectors are investing heavily in technology to improve their competitiveness.

Analysis featured in *The Times* in 1996 suggested that unions could be part of the problem by showing a clear link between areas of union strength and lower employment growth. Foreign competition is often cited as the scapegoat, because it gives people (especially those in the media) somebody to blame. A bit of nationalistic fervour never does any harm to the ratings or newspaper sales. But the truth is that the situation is not the 'fault' of the unions, or foreigners, or anyone else.

Salaries can represent the highest identifiable cost to any business. If they are too high, the company is unable to maintain its competition in the world marketplace. Britain is better placed than some to cope with increased international competition, as figures produced by the Federation of German Industry suggest. In 1996 the average German industrial worker was paid DM45.52 per hour. In France it is DM29.04 while in Britain its DM20.96. However, the UK's cost per hour is still more than double that of Asian countries such as Taiwan, Korea, Singapore and Hong Kong, and it is over 35 times that of China and more than 40 times greater than in India. In addition, many of these workers are better educated and more highly trained than the average Western worker. They want what we have and they are willing to work very hard to get it. Moreover their governments don't provide them with healthcare, pensions or unemployment benefits.

If the 19th century belonged to Great Britain, the 20th to the United States - then the 21st century will certainly belong to Asia, as it did a thousand years ago.

This doesn't mean that getting or keeping a job or career will become impossible - there will be many, many exciting opportunities for those individuals who have a clear understanding of the trends affecting them, and who create effective survival strategies to deal with the future. The secret is to plan for such eventualities well before they arise. We will go into the details of how you can do this later.

No matter who you work for, no matter how seriously they take their role as an employer, and no matter how committed you may be towards your employer, no corporation can afford to insulate its staff from the harsh realities of the global marketplace. Even in recent history, companies had some degree of certainty about their position in their marketplace, but not any more. Companies no longer have the power to make such decisions. Any employee who assumes their employer will look after them is gambling dangerously with their own future.

Avoiding exploitation in the workplace

Doing more for less is here to stay. Longer hours, less pay, fewer bonuses and no job security is becoming the lot of a growing number of workers - and they're the lucky ones! More workers are resigned to the fact that keeping a job is more important than any benefits likely to accrue from putting it into jeopardy. Make too many demands of an employer and there may not be a job for you for much longer.

The role of trade unions has declined in the past 20 years. Membership numbers are shrinking as more and more workers become too afraid to strike for better pay and conditions (and lose faith in their union's ability to do anything about it). It seems that any job is better than no job. However, there is a disturbing increase in the outsourcing of internal services such as security, catering and cleaning. To secure a contract, a growing number of rogue service companies are prepared to pitch for such contracts at almost any cost, in order to win the business. Those who do the actual work tend to suffer. The contractor blames the client for being unwilling to pay, thus justifying their exploitation. Expect this to increase as a business practice in the decades to come. Unions can serve an invaluable service to such workers by lobbying contractors and employers who behave in this way.

Exploitation is not confined to the mundane service sectors but it is rife in more 'glamorous' professions, too. Publishing, radio and television broadcasting attract a steady flow of enthusiastic young people, eager to get on in these exciting industries. As media companies continue to grow through mergers and acquisitions, and programme budgets get squeezed, the pressure is on to pare every cost down to its bare minimum. Huge salaries are paid to TV and radio executives, but an increasing number of workers are ruthlessly exploited. Graduates are often expected to work for free in order to gain work experience. As a radio reporter for BBC Radio 4, in 1994 I recorded a report on 'sweatshop' radio. Numerous interviewees confirmed widespread exploitation within commercial and community radio. One broadcaster I spoke to worked 12 hour shifts, 6 or 7 days a week, every week. He was paid less than £5,000 per year. He considered himself lucky to have a job.

But it's not all bad news. As workers become more knowledgeable, working on complex problems as part of closely knit teams, they also become more difficult to replace. Employers need to work harder in order to keep these high grade individuals. The costs of recruiting and training new people can rise rapidly. Consequently, knowledge workers are the most secure in the workplace. Clients and employers cannot afford to treat such workers poorly. If they do, they run the risk that the worker will walk. For many of these working elite, union membership is not seen as necessary, they have what they need to look after themselves, situated between their ears. Could you develop as someone like that?

My youngest brother Mike has done this. In less than a year, he transformed his own career by re-inventing himself. Using his own initiative and a home computer, he trained himself to apply technology to his job as a groundsman. This work was almost instantly rewarded with a significant promotion and additional responsibility. His opinions are now sought and valued by his superiors and elected officials. He now constantly attends training courses on computers and legal issues, adding more and more to his knowledge base. His value to the local authority that he works for, is constantly growing. The mental stimulation he receives has 'turned him on' to learning and the additional responsibilities he has been entrusted with. His life has changed for the better, and within a relatively short period.

We all earn 'interest' from each deposit of information and knowledge we add to our brain bank. The more you deposit, the more you can expect to benefit in the future. Unlike with time or money, with knowledge, you never make a withdrawal - whenever you use it, the deposit stays inside your head to be used again and again.

Are you on a corporate ladder or treadmill?

There are basically four career paths. Is yours linear, steady, spiral or transitory?

Linear: Climbing the corporate ladder, working up through a clearly defined, multi-level hierarchy. You are paid based on where you are in the pecking order, and the size of your responsibility or fiefdom.

Steady: Pick a career, train for it over a long period, and stick with it until you retire. That's the way we create lawyers, doctors, dentists and professors.

Spiral: Periodic sideways moves into different job functions (inside or outside the same organisation) to gain broader experience, before stepping up to the next level of salary and responsibility.

Transitory: Working on short term projects, these workers need a flexible approach and the ability to perform a wide range of in-demand skills. These freelance workers will soon represent the back bone of many organisations and in a growing number of industries.

The first two career variants are how our parents & grand-parents regarded all jobs. The unsettled nature of the last two types would probably have led them to believe they were not 'proper' jobs.

Those individuals who can embrace the unsettling, unpredictable spiral and transitory ways of working will be the best equipped to deal with changes in the forthcoming decades.

There will be fewer structured career progressions; you have to carve one out for yourself . You may not like it, but inflexibility within the workplace is most likely to help you jump the queue to oblivion. How do you, or your employer, know what will need to be done in 5 years? If you aren't able to, or refuse to perform the tasks which your company requires - you cannot blame any employer for finding someone else, who will do those tasks. This is a painful realisation for many. The jobs will remain with those who accept the inevitable trends in the workplace. No one will tell you what to do, although the most forward-thinking companies know that they must play an active role in helping staff to move around within their organisations. They encourage staff to work out their own medium and long-term goals and, where ever possible, facilitate an environment which takes them towards those goals. However, the employee has to make it happen. Employers know that if they don't provide this type of environment, they risk losing their best people as they become frustrated working in a flat hierarchy.

Self-employment to Self-employment; the circle is complete

Every worker is self-employed. But some entrust their lives to just one client, "the employer" while others work with many. When you look at life in this way, anyone who wants to earn more money has the following choices;

- find more customers (a part time job)
- find a better customer (apply for a better job)
- increase your daily billing rate (becoming more valuable)
- or increase your daily billing rate with more clients (becoming more valuable at many different things).

Few successful self-employed people would accept working for people they despised or who abused them. It is only when a person feels someone else is responsible for their future that they accept the unacceptable. If we do not accept the need to offer the best possible quality and value to our clients, 'market forces' might push us out. If the customer does not offer 'good value' back to you, they are responsible for your defection.

Self-employment is growing, returning to pre-Industrial Revolution times, when the very concept of a 'job' did not even exist. (self-employment is explored in more detail in the next chapter). 300 years ago, workers performed many functions, depending on what needed to be done. Being multi-skilled was essential in those days. In the earliest factories, complex products were produced by breaking down each stage of the manufacturing process into simple, easily repeatable tasks. Highly skilled crafts people were replaced by large machines operated by an army of relatively unskilled, cheap labour. Each person was taught to perform a small number of dull and repetitive tasks. This required extensive supervision to ensure workers kept working. The wage slave was born.

In the past century, hundreds of thousands of low paid, unskilled workers have been replaced, first by unsophisticated mechanical equipment, such as tractors and earth moving equipment, and then by more complex harvesters and crop-picking machines. In the United States, the introduction of cotton picking machines wiped out employment for millions of black workers who were only just getting used to the idea of freedom from slavery. In the 1920's, about five million black people migrated to the industrial cities of the North. There they worked as low paid workers in the steel works and factories. Technology evolved and machinery became increasingly complex. Over the next three decades, this, combined with increasing industrial unrest led to the widespread relocation of large factories, especially those in the motor manufacturing industry. Un-needed, unskilled workers were left behind. Today, millions of these unskilled and unemployed people remain in the urban ghettos - too poor to commute or move to the modern and sophisticated industrial parks in suburban America. Afro-Americans had been shafted again.

Traditional sources for long-term careers are evaporating as large organisations re-structure and redefine who they are, what they sell and what human help they need in order to do so. The rules have changed - and they've changed a lot.

Mechanical technology first replaced human and animal muscle. Computer technology is, and will continue, to substitute the human brain. As systems continue to become more automated, using increasingly sophisticated software-based technology, in some industries we have already reached a situation where people just get in the way and become the source of mistakes.

Tests have been conducted in technical industries where people have been brought in to solve problems of a technical nature. Invariably they make the situation worse (and take a long time to do so!), therefore high quality, and high speed diagnostics software is used to minimise human error. It's reassuring to believe that technology is unreliable. But this is yet another myth. Today's airliners have been described as flying robots, it's human error which is the cause of most collisions, crashes and fatalities!

On the subject of errors, old style industries went to great pains to eliminate errors altogether. This approach stifles creativity and innovation, the very qualities successful companies need to encourage if they are to thrive in the next century. If you are going to be punished or ridiculed for making mistakes, take the safe route, don't rock the boat and only do as you are told. Unfortunately you could also contribute to the demise of your employer and ultimately your job.

Within the foreseeable future, more people on the largest salaries will no longer be required to make certain business decisions. They too will be 'let go'. Machines will make those decisions, far faster, more accurately and less expensively. This is not science fiction; much of the technology already exists and is being used. Add to this the fact that as more and more workers are empowered to take day-to-day decisions, the need for expensive supervision has already been eliminated in many industry sectors. This is spreading, not just in Britain, but all over the world.

William Bridges in his book *Jobshift* writes of 'musical jobs' where more and more workers are forced to drop out each time the music stops. He believes commentators in 100 years, looking back at the changes taking place in the workplace, will describe them as being as futile as fighting over deckchairs on the *Titanic*.

Today, the idea that millions of people perform pre-defined 'no-brainer' tasks, while closely supervised by managers and foremen is rapidly disappearing. The 40-hours-a-week-for-40-years 'job' is dying. In some industries it is already dead. In today's global and highly competitive economy, few businesses can afford to ignore the knowledge and intelligence of its workers. The numerous executives who believe they have a monopoly on all knowledge within 'their' enterprises are making a costly mistake. Workers on the other hand, who assume that management should tell them what to do, for them to carry out the orders even if 'they don't know what the hell they are talking about' are making a similar error. Successful businesses harness the knowledge and expertise of everyone within (and others from outside) the organisation.

From pre-industrial age times, we have come full circle. Workers are expected to be multi-skilled, often unsupervised, and are called upon to work on individual projects, as and when they are needed. Workers who need supervision and those who can only 'command and control' their subordinates, are being eliminated or replaced by more knowledgeable and flexible workers. If you are not equipping yourself with new 'transferable skills' and learning to work as part of a team, or as a team leader, you will become a dinosaur.

Many of the largest corporations have now woken up to the fact that they must change radically to survive - those that don't take such steps, will slip into a coma, never to re-awaken. They can no longer predict what their customers want, and it is becoming increasingly difficult to determine what their workers will be required to do, in order to satisfy the needs of the marketplace. As the demands of business continue to change, workers must become more flexible and capable of performing a wider variety of tasks.

If, as you read this, you are tempted to think that this will (or may) only affect other people, please think again. Believing we are safe can be our most dangerous strategy, as this true story illustrates.

A police officer visited a classroom to talk to a group of 12 year olds about road safety. One of the children, who lived in a particularly quite crescent said that there was little likelihood of being run down, as few cars ever drove down her road. The police officer replied that more children get killed on these quiet roads where little if any traffic is expected, simply because they get too complacent about playing in the road. Children who live next to busy roads learn to stay and wait on the curb.

Anyone for homework?

You worked hard all day at school, and then your teacher dumped loads of homework on you. Thankfully that would end when you left school. Or so you thought. Improved technology and communications tools have led to a profound change in how and where people can work. Using telephones, computers, fax machines and electronic mail it is possible to work at many tasks without needing to go in to an office, or even a manufacturing plant. With the growing number of powerful laptop computers and mobile 'phones it is relatively easy to work anywhere, even in a different country and still remain in close touch with clients and colleagues.

This book has been written in 6 different countries on 3 continents. Working like this is a blessing for some, for others it's a curse. Working 'home alone' is not for everyone. Family issues need to be resolved. Are you naturally well motivated and a self-starter? Do you crave interaction with others? For full-time employees, who are based at home (known as teleworkers), there are other pressing issues. Anyone who needs to store large quantities of paperwork and company samples in an average shoebox sized house or flat does not welcome these developments.

Geography will not be an impediment for many workers of the future. Because of this, competition amongst workers could increase dramatically. Today there is possibly someone with a PhD in Asia who wants your job and will do it for 90% less than you are paid. In a growing number of job categories, technology can make this possible.

Employers and clients will be able to select individuals based on their skills rather than their location. This is already happening. It will escalate as 'creative' job categories such as writing and designing are performed by self-employed individuals who have escaped the rat race and live in more rural or 'remote' locations.

There is a lot of talk about the 'Virtual Corporation.' Headed by a small core of people, their products and services are provided by outside individuals and small teams of specialists, many of whom may work from home. The small core co-ordinate and lead rather than manage these ever changing teams of people. They argue, why pay for an expensive overhead which has to be charged for, when individual home offices perform the same functions at low cost? These lean operations can be more profitable and far more adaptable than their larger competitors. Could competitors pose such a threat to your existing employer? What could be done to minimise its effects?

These workers realise that much of the time they don't need to live in the big city, even if their major clients are located there. Large employers are also encouraging their workers to stay at home. It reduces commuter time and the associated stress. Damage to the environment is less as fewer cars are used by individuals travelling to and from work. But more importantly, it can save them a heap of money by freeing up, and even eliminating expensive office and parking space, as well as offering lower cleaning costs, less need for providing catering facilities and reducing a whole host of other operating costs.

When you call directory enquiries, it's highly likely that the operator is speaking to you from their home. Customer service and other 'helpline' advice is being farmed out to home workers. How could you work from home in the years to come? For many, working from home offers opportunities to improve their quality of life by spending more time with their families. How prepared are you to sacrifice promotion for improved quality of life?

The temporary & part-time option

The biggest trend in the workplace is the move towards part-time and flexible working. In an effort to reduce unnecessary costs and provide a higher level of service to ever more exacting customers, workers are being put onto flexible hours to cope with fluctuations in demand. The hotel and catering industries, healthcare, construction, agriculture and manufacturing already rely on flexible or contract workers. More industries will follow. In some of these industries, salaries are dropping as service companies are forced to compete for contracts. Of course, low pay is not confined to part-time workers. In order to provide giant corporations with the profits their share-holders and employers have become used to, many full-time employees, especially in under-developed countries, are exploited, too. Are you prepared to accept the moral responsibility for dealing with such companies?

A high proportion of these overseas workers are women. In Britain, the most poorly paid, part-time workers tend to be women too. 'Sweat shop' wages are all too common. But low pay is not limited to part-time workers. A survey by the Low Pay Unit commissioned by Unison, Britain's largest union, found that up to half a million workers in local government earned less than £4.26 per hour.

Neither is all part-time work modern day slavery. Part-time work need not be confined to women. Few men even consider it as an option for them, although this is changing. Would you be prepared to take say, a 20% cut in your salary by working four days per week instead of five? In some jobs it may not be practical. The Institute of Marketing conducted a survey which showed that up to 70% of managers would be prepared to take a drop in salary in return for more time to devote to family and leisure.

Many employers wrongly assume male staff are only interested in full-time employment, but New Ways of Working, a British 'think tank', have found a growing number of couples agree between themselves for the main breadwinner (usually the man, but not always) to negotiate a part-time role, while the other partner also finds a part-time job. There are distinct advantages for married couples with families;

- the parents can share their roles more fairly
- they can save money on child-minding services
- each spouse feels they are making a tangible contribution to the partnership and the woman benefits from improved mental stimulation and interaction with grown-ups outside the home
- stress is reduced, fulfilment increases, which often improves the intimacy within their relationship
- with two sources of income they have more job security as a couple - should one lose their job through redundancy, they are not thrown into financial trauma.

For the employers there are distinct advantages too;

- sometimes they make salary savings, although there are some additional costs incurred if other part-timers are hired to 'take up the slack'. However, this is often offset when they realise that:
- the productivity of such part-time workers tends to rise, because they are better motivated, less stressed and more energetic
- if jobs are shared with other part-timers, workers become more interchangeable. This provides employers with added flexibility.

Downshifting; the growing trend

Hundreds of millions of people all over the world battle through traffic in the daily ritual of 'commuting'. Is it all worth it? More and more individuals are coming to the realisation that there is far more to life than doing this five days a week. There is little to recommend being stressed all day and then battling through tens of thousands of commuters to reach home exhausted, where you eat a convenience processed meal because you don't have the time or energy to prepare a cheaper and healthier alternative. You slump down in front of the television for a couple of hours to 'veg out', only to repeat the whole process a few hours later, when you drag yourself out of that warm and comfortable bed once more.

A survey in 1995 for the Merck Family Foundation found that 66% of respondents believed they would be more satisfied with their life if they could spend more time with their family and friends. So how would you like to hand in the keys to your company car, hand back their company charge card and work in an environment which may pay significantly less, but where the quality of life is far superior? More people are doing this. Parents with young children want to see their children grow up. When you are on the corporate treadmill this can be difficult. People want their lives back.

"Don't give me a bonus, give me more time off."
Male employee overheard talking to his female boss in a Vancouver restaurant

How many individuals do you know who are deeply unhappy in their work. Many are in high paying jobs and feel trapped with golden handcuffs. They have sentenced themselves to a life of misery in return for money. But it takes supreme bravery to 'down shift' or achieve 'voluntary simplicity'; to step off the treadmill in order to pursue less well paid, but infinitely more satisfying and rewarding work.

Would your life be more meaningful if you accepted a lower paid job, with more time to yourself with fewer responsibilities? These and many other work related questions are being asked by more and more workers who have a nagging feeling that they no longer have a life. Are you one of those people?

Business battle fatigue

The promise of extensive foreign travel is often used successfully to attract the best graduates to the largest global corporations, but a few years later these 'road and air warriors' as they are so often dubbed, start to suffer 'battle fatigue'. They become increasingly fed up with all the travelling, especially those workers with young families at home. They miss their partners and their kids.

Stress levels in business appear to be at an all time high, and getting higher as businesses constantly try to squeeze more out of those staff lucky enough to survive the latest round of 'downsizing' and restructuring . I work with many large organisations, and find that staff are constantly being pushed into achieving more, generating higher sales, increasing their market share, cutting unnecessary and wasteful costs from their businesses. Staff in these organisations work at an increasingly hectic pace. But time and again I experience situations in which these same over-worked staff are rarely given the acknowledgement that they are producing extraordinary results. Too often they merely suffer from "moving of the goalposts". It is almost as if no one can ever do enough. This in time will take its toll on people who will burn themselves out. The most forward-thinking organisations have begun to realise that doing so is counter-productive and that they must take steps to help their staff work smarter rather than harder.

Working men

In the last few years, the traditional junior 'entry' jobs have become more elusive to school leavers and graduates. Getting a toe-hold in the job market will become more difficult - not easier. But it's not just the young who are under increasing pressures - men, those bastions of the British workforce, are beginning to feel the squeeze too. The Equal Opportunities Commission have encountered numerous cases in which men were competing in the workplace with well qualified, lower paid women. More men are having to come to terms with the fact that if they want a particular job badly enough, they will have to accept the lower rate which would be offered to a suitable woman candidate. It looks as though the employment playing field is finally being levelled - by excavation.

Poorly educated individuals, predominantly male, tend to gravitate towards physical work. Young men from steel-making or coal-mining regions still believe, based on their fathers' past that this is where they should work, despite the fact that many steel works and coal mines have closed down. In many industrial, or former industrial regions, it is the young women who are now being offered the better paid jobs. Unlike boys, they study harder and use their brains rather than their brawn.

A BBC TV documentary, *Panorama*, looked at the career progress of a group of young men and women from a particular northern England secondary school. Many of these young men were already living in the past, unaware that they were heading directly from adolescence to obsolescence. Equally 'bright' young women were going to university to train themselves for knowledge based work. One young man inadvertently pinpointed the problem when he talked about how good it made him feel to have done a hard day's physical work. Described by his teacher as a bright kid, in an area of mass unemployment he had been 'lucky' to land a job in a local factory loading refrigerators onto trucks. His future, and that of many men like him, is bleak. They fail (or refuse) to see how the world is changing around them.

Many more men in the workforce will experience a similar fate in the decades to come. Uneducated men of all races will be the hardest hit. Muscle based work will decline even further. Mind and knowledge work will increase. Much of this will be taken over by women who can compete with men on a more equal footing. Men who find difficulty working as part of collaborative teams and dealing with others in a less autocratic way, will be replaced by women. Women tend to be hard-working, more insightful, perceptive, creative and empathetic. These are the very qualities needed by a growing number of employers. Inequality within the workplace will continue for some time yet, but as more of the old male guard are made redundant or reach the end of their working lives, companies will be less able to afford the luxury of ignoring the contribution of women. Poorly trained men will experience many more of the injustices that women have endured for so long. And men will make it clear that they are not happy about it. Their protests will be ignored for the most part, leading to anger and resentment among less adequate men.

More personnel departments are coming to realise that flexible working need not be confined to the women on the payroll. Research has shown that workers' productivity declines rapidly if they consistently work long hours. Stressed-out workers are bad for business. They are more prone to sickness and absenteeism. While those who work more flexibly bring more energy, enthusiasm and motivation to their work. For some workers they invest this 'free' time studying or working within the community. A happier, more fulfilled worker is also more productive.

This option is probably not worth serious consideration unless you enjoy a relatively healthy salary. If this is you, how could you benefit by working less hours for less pay? By sharing elements of your role with someone else, how could your employer also benefit?

A 'career' for a middle class, white man was characterised by 'getting a good job' when he left school or higher education, preferably in a large multinational company, staying there for the duration of his working life, climbing the corporate ladder within a clearly defined hierarchical structure. This may have been true for your father or grandfather, it certainly isn't the case for you or your children.

"The weakness of man is the facade of strength, the strength of woman is the facade of weakness" Warren Farrell PhD

Working women: a brighter picture

Because I am a man, this section will inevitably cause some women readers to take exception to my interpretation of what is, without doubt, an unfair, male dominated society. There is not enough room here to explore why the system is unfair. Suffice to say, society and the workplace is littered with dysfunctional men; from the downright obnoxious, to the men who genuinely believe they are doing women a favour by not inviting them to business 'networking events', in order to protect them from potentially embarrassing advances by men. Those men who take on a 'caring' role fail to realise that their behaviour actually disempowers women and hinders their careers and influence amongst other men.

Women will continue to be abused and exploited in the workplace, the home and in society. In some societies, women will continue to be regarded as second or third-class citizens, but businesses and countries which exploit and discriminate against women, will be increasingly boycotted by women as well as men. For my part I have chosen never to buy another product manufactured by a particular running shoe manufacturer. This is a personal choice based on my belief that the company's manufacturing policy of using low-paid and predominantly women workers in countries such as Indonesia is immoral. I believe their products are over-priced and refuse to become a walking advertising site for the company. I am not suggesting that you should not buy their products.

The need for women to accept full responsibility for their own financial security has never been greater. More middle-aged men are being made redundant as companies continue to lay off staff. As the financial and emotional pressures build, divorce rates soar; countless women find themselves with a young family to raise, no income, no savings and little or no pension provision. Oh, the price of love and devotion!

Pensions are still based on the antiquated assumption that men support women and women raise children in a stable, long-term marriage. Therefore women don't need their own pensions. Official statistics show a very different story. Over 1 in 3 marriages end in divorce. Many of the women from these marriages suffer real financial hardship as a result. What would you do if this happened to you? Perhaps it won't, but for many women it already has. As you grow older you MUST insure yourself against financial disaster. Many women still tend to feel guilty about deserting their families to pursue a career. A personal desire for mental stimulation and interaction with other 'grown ups' is often forsaken. Many women compromise by taking part-time work. Much of this is relatively low paid, thus perpetuating the existence of discrimination against women workers.

However, there are early indications to suggest that more British employers are introducing more flexible working hours in order to attract higher qualified and better paid female workers. This means that many more women will be able to work in better paid jobs or careers whilst also being able to fulfil their other commitments. This increased flexibility also allows men to take a more active role as parents, thus freeing up more women to pursue a career. This increased flexibility in the workplace will allow women to be more independent, accepting more challenging and therefore better-paid work. Everyone wins.

Surviving 'the male system'

Feminists such as Germaine Greer have a hell of a lot to answer for. But not in the way you might suspect. In the 1960's they raised the expectations of millions of women. Poised to break through the 'glass ceiling', they waited and waited for it to happen. Progress has been made, but young women entering the workplace in the 60's, 70's and 80's were misled into believing that they would now be rewarded and recognised for their hard work. Promotions would be given based on merit, rather than gender and their voice would be heard. Feminism is often based on a female's sense of fairness. This ignores a man's sense of combat. As Frankie my wife has correctly noticed, women who want to get on in their careers 'play the game' according to men's rules believing that this is the way forward.

Unfortunately, most men say one thing, and do something totally different; some don't realise they do it while others would never admit to it. There's no point playing by the rules of cricket, when most men are playing by the rules of rugby. No matter how good you become at cricket, believing you will be rewarded for it, you are unlikely to be rewarded for those skills you have worked so hard to acquire, if male colleagues are judged by their rugby prowess and the connections they make in the locker room. But what can a woman do to survive?

For a start, men tend to define 'hard work', 'talent' and 'skill' rather differently to women. Jinx Melia in *Breaking Into The Boardroom* says *'used by women [hard work] usually applies to the amount of effort, time and energy expended in accomplishing the tasks assigned by superiors. Executive males on the other hand, most often relate "hard work" to decisions that are made, to perceptions of others that are changed, and to risks that are taken .. naive underlings commonly misperceive "hard work" as overtime; ambitious fast trackers may well do their "hard work" on the golf course."*

Male executives pay for results, results, results - they are rarely interested in the process - "just give me the bottom line" is the male business mantra. If you want to get on in business, think strategically, and don't allow yourself to get bogged down in the detail. Yes, the devil is in the detail, but whenever possible, get others to do it - just like men. Eileen C Shapiro in her thought provoking, and witty book *Fad Surfing in the Boardroom*, describes the 'internal game' as what really drives a company's culture. She recommends that everyone should *"start by identifying the factors that most closely influence actual behaviour: what is permitted and what is rewarded, versus what is prohibited and what is punished, and what is funded and supported versus what is starved and ignored."* Despite the best intentions, if staff hear executives say one thing, but see evidence which undermines those words, it will limit the potential success of the business.

Too many women de-select themselves from the best jobs. They wait to be offered an opportunity, rather than putting themselves forward. If they feel a job is 'too good' for them, they will say so. Men often feel the same way, but never say so. A superb example of the difference between men and women in business is the well known story about Anita Roddick of The Body Shop. She has been ridiculed by some men for her biggest business 'mistake'; relinquishing half the equity in her company against her husband's wishes in return for a loan. That wasn't her mistake. Telling anybody about it was. It's typical of a woman's sense of openness and fairness.

Men realise being seen to do well is often more important than getting on with the work and hoping they get noticed. Forget that you have to be brilliant at everything to qualify for the best posts. Men will apply for a senior post if they have any of the qualities being sought, women tend to apply only if they have all the qualities in the recruitment ad. Large firms often require international experience, male executives routinely believe that women are not as interested in foreign assignments. If you can't get a board appointment with your employer, build up experience on the boards of voluntary organisations.

Better still, do the same as more and more women; start up, run and grow your own company. Nearly 800,000 British women have done it. Nat West Bank discovered about a third of new companies are now run by women. And according to a French survey of 22,000 French firms in 1996, women tend to be better at it than men. From the survey, companies owned by women are twice as profitable and grow twice as quickly. These women are not reliant on the whim of male superiors. They write their own corporate handbooks; they are people like Gaynor Egan and Clare Davies, the owners of Stop Gap Marketing in Richmond, Surrey. They are typical examples of highly successful, entrepreneurial women, who set up their own business, carve out a niche for themselves within a few years, and enjoy far more success than they could ever have expected working within a male-dominated organisation - and all on their own terms.

Too many highly competent women accept the mistaken belief that they don't 'have what it takes' to run their own enterprise. Low self-esteem and a lack of self-confidence are their impediments, not the fact that they are women. Ask any successful business person (male or female) and they will tell you there is never the 'right' time to strike out on your own. If the prospect of entrepreneurship has its appeal, systematically acquire the skills you will need until you are ready for that time. Go out of your way to attend as many training courses as possible within your organisation, especially those which provide 'transferable skills'. Some employers discriminate against women by limiting their training opportunities. If your employer is not prepared to train you, pay for courses yourself or get out. And while you are embarking on such training, join and become active in male-dominated business networks as well as women's business groups. Spread your 'connections'.

In so many respects the far reaching changes in society in the 21st century represent the best news for women, but only for those who choose to seize the forthcoming opportunities. Yes, women suffer from the 'glass ceiling' (being told that they have equal opportunity whilst being unable to progress further than their male superiors will allow them) but this is already starting to change. It will change much more in the next decades. No company in the future will be able to afford to ignore, or discriminate against, any sector of their workforce. I am not suggesting that businessmen will suddenly get attacks of conscience and start helping women altruistically. The demands of business will dictate these changes. As competition intensifies in the business sector, the more forward-thinking organisations will actively seek to harness the intellect and the 'softer' qualities of women.

As we have shown in this chapter, the workplace continues to change. How we respond to these and future changes will determine our employability. This requires a totally different mindset and behaviour from millions of workers and business owners. Many companies and executives have demonstrated the necessary courage to prepare themselves for the new millennium. The next chapter outlines the many alternatives available to you to safeguard your employability.

Chapter 10
New Ways of Working

Why it's important to know how fleas are trained

Fleas are remarkable creatures. If humans could jump as high as fleas, we would all be jumping over skyscrapers!

Professional flea trainers will tell you that the first thing they do when training fleas, is to put them in a large glass jar. The jar has a lid. The fleas will keep jumping and banging their heads on the under-side of the lid, until they finally realise that if they stop just short of the lid, it won't hurt. After a few days, the lid is removed by the flea trainer. Interestingly, none of the fleas will jump out of the jar; they have been conditioned into believing that if they jump too high, they will get hurt.

Most employees are capable of achieving far more than they are allowed to within the confines of their organisation, but many have been conditioned to 'jump short' of this potential. For managers to expect staff to behave differently just because it has been decided to 'take off the lid', is an unrealistic expectation. By deciding that their staff are now 'empowered', not only have senior management taken the lids off the jars in which they keep their staff, they are also urgently trying to coax these people to jump high into the air; to apply their intellects and creativity for the benefits of the business. But it's proving difficult. Employees feel frightened at the prospect. They are afraid of banging their heads on that lid. Many don't trust their managers when they are told the lid has been removed. They still remember how much it hurt when they tried to think outside of their jar. They fear reprisals if they jump too high and worry that they will hurt themselves when they fall to earth. Perhaps fleas think the same way?

Businesses desperately need to harness the ideas and full potential of their workforces if they are to survive and thrive in the 21st century, but such resistance from workers is understandable when you consider how well they have been trained NOT to jump too high.

Corporate flea trainers must learn to develop new training programmes which inspire and provoke their 'fleas' to outperform their jar - even if those fleas start to make their senior managers want to scratch!

- Have you been conditioned in this way to ensure you never fulfil your true potential?

- What are you most afraid of if you tried to jump too high within your existing job?
- How sure are you that such obstacles to your future capacity are real rather than imaginary?
- What should you do about it?
- Who can help you?

Self-limiting beliefs among employees are often reinforced by some middle managers who see it as their role in life to be the lid of the jar. If you run a company, are your middle managers 'keeping the lid on things' by restricting the innate abilities of your staff? More business leaders have come to realise that the future success of their enterprise will rely on harnessing the knowledge, ideas and enthusiasm of the workforce.

Anyone who is serious about creating an entrepreneurial environment within their business must first acknowledge that people have been conditioned over a long time to 'do as they're told'. It takes time, patience and encouragement to create an environment in which people feel comfortable about taking the initiative, making mistakes, looking for new business opportunities and implementing improvements to a business.

As in the 'flea training' example, people are often capable of greater achievements, if only they were allowed and encouraged to 'get on with it'. Dr. Stephen Covey often asks the following question at conferences *"How many in this room would agree that the vast majority of the workforce in your organisation possess more talent, more creativity, more initiative and more resourcefulness than the present jobs require or even allows you to use?"* Most hands go up. Managers and business leaders need to create an environment which harnesses these untapped resources. If they fail, they will lose their best people, and will be left with an organisation totally incapable of competing in the marketplace. Life may get tough for the workers, but things are getting very hot indeed for managers too.

Before this can be achieved, however, it is worth investing a little time in looking at some of the obstacles to entrepreneurialism which almost certainly exist within every company.

- Who within your company has a vested interest in maintaining the status quo? It is not always in the interests of your bosses to change the status quo simply because they are the one's responsible for creating it in the first place.
- What would need to happen to persuade those people to embrace important changes and potential improvements?

Empowerment

No organisation can become 'entrepreneurial' if the overriding culture remains one of 'command and control'. People need to operate in an environment of trust, personal initiative and collaboration. The word 'empowerment' is probably bandied around in business even more than the phrase 'paradigm shift'! But what is empowerment? A misunderstanding of what empowerment is can lead to utter frustration and increased cynicism amongst staff and executives alike.

Empowerment 1: "The result that ensues when employees understand what "doing a good job" means for their position, are motivated to do so, and are given the tools and autonomy for using their hundred decisions a day toward this purpose; 2: New name for what used to be known as "delegation"; 3: A process, now also sometimes called "employee involvement" or "employee satisfaction" (but never "delegation"), that when done well can scare the living daylights out of corporate chiefs and union executives alike"

Eileen C Shapiro from *Fad Surfing in the Boardroom*

Empowerment is all about sharing power, authority and responsibility. If you are a boss, that means yours! Are you prepared to accept the advantages and disadvantages of involving your staff with fundamental decisions about how your business is run? If not, you need to look more closely at why you do not trust them. Many middle managers resent subordinates being given authority to make decisions about how they conduct their own work. Some of these managers try to protect their own positions by putting a "spanner in the works" of empowerment.

If you are a business owner, what can you do to encourage middle management to agree to hand over even more of their power to subordinates? If your senior and middle management are not given sufficient reasons to share their power, then empowerment and the benefits that derive from it will not be forthcoming. Charles Handy, in his book *The Empty Raincoat*, favours the concept of 'subsidiarity' rather than 'empowerment'. Empowerment implies that power rests at the top of an organisation and that it is the bosses who have decided to hand over this responsibility to their underlings as an act of largesse. Subsidiarity, on the other hand, assumes everyone already has all the power, which they exercise as a matter of course, handing over duties and responsibilities to their superiors only when they feel incapable of performing them to the standards they have decided for themselves. This obviously involves a massive shift of trust on the part of management and a hike in the level of knowledge required by workers to perform in this way. But ultimately it removes the frustration experienced by so many employees, as well as increasing the potential fulfilment they can experience in their jobs. It also frees up managers to do more planning and pursue the strategic aspects of their work. The most successful companies such as Asea Brown Boveri (ABB), the $30 billion Swedish engineering group, are already working in this way.

Entrepreneurial staff must have the power and authority to make decisions and carry them through. Without such power, they are not 'empowered'. If they are not empowered, they cannot operate entrepreneurially.

Decision power

The best staff are paid to make decisions, solve problems, minimise unnecessary expenditure, and increase revenues. Each decision you make can be good or bad for your employer. What do you need to do in order to maximise the possibility that every time you make a decision, it is good for the business, as well as good for you? Do you have sufficient knowledge to make appropriate decisions? It is dangerous for bosses to assume that people will always make the same decisions in a particular situation that they themselves would make. It is therefore the bosses' responsibility to ensure that each worker is armed with the best, most up to date information. This cannot be achieved within an organisation if people horde information and knowledge under the old belief that 'knowledge is power'.

No business can expect to be successful in the future if its senior executives believe they have a monopoly on all knowledge, wisdom and expertise within their organisation.

The courage to ask

We all know that businesses must be leaner, faster, and more responsive to market changes and developments if they are to survive in the future. The individuals best positioned to offer added value to any business are the staff - many of whom are frustrated at unnecessary waste, lost opportunities, and what they see as ludicrous regulations. In almost every business I have ever worked with on a consultancy basis, people are grossly under-utilised as a resource, even though executives routinely describe their people as their 'biggest asset'.

No wonder business leader Julian Richer, of Richer Sounds, the highly successful British chain of hi-fi retail stores, has a 'Cut the Crap' committee amongst his staff.

"What 'crap' needs cutting in your organisation?" All bosses and managers should encourage their staff to tell them, but it takes courage to ask. Fear of hearing, or being the bearer of bad news strangles entrepreneurialism within any business. Simply asking everyone in the business the above question and REALLY listening to the answers will generate tangible savings.

That's not the way we do things around here

The combined intelligence within any organisation can turbo-charge a business and safeguard everyone's job, but only if it is used. It staggers me how many companies place such importance in recruiting workers with a high level of experience and knowledge, and then don't use it!

Instead of recruiting the best and learning from their experiences in other organisations or industry sectors, they devote the first few months of their time at the new company, moulding them into clones of the workers they already have or those who chose to leave. Such companies miss a golden opportunity to capture and use the 'insight of outsiders'.

What did their previous company do well? How could it be applied here? How did those companies save time and money? What were the most effective training programmes? Countless other questions can be used to generate invaluable input from people whose experience should be harnessed.

When I ask business leaders what their staff think and feel about particular issues, they usually provide me with an instant and comprehensive answer. Only after closer scrutiny do they accept that they don't really know. This is often because they have never thought to ask. So, if you are a business owner or senior manager in a firm, what do your staff think and feel about working within your company? If they have no clear understanding of where they are today, it is unlikely they will buy into what you think needs to be done tomorrow and beyond.

Below are a number of questions which you would be well advised to ask yourself and key members of your management team and staff. This list is certainly not meant to be comprehensive, but rather is aimed at helping you to question any assumptions you might have about your people and the core beliefs within your organisation.

- What is really stopping you from improving the company's results?
- Every organisation creates an element of fear within its workforce - what are your staff most fearful of?
- What is the overriding management style within your company? Is it authoritative or collaborative? How closely would your staff agree with this?

- How could you improve trust within your organisation?
- What should your staff know about the business?
- What do they actually know about it?
- What are the top five priorities in your business?
- What must you do to ensure that everyone is aware of these fundamentally important business priorities?
- Where is the hidden profit inside your organisation? Who knows? Ask them.
- It is easy to see how business owners might want their staff to be entrepreneurial, but what's in it for them? Why should they bother?
- You'll always get the behaviour you reward. Which behaviour do you have within your organisation that you do not want? Look closely enough and you will find that this behaviour is somehow being rewarded.
- Which factors drive the actual behaviour within your organisation?
- Are people actually punished for showing initiative or for any other 'positive' behaviour?

When making mistakes can be good for business

Few entrepreneurs get things right first time. An organisation with a 'blame culture' inhibits exploration and development because staff will always choose the 'safest' options and, wherever possible, avoid the unknown which may yield far better results. Fear of making mistakes is often cited as a prime de-motivator in business. We protect ourselves against failure whenever possible. But it is only through making mistakes that people learn. This is not to suggest that people should be encouraged to make more mistakes, but mistakes can often create massive opportunities within a business. How are your staff treated when they make mistakes? One particularly impressive leader I worked with treated people who had made a mistake in this way: the first time an individual made a mistake he regarded it as his own personal mistake - this gave his people permission to experiment. If they went on to repeat the same mistake - it then became their fault!

Just suppose you were responsible for developing an adhesive - eventually you have to report to your superiors that the glue you and your team have been working on doesn't actually work. In many companies criticism and ridicule would be the result. But not at 3M. They created the concept of 'Post It notes' - a huge global business success, resulting from a glue that they were developing that didn't work well enough.

This is the essence of being entrepreneurial - seeing opportunities where others can only see failure or problems.

What it takes to be an 'Intrapreneur'

We are living in a world in which those who master the skills of entrepreneurship achieve remarkable success. If your main preoccupation is how to hang on to your job, learn how to be an entrepreneur. Setting up and running your own business is not everyone's idea of fun. Most ordinary people look to successful people like Anita Roddick of The Body Shop and Virgin's Richard Branson as role models we admire; but we probably feel that, quite honestly, what they have achieved is almost certainly well outside the reach of most 'realistic' or 'sensible' people. It takes a rare breed of person to risk everything in pursuit of a business idea on his or her own. However, you don't have to leave an organisation to set up another business. Indeed, setting up a new enterprise is not essential either. As already discussed, with increased local, national and international competition in most businesses, few enterprises can afford the luxury of ignoring or suppressing cost-saving or profit-generating ideas from staff. But, based on widespread experience working within many medium and large companies, the majority of staff usually believe that they are not listened to, that they are not valued, trusted or encouraged to take a more active role in the future development of the enterprise. As any successful entrepreneur will tell you, success is down to spotting opportunities and finding ways to make them happen. Where are the most profitable opportunities that your company is currently overlooking? By coming up with workable ideas within your business you can establish yourself as an intrapreneur.

Enlightened business owners tend to realise that the brightest and more entrepreneurial staff will eventually want to leave to set up their own businesses. These executives have a choice; to let them go, or find a way to keep them. By letting them go, they risk turning a valued past employee into a new competitor. And who needs even more competition? Richard Branson is well known for encouraging his staff to find new business opportunities. He and his executive team have grown the Virgin empire by providing these would-be entrepreneurs with start up capital, support and expertise, as well as an equity stake in the fledgling business. This way everyone can benefit.

All businesses need a constant flow of good, workable ideas which attract additional new business and clients, or help reduce unnecessary costs. And you don't have to work in the sales or marketing department to qualify for this role. Indeed one of the biggest problems in business today is the assumption that you should only ever do what your job description dictates. This belief is slowly disappearing as more business leaders realise that old compartmentalised 'jobs' must be replaced by more flexible, solutions-orientated workers. However, it would be naive to assume that all businesses have seen this particular light. If you work for (rather than 'with') employers who actively discourage staff to contribute to the business in the ways described, what can you do?

Firstly, any business which continues to overlook or ignore internal knowledge is probably doomed. You have two choices; create an exit strategy, or you you could try educating your bosses. All too often, business owners assume staff have little or no interest in the future well being of the enterprise. What owners sometimes fail to realise is, that if the business fails, they are all out of a job. Owners in some firms are simply not used to staff taking the initiative to help the business grow. Anyone who shows such an interest in this way can strengthen their position quite considerably.

Before you rush off to implement your new ideas, there are a few points to consider. The first is; do you really know enough about the problems facing your company, the environment in which it functions and its future developments and challenges? These are important questions that you must know the answers to, before you can expect to be taken seriously.

Why company suggestion schemes don't always work

When working with some organisations, I occasionally recommend that the company abolishes the suggestion scheme. Why? Because they aren't sufficiently focused. Most suggestion schemes fail because senior managers and staff don't take them seriously. The word 'suggestion' is too flaccid. It doesn't convey any sense of urgency or a desire on the part of the bosses to implement them. But business 'Improvements' seem more tangible. Who could refuse a business improvement? Therefore, many suggestion schemes should be replaced with 'Business Improvement Schemes'. In order to make an improvement, you have to be well informed. You have to understand the problem fully in order to create an improvement or a solution. Better knowledge is essential if future improvements are to be made. Many managers who oversee suggestion schemes complain that so many of the ideas supplied show a chronic lack of understanding about their business. They become jaded by what is seen as petty 'non-value-add' suggestions, and then don't respond or inform well meaning staff why their suggestions have not been implemented.

But suggestion schemes usually illicit a response from those most interested in the business and their role within it. These people care about the wastage, missed opportunities and unnecessary duplication of work. By submitting a suggestion they are saying "I care about the company." And "I care about my future job."

Receiving a lot of ideas can result in processing delays. Therefore, companies should expect a lot of ideas from the outset and set up a system to evaluate and implement the best ones rapidly. It is important that staff are made to feel that their ideas are valued. Each time an idea is accepted and implemented, it will encourage those individuals who submitted ideas to submit more. It will also go some way towards encouraging the cynics to get involved. The most successful improvement schemes include a mechanism for acknowledging each improvement.

Imagine you were the person who made an improvement. If the evaluation process is time-consuming, it sends the signal that executives are not really that interested in your ideas.

Suggestion schemes tend to encourage the obsession in business today for cutting costs and eliminating waste; this is only a small part of the solution. Cost-cutting does not grow a business, it merely helps you survive longer. Business success is only made possible by increasing revenues. This requires innovation and the implemention of more profit-generating ideas than your competitors.

Nothing promotes an active interest in the future success of any enterprise than a full understanding by everyone of how the business works, what the particular challenges are and a shared desire to solve the problems.

At least 10-15% of the people in any workforce don't care about any of this stuff - nor will they ever do any more than what they feel they are badly paid to do. All too often, senior managers waste valuable time trying to 'convert' these cynics. Forget them; concentrate only on the 85%. Sooner or later, the 85% will realise that they are 'carrying' the cynics - perhaps they will then do something about it.

Every successful entrepreneur will tell you that business is fun. If you are a business owner and your business isn't fun and exciting for your staff - what are **you** doing wrong? And what are you going to do about it?

Everyone likes to perpetuate the impression that they are constantly busy at work. If you are not, your job may be eliminated, made part-time or incorporated within another function. What will you do when it is? Prepare yourself NOW. Acquire additional skills and competencies.

Generating ideas

Thinking about hidden opportunities and how a business can be improved can be difficult when you are under increasing pressure to do more. Doing more may not be the best answer. Doing something different may be the better alternative. A constant supply of ideas is the foundation for any entrepreneurial organisation. Ideas come to those who ask questions and to those who refuse to accept the status quo. The most valuable employees ask, *What would happen if..?'* Regardless of what role they have, staff should be encouraged to look closely at their job and ask these and other questions:

- Why is each task (within each job - not necessarily just their own) done the existing way?
- What are the simpler, quicker, cheaper, more effective and interesting alternatives?
- What and where are the bottlenecks?
- How could you smooth out the problems?
- What would happen if you did tasks at different times, or in a different order?
- What if you changed where you performed a given task?
- How would the task be affected if more (or fewer) people were involved?
- What internal and external needs are currently unmet?
- If you are involved in manufacturing, ask what would happen if your products were made larger, smaller, from a different material, in a different colour, upside-down, inside-out, back-to-front or in any combination of these alternatives.

With a little practice and encouragement, you will begin to develop more and more ideas. The more ideas you generate, the easier it becomes. The more your confidence grows, the more that thinking will become fun. As your self-assurance grows, ask increasingly outrageous 'What if . . . ?' questions.

Brainstorming sessions can be highly productive. Set a time limit of say, 10 minutes. Put together a group of people and encourage a free flow of ideas - criticise nothing. Even the 'silliest' ideas can be highly useful in stimulating more practical solutions to problems. No one expects a footballer to score a goal with every shot, but the more shots you aim at goal, the more likely you are to increase dramatically the number you score. One thing is for sure: anyone who is afraid to take these shots is not going to score at all. Suggesting ideas is exactly the same.

"You see things that are and say, "Why?" But I dream of things that never were and say, "Why not?" George Bernard Shaw

Are you at risk?

Look at the way you work. Do you operate in an old fashioned way? How could you change to become more efficient and more productive? This does not necessarily mean being able to do more of the same. Think about what you do and why you do it. If you suspect that it is becoming unnecessary or if it does not provide tangible, additional value, it could be just a matter of time before you are forced into changing.

Get real

The first set step towards changing your life for the better is to "get real". By facing reality, you are far more likely to be successful. Developments in technology and increased national and global competition will mean that more change is likely rather than less.

If you work for an organisation where senior staff and directors do not see the need for change in an industry which is under attack, you have a number of choices: bring this need to their attention, offer to help implement such changes, or if what you say falls on deaf ears, find a way out of that organisation.

If you do not get out of such a company, you are sentencing yourself to death because once it becomes widely known within your company that things are dying, you could get crushed in the rush to leave.

What you are REALLY paid for

Employers and customers buy your time. You work from (say) 9am-5pm and are given short breaks for food and drink to keep you going until you race out of the door to 'freedom'. Your employer effectively 'owns' you during those working hours. In the future, for many workers, this relationship will change quite fundamentally. The knowledge and proficiency you can bring to the projects and assignments you get involved in, will determine your value to an employer or a client. This will be based on your knowledge rather than the time you exchange for a salary.

So, what do you get paid for? Every penny and pound you earn is in return for the 'time' you offer your employer or clients. At my seminars for freelancers, I recommend that workers in the 21st century will generate additional revenue by moving away from merely selling their time, towards selling their knowledge and expertise to become what management guru Peter Drucker defined as 'knowledge workers'. The most forward-thinking workers who have transformed themselves into 'knowledge workers' receive fees and salaries commensurate with the time they have invested in themselves while acquiring knowledge and learning new skills. They are almost certainly paid to solve problems, and provide solutions.

More and more workers are needed to solve problems rather than merely performing a clearly defined and narrow range of tasks or functions. The individuals who will be of the most value to an employer or client will be those who have the confidence, the knowledge and the skill to take the initiative.

The provision of knowledge is subject to the oldest laws of supply and demand, but information, however valuable, is often taken for granted by those who supply it as well as those who use it. If you share a tangible resource with someone else, you will end up with less of it. But share knowledge and its value is doubled.

There are still too many organisations which assume that information and knowledge should be provided for free. They prefer to place a value on someone's time, but this will change. Those individuals with the best knowledge (or access to it), will increase their employability and value.

"...the same knowledge can be applied by many different users at the same time- and if used cleverly by them, it can generate even more knowledge. It is inherently inexhaustible and nonexclusive." Alvin Toffler, *Powershift*

In 1995, 14 out of 15 of the richest people in North America, according to *Forbes* magazine, work in industries based on knowledge, communications and information. How much 'knowledge' exists within your company? How much is it worth? It's worth everything - but it rarely, if ever, shows up in a company's accounts or assets. But what would happen if the brains walked out? Firms would eventually fold. Brains are vital to any successful enterprise. Become a valuable knowledge worker and your employer or clients will want to keep you. Specialised knowledge-on-demand is a growth industry and will continue to be so in the decades to come. The suppliers of up-to-date knowledge represent the most secure workers. Don't assume you do not have valuable knowledge, equally though, don't assume your knowledge necessarily has a high value.

The following knowledge-based skills are essential for the current workplace. You must be able to communicate, to persuade and to speak and write clearly. Empathy with those you work with and sell services and products to is an essential quality. This means understanding the anxieties, fears and concerns of others. Clients and employers need to be sure that you are dependable and professional. This requires a deep knowledge and understanding of how people behave, as well as the tools to deal with others in a collaborative and non-confrontational manner. The most successful individuals will be capable of questioning the status quo and offering new and innovative solutions to problems. In the very near future, it will be essential to add computer-literacy to this list.

Choose your training courses carefully. How up to date is the information you will be taught? Are the teachers at the leading edge of their subject? Or are they dinosaurs who continue to trot out the same material they have taught for decades?

Where should you work?

This section will be of particular interest to people in the earliest stages of their career, although anyone experiencing a career change (through choice or necessity) will find this information invaluable.

Nuala Beck, the Canadian author and economist, defines a future business environment comprising growth industries which are part of the New Economy, and those fading industry sectors from the Old Economy. The most powerful future industries are what she calls 'the four engines'; communications and telecommunications; computers and semi-conductors; health and medical care; and instrumentation. These engines, she predicts, will drive the economy in the 21st century in the same way that the mass production of cars, machine tools, housing, and widespread retailing drove the 20th century engines. In the 19th century the economic engines were the production of commodities such as steel, coal, textiles and the building of the railways.

The future 'engines' will create new wealth throughout the world, and they will be based on the combined knowledge of individuals, rather than the transportation and processing of raw materials. In the past, vast wealth was created by those who owned land, resources and distribution rights. This is changing. Increasingly, in the future, successful businesses will demand high levels of specialised knowledge from their workforces. The more up to date it is, the more likely you will be to remain employable.

One of the most profound yet simple questions asked by Nuala Beck in her books *Shifting Gears* and *Excelerate* is, *"What industries are growing and which are not?"* By finding out the answers, you will be able to minimise the risk of working in the shrinking industries most likely to lead to widespread cost reduction, downsizing and redundancy. This does not mean that you must choose one of these four industry engines to create a secure future for yourself, nor does it mean that you will be guaranteed a higher salary in those sectors. Your income will be based on the level of growth in your chosen sector combined with how your knowledge can be harnessed.

These strategic engines will create massive opportunities for other support industries which will grow as we move into the next phase of economic development. Excellent career opportunities will exist for knowledgeable people who invest the time in identifying growing industries rather than slipping into fading industries from the Old Economy.

Recently someone told me that their son was training to be a car mechanic. My heart sank. Yes, we will continue to sit in traffic jams for many more years and cars will need to be repaired, but vehicles are now fitted with so much technology that they are more reliable than ever and require sophisticated and expensive diagnostics equipment to isolate and correct faults. Newer technology is already eliminating the need for so many auto mechanics. Highly trained mechanics were replaced by less well trained auto parts fitters decades ago. Small independent garages are going out of business every week, as the larger, better-equipped (and fully approved and accredited) car dealers focus more on attracting potentially lucrative servicing business. They realise that the sale of new cars is declining and will continue to do so, therefore, if they are to maintain their profits, past customers must be retained. The money they can earn from each customer over many years is potentially far greater than the profit from selling them a new car or two.

Training to be an auto mechanic in a declining industry may not be such a smart move in the longer term. Many other Old Economy industries such as coal-mining, steel-making, mechanical engineering, agriculture, oil and gas production and refining, ship-building, retailing and banking should be included in the Old Economy. There are far more industries which could be listed here - but it would fill many pages. These industries will continue to lay off workers by the thousands.

What to do

For you, regardless of your age, the secret is to identify New Economy businesses and avoid the old ones. If you are young, don't be seduced by relatively high starting salaries in old industries which could 'let you go' relatively soon. Then where would you be? This doesn't mean you should always refuse a high salary, but be aware of what you are getting into.

By focusing on business sectors set to grow in the coming decades, you will be far more secure in the workplace. A report by IDPM, *1996 IT Skills Trends Report* forecasts a shrinking skills base in the information technology industry. The number of under 25's has dwindled from 20% in 1987 to just under 7% in 1996, while those over 35 have risen to nearly 50% of the IT workforce. This means that well-qualified, young individuals will be in great demand in the future. The best people will command high fees. It is also indicates a further failing of the education system if we are not producing enough good engineers and technicians. Equally, British 'society' is guilty of under-valuing the technical professions. In (say) Sweden or Germany, engineers are held in similar regard to doctors or lawyers. But in Britain, if you say you are an engineer, most people still look for your oily rag and spanner.

But what if you are already working for one of these old industries or rely on them as customers? You could be in a weak position, but it is not insurmountable. If or when such employers or clients are forced to cut costs by restructuring or buying less from their suppliers, it often sets off a downward spiral of blood-letting. This is yet another scenario which demands the creation of an exit strategy. Start to re-train yourself now, but make sure it is not in another old industry. Ask Nuala Beck's question *"What's growing and what's not?"* , and then act accordingly.

You are far more likely to be successful if you have an on-going survival strategy. It should be updated on a continual basis. This is not the same as merely keeping your CV up to date.

Take a close look at the industries and companies which operate in your area or region. Are they new industries, or predominantly old ones? Try to assess what will happen to your community in 10 or 20 years from now if a significant proportion of these companies are forced to relocate or close down. Many communities have already suffered economically. More will suffer in the coming decades. My own home town is a classic example of how a local economy can be devastated by 'progress'. Haverfordwest is in rural Pembrokeshire, West Wales, and has been hit badly on a number of different fronts and at practically the same time. It is heart-breaking to see a community suffer. Agriculture has declined there as it has everywhere, the tourist industry has been hit badly by overseas competition where accomodation and airfares are cheaper and where sunshine is practically guaranteed. The deep natural harbour at Milford Haven was perfect for offloading giant oil tankers of their precious cargo. The oil refineries have been closed down and dismantled. The highly paid workers at the refineries were laid off, their incomes have dropped considerably and the money they used to pump into the local economy has gone. Consequently, other businesses folded.

Thousands of other high-spending families left the area when 'bad' Russians became 'good' Russians. Defence cuts meant the closure of the RAF's tactical weapons training base and the US Naval submarine tracking facility at Brawdy.

The above description is not a criticism of those who run the community. It is no one's fault, it is merely a symptom of our times. Many other areas are suffering in similar ways. As an individual, you have a responsibility to yourself and your dependants to identify potential threats to your future employability and to take what ever action is appropriate.

This does not mean by definition that everyone should leave a small community in favour of larger cities. New technological developments as described earlier, allow a growing number of people to work anywhere, connected electronically to their customers and clients who may be hundreds or even thousands of miles away.

More people are moving back to rural areas to combine their work with a better quality of life; a slower pace, cleaner air, sometimes beautiful scenery, safer streets and better schools. The more forward-thinking communities are actively trying to attract such workers by creating an environment which will allow them to gain easy access to state-of-the-art telecommunications systems. Communities such as the ski resort of Telluride in Colorado have done this very successfully and enjoy the added economic benefits which go with attracting high-earning (and therefore higher-spending) professionals to their area.

Why do we work any way?

Here are a few reasons - may be you can think of a few more.
- to earn a living to pay bills for food and shelter
- to enable us to do the things and own the grown-up toys we would like in order to feel good
- to spend quality time with those people who are most important to us
- to get involved with our chosen leisure activities
- to provide the best for our partner and children
- to make a contribution to society
- to meet people
- provide mental stimulation/avoid boredom

Few full-time employees can obtain all these qualities from one job or career - but if you are self-employed, it is quite possible, with a little forethought and planning, to construct a 'workstyle' which offers many of these life enhancing qualities.

The 'Portfolio' approach

A well known British TV commercial for instant coffee features a bland, middle-aged couple who live in a grey house, wear dull, greyish clothes and live next door to a young, vibrant, colourful couple, who seem to enjoy life to the full, no doubt over-stimulated by all that caffeine. The miserable woman accepts her husband's view that they have enough excitement in their life, although the final shot of the commercial shows her holding up a jar of coffee behind his back with a broad, wicked grin across her face. The woman in the commercial is actually a very happy person indeed. Her name is Geraldine McNulty. Gerry is a highly successful freelancer. You can learn a lot from the way she works.

I first met her in Berlin when I presented a three-day multimedia conference for Hewlett-Packard. Gerry was working as a floor manager-ensuring that everyone knew what they had to do; when to come on and off-stage, as well as directing business scenarios with a group of actors who were performing live on the day. She was also coaching senior executives prior to their presentations. I found out that Gerry:

- is a director of a successful video production company
- she works as a trainer, presenting seminars for a well known training company
- she offers executive coaching for presentation skills
- she is co-founder of a company which develops new comedy writing for TV and Radio
- she works as an actress on TV and Radio - hence the commercial
- she writes and performs her own comedy stage shows - winning awards at places like The Edinburgh Festival. If you ever have the opportunity to see any of her one woman shows - get tickets - she's incredibly funny and highly talented.

Gerry is a wonderful example of a portfolio worker. It's a phrase coined by the writer Charles Handy and is based on the way a financial investment portfolio is constructed. If you have investments - you'll know that some savings or investment plans have a higher return than others - those are usually more risky, so it doesn't make sense to put all your money into those areas. Instead, you would spread the risk by including other 'safer' investments which are unlikely to generate as high a return on your money, but on which you are less likely to lose your shirt. The way you combine your collection of stocks and shares, pensions, gilts, PEPs, TESSAs, ISAs building society and bank accounts, represents your financial portfolio. In the same way, a successful self-employed person will deliberately put together a 'portfolio' of different (but often related) jobs which satisfy different personal criteria. They can be personal fulfilment, excitement, meeting new people, working on a solitary project, an opportunity to travel and of course - earning money.

For Gerry there are opportunities in her portfolio for her to work for a couple of days with a high return (such as appearing in that commercial) which she can then use to finance her other, less lucrative, but more enjoyable and fulfilling activities. Portfolio working provides Gerry with many choices in her life; it's always varied, all the parts feed from and enrich one another. And to a large extent she can pick and choose what she does. Can you imagine what effect that has on how she feels about her work? And can you imagine what a work portfolio could do for you?

A portfolio worker is someone who, like the financial investor, spreads their risk and increases the choices they have available to themselves.

Charles Handy describes portfolio living as "*Something like a pie chart with different segments marked off for different occupations, each coloured for kind and degree of hoped for remuneration. Some occupations will be paid in money, some in other kinds of reward; love, creative satisfaction, power, joy and the like. And of course the chart will be constantly changing, the dimensions of the occupation segments expanding or contracting according to time invested, the remuneration colours fading or brightening according to the returns on the investment, and this not only over the years of one's life but from week to week, even day to day.*" All his books are well worth reading; notably *The Age of Unreason*, *The Empty Raincoat*, *Beyond Certainty* and *The Human Spirit*.

You do not have to be self-employed to benefit from this mindset change. If you are in full-time employment, what projects could you create or volunteer for, which would provide you with invaluable 'transferable skills', whilst providing deep personal satisfaction and adding value to your employer's business? Proactively developing a work portfolio, rather than merely responding to whatever work you are required to perform, can and will make a big difference to the way you feel about your work. You will also benefit from the added 'security' of knowing that if the unthinkable were to happen, you could turn your hand to other tasks and increase your chances of other employment.

Why 'Tiny is beautiful'

Technology is now allowing tiny companies with fewer than five employees to spring up and compete on an equal footing with larger, well established organisations. These entrepreneurial micro-businesses are often capable of out-manoeuvring their larger, less nimble competitors. "*The days of the large bureaucratic disorganisations are over.*" proclaimed Dr. E.F Shumacher in his book *Small is Beautiful* way back in 1973. Not even he could have predicted the huge growth in the number and success of these enterprises. This is yet more proof that self-employment is becoming the preferred, rather than the last option for more and more people. Each of these micro-businesses is headed by one or two individuals who have a dream, pluck up the courage, embark on a steep learning curve to run their own business and create their own future.

Self-employment as a first option, not the last

As a last resort, if all else fails, you could consider becoming self-employed. But why a last resort? It was certainly never even offered as an option when I was at school. Self-employment is the least attractive option for a significant proportion of the workforce. But self-employment has many distinct advantages, although it does require a fundamentally different attitude and mindset to deal with what can appear to be a tenuous and insecure workstyle. As mentioned earlier, self-employment, when practised effectively, can be far more secure than most full time jobs. As someone who has advised thousands of self-employed people through self-employment seminars, taped programmes, newsletters and personal consultations, one of the most serious obstacles I have encountered facing people is not their ability, but their low self-confidence and self-esteem. Self-employment requires a lot of guts, determination and ample quantities of self-esteem and confidence. Could a lack of self-confidence be the sole reason holding you back from branching out on your own?

Self-employment will continue to spread as more employers see the advantages of calling on freelancers only on those occasions when they are needed. For years, many of the creative jobs in broadcasting, publishing and design have been carried out using freelancers on a daily, or project basis. More industry sectors are following down this 'casualisation' route. Everywhere, permanent staff are surrounded by freelance, part-time and temporary staff. Some of whom are better treated and seen to be better paid, although in reality they may not be, when you take into consideration the overheads they too must pay for in order to function in their self-employed capacity.

Freelancers realise they are 'only as good as their last job'. As competition for projects amongst freelancers and consultants increases, they too will experience increased pressures in the workplace. Already, many experience real fear about where their next job will come from. But equally so, those who have learned to market themselves accept such feelings as merely a part of life. It never goes away entirely but you do learn to live with it.

Let me declare my bias; as someone who chose to become self-employed on a full-time basis in 1984, I simply cannot imagine that I will ever be employed in a full-time capacity by anyone else for the rest of my working life. Earnings rise and fall like the oceans, although on balance I am far better off financially. For me, the loss of independence and freedom to choose what projects I want to work on, with whom I choose would drive me nuts! Eight years at the BBC put me off company life for ever.

Self-employment certainly has its shortcomings; namely uncertainty, although this in itself can represent an element of excitement, not knowing exactly what you will be doing a few weeks or months down the line. Chasing payment from clients with financial constipation is another problem. This can make financial planning and cash-flow forecasting well nigh impossible. But at least you can go to the cinema, the park or supermarket shopping while everyone else is at the office!

Three times a year, I stage a one-day seminar for freelancers on how to improve the results they get from their self-employment. This seminar is based on the 20 most common mistakes you can make in self-employment. There simply isn't enough space here to go into all the details, but here are some of the ideas covered at the seminar and the 6-part audio cassette programme, *"The Secrets of Successful Freelancing"*. They deal with every aspect of marketing yourself as a freelancer. Ordering details for the tape programme can be found at the end of this book.

With more and more freelancers coming into the market, either through choice or redundancy there has never been a greater need for freelancers to understand more fully the marketing options available to them. The best paid freelancers are not necessarily the best at their job. Highly paid freelancers are almost without exception better organised, better marketers and better sales people. They have a realistic and workable plan - they simply refuse to accept that they have to muddle through and hope for the best.

Many self-employed people needlessly lead a hand-to-mouth existence:
- the money they earn is less than they deserve,
- the hours are longer than they might choose to work,
- they don't receive perks such as company pensions, holidays or health insurance.
- they are constantly scrambling around for work and
- some are willing to accept almost any assignment, at almost any fee, just so long as they are kept busy.

The following have been identified as some of the most common mistakes made by freelancers and the self-employed. Just by avoiding these mistakes, you will improve your results.

MISTAKE #1 Assuming past customers will automatically book you again without any help and encouragement from you

A writer/director who attended our seminar wrote shortly afterwards to say that this idea generated "a level of work I've never known before". You simply get in touch with every previous employer (this must be done systematically for it to have the best effect) that you would want to work with again. Assuming you did a competent job, you are practically guaranteed to end up with new work. Why? Because previous happy customers are always the easiest people to sell yourself to. It costs money to attract a new client, sometimes it can cost quite a lot in terms of time invested, too. Working again for past clients is more profitable than constantly spending time and money to find new ones. Forgetting about clients you have worked with in the past is a costly mistake for any freelancer.

So maintain a relationship with all past clients and customers. If there are past clients you haven't spoken to in a while - get in touch again. Re-awaken the relationship. Assume the responsibility of contacting them, you will find that a significant amount of repeat business will come your way. It's known as 'top of the mind' marketing.

MISTAKE #2 Not marketing yourself proactively

If you continue with the same behaviour, you are GUARANTEED to get the same results. Failing to actively market yourself effectively is the most expensive mistake you can make. Many freelancers believe they don't have the time. This is usually an excuse because they don't really understand what they need to do, what it entails and where they start so they convince themselves that it is better, or OK, to do nothing.

"WHERE DO I START?" is a common question.

The biggest obstacle to success for many freelancers is that so many look upon themselves as crafts people first, and business people last. They mistakenly believe that the high quality of their work should be enough to sell them. It **should** be enough, but it isn't - nor will it ever be - and it will be less so in the future. They like to think that a professional doesn't need to resort to the dirty world of marketing or selling.

But you cannot **not** market yourself. If you don't market yourself actively, by definition you market yourself passively. Most passive marketing is poor, needlessly costing you money and lost business. Effective personal marketers make sure that their customers and potential clients perceive them in the best or most appropriate way - rather than allowing them to make up their own minds about them. Look to see precisely who needs your services. Brainstorm with others if possible; preferably people in different industries. Your customers are not always who you think they are and don't always want what you think they want.

Think about your business or what you do from the employers

perspective. Ask yourself how you can satisfy **their** needs - for the time being forget about your own. How can you help your clients to save money or to make more of it?

By really understanding what happens before a freelancer is hired, you can dramatically improve your chances of winning the business. They want a result. People hire you because of the result you can provide them with; the better the result, or the quicker you can produce that result - the more appealing you will be to any employer. How can you give your prospective clients a better result than your competitors?

The secret is to take a systematic approach. Most people don't do this; looking for work in a very ad hoc way and failing to go through every resource, skill and option open to them. They merely rely on luck.

This is a simple process for finding new clients; the more potential new clients you have, the more choices you have in your life, and this will help you become more confident about your freelancing. Prepare three separate lists of people: Your first list should include every person and organisation you know who is personally capable of offering work. Include everyone you have ever worked for in the past. This list represents your hottest prospects.

Your second list should comprise everybody you know who might know someone else who might be able to offer you work. There are lots of 'coulds' associated with this list. Dismiss no one. Include people you haven't spoken to in months or even years. Go through your old address books. Don't deselect anyone at this stage.

Your third list should comprise the most detailed list of people or organ-isations who you do not know personally, but who you would want to work with or work for. They might include the leading companies in your industry, or if your clients are members of the public - they could be the rich, famous or the most powerful and influential people in your locality or your city. This third list is a 'wish list' of possible clients. Go through the telephone book, Yellow Pages, the Thomson Directory, and the Business Pages for the local-ities you are interested in. Go to your local reference library. Treat your visits as though they were days at the office - they could easily represent the most productive marketing days you spend. You will find a variety of trade and association directories. These can be a goldmine for prospective clients. Look for associations which use your products or services. Try to think laterally.

Contact clubs and, if appropriate, offer a special deal to their members - the club is seen to offer extra value to their members while you get new business at little or no cost to you.

Once you've identified all these people, you need to contact them - but

don't ask for any business! Instead, do the following; ask them for some advice and feedback. There are two reasons; firstly, it takes the pressure off them if they are not in a position to offer any work, and secondly, you will be seen as someone who cares about what they think and have to say - everybody likes to be asked for advice.

By talking with a number of existing and potential customers you will get a clear idea of what motivates people to employ freelancers in your industry. Go through your notes and extract the most insightful comments from this research.

Think deeply about the information you have been given and start to write down how you can address those concerns, how you can and will solve their problems. This approach is the opposite way most freelancers operate; the only time they ever make contact with someone is to ask for work. If you think about what you can do to help an employer to solve their problems and allay their fears or anxieties, then a letter or brochure which addresses and answers those concerns and is conveyed in a sincere but professional manner will gain you more business.

MISTAKE #3 Asking for work

This is the biggest self-employment sin. A successful freelancer **never** has to ask for work; instead they present a prospective employer with an offer or a series of offers so powerful that they will ask the freelancer to work for them. Don't be one of those freelancers who only ever contacts a client if they want work. Yes, you want work, but prospective clients don't care about you - they care about themselves. So help them by developing a habit of offering them something every time you make contact. This is very important. You can even send a newspaper cutting which you think is relevant to their job/interests. If you can't think what you have to offer - you simply cannot expect a client to.

Inexperienced freelancers say they don't maintain contact because they think they will be seen as a nuisance. They don't want to pester but only freelancers who fail to think of themselves as people who provide solutions to clients' problems think in this way.

MISTAKE #4 Believing the money you earn represents 'take home' pay

It costs money to earn money. Many freelancers mistakenly think that money spent on promoting themselves or attracting new customers comes out of their pay packet - so they tend not to do it. This means that attracting new clients is perceived as being a 'cost' and is therefore probably not worth doing. After all, why spend money you've worked so hard to earn and risk losing it, if it doesn't succeed in producing more business? Such an attitude is guaranteed to cost more money than it saves. It is a fact of freelancing that if you are not confident about exactly 'how' to promote yourself, it is most likely that you will not do it. Depending on how much you earn annually, it can cost anything from 10-35% of your income to earn your salary. And of course, any freelancer who does not put away up to 25-30% of all their income into a high interest 60 day account for their income tax liability is headed for trouble!

MISTAKE #5 Not Charging Enough

An obvious mistake perhaps (no one does it unless they feel they have to) but look at why so many freelancers don't charge enough. Fear and lack of self-confidence are almost certainly the biggest culprits, followed closely behind by a lack of information either about their own finances or the industry they are working in. Too many freelancers are afraid that they won't get a job if they charge too much. This fear is very real if they aren't earning enough from the jobs they are doing already. This in turn forces them into accepting more poorly paid work, which in turn means they need the money so much that they can't afford to risk missing out on future work, so they keep their fees low. If you do this - this fear is slowly strangling you. It will never improve unless you do something about it.

Any self-employed person who uses the above tips should improve their results, and more than justify the cost of this book many times over.

Chapter 11
Managing Yourself

Your personal marketing survival guide

In previous chapters we have explored the need to become more self-reliant, knowledgeable and forward-thinking by adopting continuous learning as a way of life; the need to understand and accept change, embrace new technology and to think differently about the ways you invest your time and money. Much of this preparation for your future will lose its full impact if you are not proficient at managing and marketing yourself.

You must learn to run your own life as a business. Like it or not, you are the product. You are the service. Society is changing; clearly defined jobs and work roles are disappearing. No longer can anyone rely on employers to look after them in return for 'company loyalty'. Employers do not have the power to deliver on such promises. The most sensible and potentially secure individuals in the future will develop "You Incorporated" as an integral part of their lives. If you don't do this, no one else will. This requires a fundamental re-think for many people.

To survive in the 21st Century, being confident about selling yourself and becoming skilful at it will improve your choices. The long term benefits to you and your dependants for developing and maintaining a self-marketing campaign will be to increase the likelihood that you will remain employable during your entire working life. If job security is an issue for you, a self-marketing campaign is worth serious consideration.

As a nation, the British exhibit a widespread lack of ease about 'Self-marketing' and selling themselves. It conjures up images of conceited, egotistical, self-centred people who we either envy or despise. We see too many smooth-talking, self-focussed salesmen who show little or no interest in others, constantly telling everyone they meet how wonderful, successful and wealthy they are. In short, marketing yourself must be about learning to bullshit.

No, this is **definitely not** the case!

Marketing is simply about ensuring that others know of your talents, skills and capabilities. Until they fully understand the long term benefits of self-marketing, most people believe it is not for them. Women in particular tend to believe that excellence should not need any help.

You don't have to be a nationally known celebrity to benefit from self-marketing. Your employment prospects, and your ability to persuade and influence others in your local community will increase when you learn how to improve how others perceive you. The combined effects of developing such skills over many years will repay your attention many times over.

Marketing yourself effectively is nothing to do with learning to brag. Nor is it about learning to convey an image which has no foundation in truth. Self-marketing can and should be totally ethical and honest. Anyone who tries to deceive or manipulate others deserves to be found out, as so many publicity-hungry celebrities and politicians discover on an almost weekly basis.

This is not about how to create an acceptable veneer for a scumbag character.

Having total control of your life is obviously impossible: outside pressures and responsibilities to employers, clients, family and friends make sure of that. But you can exert far more influence and control than you may realise.

Professional manipulators learned a long time ago that we are what we are perceived to be, not what we think we are. This realisation and the amount of money to be earned from it has led to the massive growth of the public relations industry, which actively creates positive images for all kinds of public figures. These day's politicians, professional businesspeople and the stars of sport, film, television and pop music avail themselves of the publicist's expertise. Images are created deliberately and are carefully nurtured.

Countless individuals don't realise the additional opportunities they are missing simply by not being in control of this area of their lives. Understanding the way you are perceived by others can make a staggering difference to your lifestyle: this knowledge can bring you more respect, power, friends and a significantly higher income. When others perceive you as successful, self-assured and firmly in control of your life, it is far easier to influence them.

So what 'vibes' do you give out to others? If you can persuade others to perceive you as someone who is special, you will be treated better, your opinions will be sought more often and you will increase your perceived value. It is a common mistake for people to think that financial success is based on expertise and qualifications. Employers and customers are prepared to pay more for something they believe is worth more. It is also a common myth that successful people are more intelligent and better educated than the less successful. All too often, successful people are just more effective at positioning themselves and persuading others to give them the opportunity to 'shine'. Then, when they are seen to be doing well, they use each new opportunity as it arises to progress even further. You can do the same.

The career of movie-star Arnold Schwarzenegger is widely regarded as 'textbook self-marketing'. From humble beginnings he made a name for himself in his native Austria as a bodybuilder, before moving to the US - a larger market where he was able to raise his profile even further. Once he'd reached the pinnacle of his bodybuilding career (winning the *Mr Universe* title), he made the most of it by writing definitive books on bodybuilding and securing lead roles in films such as *Conan the Barbarian* and *The Terminator*. Over the years he has consolidated his position and reached an even wider audience by developing another, more loveable public image in movies such as *Twins*, *Kindergarten Cop* and *Junior*. This professional success and 'box office' appeal has made him one of the most powerful performers in Hollywood. Capitalising even further on his fame as a movie star, together with fellow actors Sylvester Stallone and Bruce Willis, he has become an international ambassador for *Planet Hollywood*, their fast food money-making machine.

His much-publicised marriage to Maria Shriver, a member of the famous Kennedy clan, has given him access to American politics. Who knows what else he wants to achieve? It's probably fair to say that whatever it is, he has certainly built a solid foundation for it. Not bad for someone who was told that he'd never make it because no one could pronounce his name!

But what can we all learn from Arnie? A great deal. The principles he has used to build his career are universal and can be copied by anyone who decides to devote the time and effort to it. This doesn't mean you have to take up bodybuilding or try to become an international movie star - there are enough wannabee celebrities in society already. One of the keys to his initial success was a relentless devotion to making the most of what he was best at. Schwarzenegger took a proactive, rather than a passive, approach to developing opportunities in his life. Using his obvious success at bodybuilding, he 'leveraged' this expertise and prowess to move into higher profile arenas. Is he the best actor in the world? Hardly. Does it matter? In his case - no. This is certainly not to damn Schwarzenegger's acting skills (in any case he's a lot bigger than me!) 'Serious' actors are keen to promote their craft and expertise - but when you think about it, acting is only about 'pretending' to be someone else. The best actors and actresses are without doubt, remarkably skilful at pretending. Where you are positioned within the 'pretending spectrum' is only important to others who pretend for a living, or would like to if they were given the opportunity. In Schwarzenegger's case he has other talents and skills - it is these which we are showcasing here.

Behind Schwarzenegger is a team of highly skilled professional's; managers, photographers, image and wardrobe consultant's, public relations consultant's and publicists. Most of the population is largely unaware of the machinery behind the gloss and glamour. Nor do they care, even though it is all focused with laser accuracy towards persuading us to hand over our money at the cinema box office - a proportion of which goes into Arnie's bank accounts. Conveniently for him, the film companies who have an interest in promoting the movies he appears in will pay for many of these high-earning professionals. Experienced self-marketers work out ways for others to promote them too. By developing a core team of people who support your interests (this can often be achieved by helping others on a reciprocal basis) you can become aware of opportunities which might not be made available in any other way.

Unlike Schwarzenegger, your on-going campaign would focus only on the relatively tiny number of individuals you would choose to influence. Anybody can do this stuff if they choose to build a valuable network of people around them (there's more on 'networking' later).

Self-marketing is about identifying, anticipating, supplying and ultimately satisfying the needs of decision makers and those who are interested in the product or service you can provide. Once again, self-marketing is described here in the business context but it is equally applicable on a social level. And it is most effective when camouflaged!

You, as a supermarket product

Try, for a moment, to think of yourself as a product in a supermarket. There are a number of simple options open to you. You can sit there quietly and anonymously, tucked away at the back of the bottom shelf waiting for someone to notice you, or you can choose to position yourself at eye level in front of those people who may want to buy you. Selling yourself in much the same way as a professional marketer would sell a packet of washing powder is not as outlandish as it might seem. There are many similarities. To sell any product it is essential to display it in its most desirable light in front of those most likely to be interested in it, at the price specified. Positioning on the shelf is therefore very important. You won't be alone on that shelf; millions of others will be jockeying for position and ultimately for the attention of employers, friends or potential partners. Because of this intense level of competition, companies invest enormous amounts of time and money ensuring that a product's image and packaging will 'flag-wave' to attract enough attention to stop a prospective consumer so that he or she takes a closer look. This must happen before anyone makes any sort of commitment to buy. The experts also know that if they put the product under the noses of enough potential buyers, statistically they have a much greater chance of selling it.

Any company that left this process to chance would soon go out of business. The principles are the same for individuals. How much of your life is left to chance in this way?

A passive approach to the future is certainly easier (which is one of the reasons why millions don't plan). Planning requires effort, an investment of time to develop specific knowledge and new skills, as well as the determination and self-confidence to follow the plan through. As we discussed in an earlier chapter, fear, in its many forms, is an over-riding factor which imposes self-limiting beliefs and behaviours on people who are invariably more capable than they think. It's what Zig Ziglar, the American sales trainer, describes as the difference between being *"a wandering generality or a meaningful specific."*

Leadership qualities for the 21st century

A self-marketer is a leader rather than a follower. Being a leader no longer has to be confined to those at the top of a company. And you can still possess leadership qualities even if you are not involved in business at all. But as so many organisations are evolving into collections of independently run teams, there have never been so many opportunities for individuals to become leaders. 'Command and control' techniques are being replaced by 'collaboration and coaching', while collective leadership is superseding individual leadership. A few words of warning - don't believe that 'management' experience automatically qualifies you as a leader!

Anyone who takes the initiative to acquire and develop leadership skills will improve their future prospects. 'Taking the initiative' is obviously crucial; waiting to be invited to lead is hardly a demonstration of leadership potential. The conventional view of leadership (as exemplified within the military) is the ability to create a strategic plan and instruct subordinates to carry it out. Historically, subordinates rarely had much say in the process. However, the best leaders focus on leading a) by example and b) by consent. Authoritarian bosses mistakenly believe they demonstrate leadership by striking fear into those who report to them. Tyrants tend to lose good people, who will simply go elsewhere, refusing to take any crap from anyone who makes their lives more stressful than it needs to be. Usually, it's only the frightened followers who stay.

True leadership skills now involve learning how to listen, inspire, coach, mentor, persuade and motivate colleagues. Anyone who can initiate conversations and constructive discussion within an organisation, and facilitate the application of the knowledge produced by such discussions, will improve their personal standing within any group. Your reputation as a 'hub' of information and knowledge will grow.

If your life is governed by fear (as described in earlier chapters), you will be unlikely to take on many roles as a leader. Leaders still experience fear, but don't let it stop them from sticking out their necks and saying what needs to be said in order to get a job done.

This type of courage is a pre-requisite for anyone who is serious about self-marketing. To overcome fear, take small steps by taking initiative in ways you may not have attempted in the past. As you gain more recognition and validation for your efforts, you will gain more confidence and the encouragment to continue with this approach.

How are you perceived?

One of the secret keys of effective self-marketing is that you can determine so much of what others think about you. It is possible to direct those who come into contact with you to think what **you** want them to believe. Very often, our clients, friends and partners have particular beliefs about us which would probably shock us. This does not have to be the case.

- How do others perceive you? How do you know this to be true?
- How valuable are you to others?
- What qualities do you possess which others find unappealing?
- What could you do to eliminate these traits?

In short, most people don't know what others think of them - and are often too afraid to ask. It can be painful, as I discovered when I carried out this exercise for the first time many years ago. But the feedback can be invaluable.

One of the reasons people refuse to pursue or develop a self-marketing campaign is their fear of being noticed. When you step into a spotlight there are a number of things that can happen; your face will be kissed, slapped or ignored. No one wants to get their face slapped. And who likes to be ignored? More importantly, others may not be as bashful as you and could end up getting not only the credit they deserve, but the credit you deserve as well.

Communication mistakes

Our ability to market ourselves effectively is often linked to our skill in communicating with others. Poor or mis-communication is invariably at the heart of most people-related problems; improve the communication and you will inevitably improve the situation and the eventual results. As part of my work I often find myself discussing with company directors of large international corporations the difference between what they want from their staff and clients and what they actually get. This is equally valid on a personal level between colleagues, friends and family.

How many of the messages you convey to others are not the messages received? If you believe that the results you are achieving in your life are not what you had in mind, it is highly likely that this is one of the problems.

No matter how keen you are to market yourself, your efforts will be wasted, if you do not improve the effectiveness of your communication.

Much of the time you may use the correct words, but the way you convey the message could be inappropriate. Detailed research by Professor Albert Mehrabian of UCLA has confirmed that effective communication consists of the following components: body language, tone of voice, and the words you use. But surprisingly, body language accounts for 55% of the effectiveness of the communication, voice tone 38%, while the words you use contribute only 7% to the process. So, using the right words does not, in itself, guarantee successful communication.

Imagine the following scenario; a confident and skilful skier is gliding gracefully down a steep slope in the brilliant sunshine. On one side of the slope is a novice skier nervously inching his way across the snow, trying not to fall over. As additional insurance against a potentially painful mishap he has surrounded himself with a large number of well meaning advisers and underlings, each one closely on hand to catch him in case he falls. He can be sure he will never be allowed to fall - because when he does, they all get fired.

The latter approach to business communications seems to apply to a significant sector of British business. You cannot learn to ski by making sure you never fall over. But, as every skier knows, a face full of snow does not hurt; you can often have a good laugh about it - unless, of course you have been behaving irresponsibly, in which case, limbs tend to snap!

The fear of looking foolish and a lack of self-confidence when communicating with staff, suppliers and customers often hinders the communications process. Personal communication skills will always impact directly on the effectiveness of 'corporate' communication. They are inextricably linked. In short, 'backfoot' behaviour costs money and creates frustration, slowing down productivity and stopping the business reaching its full potential. But developing your communication skills is not only applicable to business - the way you behave in every interaction you have with others, affects the outcome and the subsequent results you achieve - with your spouse, your kids, extended family and friends.

Here's a good business example of how poor communication can affect the results you achieve. At an international senior management conference in Madrid, it became apparent that no one felt they knew what was going on within the business; if they wanted information they felt the need to ask a junior. They were not happy. Although the company had a sophisticated electronic mail system, it was not used by senior executives. As the conference facilitator, I suggested implementing a weekly bulletin from the managing director. His initial response illustrated what I believe is the most common mistake in business communications.

The MD felt that with so many 'delicate' developments in the business, it would be premature to 'announce' anything until deals were signed. But, by not communicating information he was communicating the message to his managers that they were not important enough to know about present and future developments. Worse still, his belief that confidentiality could be jeopardised sent another message - "I don't trust you!" a great example of how the message 'sent' is not always the message 'received'.

As a result of the conference discussion he began to understand why he was failing to get the co-operation he both wanted and needed to implement new business processes. When he saw the effect he was having, he instantly agreed to send out a weekly confidential bulletin on all developments affecting the business. This bulletin also encouraged feedback and requests for help from those 150 executives. This fundamentally improved their relationship with this rather autocratic manager who, in turn, benefited from more co-operation. He was also able to use valuable knowledge and insight from his management team. This MD was not communicating effectively - therefore he was not marketing himself effectively.

When you don't get the response you want from someone, your communication has been ineffective. But few people devote much time thinking about the response they want to evoke in the first place - too much effort is put into the initial composition or delivery of the message.

"If I tell you something and you do not understand it - who's fault is it?" Without a doubt, it is my fault. Why? Because you are not stupid - or probably not! However, it is surprising how quickly this view changes when someone is impatiently trying to explain something complex to a 'slow' subordinate.

The best and most effective communication is based on improved listening skills. Really listen instead of using the time to work out what you plan to say next. An effective communicator concentrates more on being interested, rather than being interesting. Isn't it strange that everyone is taught from the earliest age how to talk and yet we don't meet anyone who attended classes at school which shared the secrets of how to listen? We have two ears and one mouth - they are most effective when used in the same ratio.

By minimising such errors of miscommunication you will fulfil the first part of a personal self-marketing campaign.

Learn from 'corporate' marketing

No professional organisation can hope to be successful today or in the years to come, without having a clear and detailed understanding of who their customers are, why they buy their products or services, what their needs are and how those needs can be satisfied. Gone are the days when businesses simply made products and provided services and vaguely hoped that enough people would be willing and able to pay for them. Every business MUST learn about the needs of those most likely to buy from them and set about satisfying those needs - if they don't, customers who are becoming increasingly demanding, will go elsewhere. This is exactly the same for people. If you have no idea, or do not care about what your customer (or your employer) wants from you - you are not as valuable to them as someone who makes it their business to find out and deliver what is wanted.

The individual can learn a lot from this professional approach to business. The same marketing principles can be taken and moulded to form personal strategies for business and social success.

The most successful individuals have a very clearly defined understanding of what everyone in their life wants and needs from them. In an interview with Lord Sheppard of Didgemere, the former CEO of food and drinks giant Grand Metropolitan, he spoke to me about his attitude to business leadership and the role of the individual within a large organisation. He offered his own simple personal business motto, *"Add value or get out"*. Increasingly in the future, businesses will be forced into demanding added value from their staff and suppliers. It will be a case of add value or you will be pushed out, to make way for someone (or technology) that does.

But how do you add value to your colleagues, customers, your family, friends and your spouse? This is at the heart of effective personal marketing. By taking the time to understand the differing needs of those around you, you can 'position' yourself as someone who helps to provide them with solutions to their problems. It is only by finding out what those problems are, that you will be able to do something about them. Hence the importance of developing a mindset of being 'interested' rather than 'interesting'. For many, taking care of the needs of others **first,** may seem strange. This does not mean becoming a doormat whose own needs are relegated to the bottom of a priority list. It is merely focusing attention on the needs of others, so that your needs are satisfied, almost by default.

First define the skills you have, assess the demand for those skills, identify areas where your skills are deficient and make moves to acquire such skills. Research who is most in need of the tool kit of skills you possess, find out who is competing with you for that business, and research what your competitors charge for their services. My audio tape series *"The Secrets of Successful Freelancing"*, provides ideas and strategies to find the answers to these questions and many more.

The most effective marketing is based on detailed knowledge of your existing and potential customers; their needs, problems and aspirations. Quite often they are not always fully aware of these things themselves. It is your job as a personal marketer to uncover such concerns. When you can literally 'walk in their shoes', by empathising with them, then you can lead them towards solutions.

Your image

The first step to successful personal marketing is to list all your strengths and weaknesses.

Your strengths might include:
- reliability
- honesty
- integrity
- particular skills and qualifications
- working well as part of a team
- being good at thinking up innovative ideas.

Weaknesses could include:
- a character lacking in honesty, integrity and reliability
- poor attention to detail
- being too meticulous
- a habit of criticising others
- being too confident or not confident enough
- interrupting people
- a lack of specific qualifications or experience

This information will help you to concentrate on your strengths in the future and give you a clear and realistic understanding of your own potential and limits. If you discover a number of negative aspects to your personality, appearance, or behaviour, at least you will know about them and, if you choose to, you will be able to do something about changing them.

Look at yourself again as if you were a product. Take a long hard look and ask, 'Do I like what I see?' If you do - look again! Be a bit critical and try to assess what other people would notice about you if they were meeting you for the first time. In the context of self-marketing it is important to remember that, regardless of what you think of yourself, everyone you meet will respond to you, whether positively, negatively or with disinterest. If you want to persuade or influence the behaviour of someone, you must control the way they perceive you. If someone thinks you behave nervously, for example, it is irrelevant that you don't agree. It's how they perceive you that matters, not what you think.   An impartial appraisal is needed, so conduct a bit of 'market research' by asking trustworthy friends and family to tell you what they notice about you - good and bad! It is easy to dismiss what you don't want to hear, but if different people tell you the same things, don't ignore them. Write down everything. Such notes will provide you with a unique insight into the real you - as seen through the eyes of those closest to you. Be methodical in your approach - if it helps, start at the top and work down to your feet.

It's no longer good enough merely to be clean and reasonably presentable. Invest time and effort in yourself and it will pay off. Employers and clients associate high personal standards with high business standards. Put yourself in their place. Look at yourself from their point of view. People want to deal with individuals who are smart and well groomed. Computer programmers are an exception, they will be more likely to get a job if they turn up blinking in the sunshine, wearing jeans, a pizza stained T shirt and carrying a can of coke. However, each of these people will have e-mailed details of their academic qualifications first. It will include a string of firsts from the best universities!

Being good at your job is no longer enough. The way you look and behave have become crucial parts of the job. The signals you send out to others will be judged by everyone you meet. One or two shortcomings may not spoil a generally good impression, but an overall sloppy look will.

A man in his early fifties was experiencing severe professional problems. He was extremely handsome, with immaculate silver hair, a chiselled jaw, a deep tan and blue-grey eyes. He looked like a highly successful chief executive. But all of these positive attributes were eroded within the first few moments of meeting him. Shaking his hand was like holding a wet, limp fish.

Both his shirt cuffs were slightly frayed. His blazer was probably 25 years old. He was proud of the fact that he could still fit into the trousers he was wearing, which he had bought 20 years before. The trouble was they were slightly too short, revealing his white socks emerging from vinyl shoes.

OK, looks aren't everything, but he was also soft-spoken, apologetic, nervous, and lacking in self-confidence. The combination of the clothes he wore and his behaviour had a very damaging effect on all the good looks Nature had blessed him with. When I told him what signals he was giving out, he found that with a bit of practice he was able to start behaving in a way that reinforced his positive attributes. In so doing he actually became more distinguished, authoritative and confident. Not everyone is naturally good-looking, but with just a bit of thought and attention to detail anyone can help transform themself. The change may not be radical but it could make the difference. This difference, however small, could be all that is keeping you from winning that promotion, new contract or the heart of someone you find attractive.

Systematically creating a positive image will provide you with more opportunities in all areas of your life. You will increase the esteem in which you are held by others. This in turn will provide you with even more opportunities. It becomes an ongoing process. The more you are seen to be in demand, the more people will want you. Film and television stars have known this for years. Obviously we can't all be stars, but there is no reason why you can't be seen as one within your own circle of activity. Your self-image is too important for your future success to allow it to take care of itself. In a fair world it would not be necessary to consider how you are perceived, but unfortunately we don't live in such a world.

Who do you know?

Who you know now, and who you get to know in the future could make the most positive impact on your future success, fulfilment and happiness. One new contact has the power to alter your life dramatically and for ever.

How well connected are you? Everybody has a network. For many, it is an untapped goldmine of opportunities - not just for them, but for everyone else they may know. Actively building your network could be one of the smartest career moves you ever make. Don't believe, as many do, that networking is a manipulative abuse of other people. Sadly, many so called networkers are insincere, selfish individuals who give networking a bad name. We all know individuals who attend everything - they'd even attend the opening of an envelope if they got the chance.

Many flit like a butterfly from person to person handing out and collecting business cards whenever possible, before moving on to their next 'contact'. How many times have you been approached by a stranger, who within 30 seconds of meeting you, tries to sell you health insurance? Or what about those people who claim everyone is their 'best friend', when they barely know the individuals concerned?

These people are not good networkers. They just think they are. You can tell a good networker at a party - they attract people like a magnet because they are worth knowing. They are interested in others, and they respect people deeply. They actively put individuals together. When they meet someone new, a poor networker asks the question "How useful is this person to me personally?". A distinguished networker will ask themselves, "How useful is this person to my network". Poor networkers for only looking after themselves, good ones develop a reputation for helping others. The interesting point is: good networkers not only build an admirable reputation, they benefit more than those who take the more selfish approach. For some readers this may require a leap of faith - but every good networker will confirm this to be true.

ANYONE can be a good networker. These are some of the benefits for those who build and maintain a good network of people:

- You will always be employable because you'll find the best jobs and freelance projects before they are advertised
- people in your network can provide you with a sounding board, guidance, support, priceless information of all types, inspiration, financial help, a more enriching social life, access to powerful and influential people who can help you and your other contacts and
- it's a lot of fun.

Actively develop your network as part of an exit strategy from a job, just in case you are made redundant. When you know you have a parachute already packed and ready for use, it will also improve the way you feel about yourself.

The power of networking; case studies

When I worked as a broadcaster, the most common question was, "How did you get in?" The answer demonstrates the value of networking and why it is a mistake to overlook help from anyone. In my youth, like many thousands of others, I was desperate to work for the BBC. And got nowhere in my efforts to gain a foothold there. Perhaps it was because I didn't go to either Oxford or Cambridge University.

Four years into my hopelessly inadequate pursuit of a break at the BBC (I had written literally hundreds of letters), in one of my many despondent moments I mentioned this to my mother, who very matter of factly suggested I speak to her cousin Phil, who was a well respected programme director at the BBC! She had never mentioned this before. Imagine my disbelief. But she had a point when she said "You never asked." She called him. He immediately invited me to meet him at the BBC in Cardiff where I was actually living at the time. While on my visit, he took me to the office of a senior BBC radio producer for an on-the-spot informal meeting. Within three weeks I was presenting my own Saturday breakfast programme on the BBC national radio service, Radio Wales. I hosted that show for over two years before going on to work as a BBC radio & TV announcer. There I met a producer called Bernie Newnham who returned to London to produce BBC1's *Points of View*.. He gave me a regular job as one of the letter readers (for some reason as the young 'cheeky chap' voice - why oh why?!). In parallel, as an announcer, I worked with a young and ambitious TV director, Mark Killick. He was highly skilled and very professional. On one particular night when he directed a live TV show and found himself in a hole, I helped him out. Years later he moved to Manchester and remembered my favour. He recommended me to Peter Weil the editor of the new programme he had joined. Peter agreed to meet me. His first comment was "Unfortunately I don't have a job for you." I was quite disappointed but he went on to suggest I contact a BBC friend of his, Jane Drabble who was, at the time, programme editor at BBC TV's South East News. I then met Jane soon afterwards, but before I had time to say anything, I was whisked into a TV studio for an on-camera newsreading audition. No time for any preparation: I read the news on BBC TV in London to an audeince of 2.2 million for the first time, about four days later. I stayed for about five years. While there, I met Julia Brooke, a radio producer who was visiting the studios. Six months later, out of the blue, she called to offer me a jobpresenting her Sony Award winning BBC Radio 4 programme, *In The News*.

My mother also sent me to Sunday school as a child of nine where I met Peter Wynne Davies. We've kept in touch ever since. He invited me to a high level networking event at the top of the BT Tower in London. I was invited so he could introduce me to Frankie, a remarkably intelligent and gorgeous political lobbyist. I'm glad he did because in December 1996, I married her! What more proof do you need that networking can have a hugely positive impact on your future? Thank you mum, Phil Lewis, Peter and everyone I've met in between.

The moral of the story? 1: don't assume that family and friends can't help you. 2: you already know people, who know other people, who could give you a great deal of help. If only you asked!

Think back to the turning points in your life. It's highly likely that they also came about because of the people you knew. Doesn't it therefore make sense to develop your network proactively rather than leaving it all to chance?

Develop a networking system

What you will read below is a summary of some of the material from my seminar*How to Unlock Your Full Networking Potential.*. Of all my professional activities, presenting this talk at conferences is certainly the most enjoyable and fulfilling. It's such a lot of fun, it brings people together, and delegates seem to improve and enrich their lives whilst simultaneously acquiring useable skills which can be used immediately within their work. They win and their employers win.

At most of my networking talks, everyone agrees that the majority of their business is generated through the relationships they build with customers and suppliers. These businesses have highly complex and sophisticated systems for just about every aspect of their business, but very few organisations have a system for networking. The basis for building a valuable network is a systematic and organised approach.

No one can operate a network if they cannot gain easy access to the contact details of those they know. List everyone you can remember and find their current contact details. If you can't find someone's details, who do you know who can furnish you with the information you need? This question is a key to networking. Collect together and record (on paper or electronically) every business card and useful contact you have met both in business and socially. Search everywhere - old correspondence files, diaries, address books and delegate lists from past seminars you have attended. Some networkers colour code contacts; family, friends, business associates etc. All these people represent your initial network. Take your time - do it methodically. Once completed - make a copy of every page or every entry. Do it regularly. Computer databases in particular **must** be backed up often. Your personal network will become your most valuable possession. Look after it.

No network would be complete without the following; a good accountant, lawyer, doctor, plumber, electrician, carpenter, gardener, cleaner, architect, a travel agent, a headhunter, a high ranking police officer, a brilliant divorce lawyer, print, radio and TV journalists, a couple of celebrities, a team of reliable baby sitters, a trustworthy car mechanic and competent computer 'fixer'. I'm sure you can think of others. The secret is to find these people before you or members of your network need them. You become useful to others if they know you can be relied upon to know other useful people.

Meeting someone new

Make a point of connecting with someone new every day. And re-acquaint yourself with anyone you have not spoken to for some time by going through your address book.

Approaching new people is often perceived as being dangerous. Our fear stops us. What if they refused our advances? Perhaps it would be better if you didn't bother in the first place, that way no one can reject you. The only problem is that by taking such a course of action you are actually rejecting yourself.

So, when you meet someone for the first time, overcome any initial nervousness you may have by taking responsibility for making the other person feel at ease. This will help you forget to be anxious yourself. Make the first move by offering your name first. Speak your name clearly. This puts others at ease and leads naturally into a request for their name. Really listen to what you are told. Many say they can't remember names - untrue, they don't make the effort to learn them in the first place. If you didn't catch it first time around, ask for it to be repeated. Incorporate their name into your conversation until it has been lodged into your mind. If you are ever talking as part of a group and you spy another individual listening in to the conversation, waiting for the most appropriate time to jump in- take the initiative and actively bring that person into the conversation. Introduce yourself, and if possible go around the group, saying everyone else's name whilst summarising the topic of conversation so far. If there are any people whose names you don't know, simply ask them to give their name. The rest of the group will almost certainly appreciate it too because it can be so easy to get involved in a conversation with someone you don't know, but feel you cannot ask their name so deep into a chat. By taking this approach, everyone within the group will appreciate what you have done. This is one of the keys to effective networking; putting others at ease and taking the initiative to introduce everyone.

Train yourself to be observant about people. Learn about body language. It is said that we always talk with our bodies. Seek to understand people, what motivates them, what fears and anxieties they have, and provide help to overcome to them.

Should you offer your business card? That depends. Personally, I usually wait to be asked for my card. This is a sign that I have earned a place in their life by demonstrating potential value to that person in the future. Unless you can do this, why should someone bother to remember you?

Inexperienced networkers fail to realise they do not need to learn how to talk, merely how to listen. Listening requires one powerful technique: asking questions. This doesn't mean you should become a grand inquisitor. All you have to do is get them started. Listen attentively and pick up on some of the things they say, showing interest. Why are they attending the meeting? Who do they know? A technique you could try is to ask someone for help in meeting people. Most individuals are keen to do their bit. If that individual doesn't know anyone either, you instantly have a topic of conversation; how neither of you knows anybody else!

Networking mistakes and how to avoid them

Failing to see the value of a network is the biggest mistake. But it's worth looking at why so few individuals proactively make the most of their connections. Hopefully by now you can see that it is not manipulative.

Networkers make the effort to accept invitations and organise events where they can grow their network. If you accept, show up. Develop a reputation for being reliable. You will become known and respected for helping others to do well. This costs little and repays rewards by the bucket load. Attend trade shows and exhibitions. Go to seminars and external courses. Attend night school. Are you involved in any charitable work? Not only is voluntary work very satisfying in that it helps people who are not in a position to help themselves, but you will also often meet others helpful to you. Join special interest groups. Don't just join and then hope for the best, get involved.

Create or join inter-departmental work teams. Get to know colleagues in other departments. Learn about their problems. Understand the pressures they work under. Offer help to resolve them.

Look out for everyone's best interests. It is so satisfying when you hear of an opportunity which you feel would be appropriate for someone within your network. By tipping them off you will make a friend for life. If those people go on to bigger and better things, their value to you within your network will rise as their power and authority increases.

Always be on the look-out to make connections; putting people together who have complementary skills, knowledge or interests. By doing such favours without requiring an immediate pay back, you will build up deposits in your networking 'bank'. Over time, you will be able to call upon others for return favours. That's the mercenary way of describing the process - in reality, favours are given and received in a far more random and altruistic fashion. What actually happens is; by helping persons A, C, E, S and T, you could benefit from persons B, D, F, G, J, R and U. It's a mistake to believe that this wouldn't happen. It does - trust me.

Networkers collect good people. In doing so, you become a more useful and valued individual to those who know you. They want to be a part of your network because they know they will benefit from the connection. Everyone knows approximately 200 people, who in turn know another 200 each and so on. Get into the habit of re-connecting on a regular basis with those you know. If you have ever been involved in a team effort, perhaps a short-term work project, make it a point to keep in touch with those people.

If you see newspaper or magazine article which someone would be interested in, photocopy it and send it off. If you find yourself thinking about someone in particular, write a personal handwritten note to tell them.

Francis Bacon asserted that "Knowledge is power". This belief stops some people from sharing it. They believe that if they keep information to themselves, they will maintain power; the opposite is true. People who keep information to themselves get bypassed. They are left out of the loop.

If someone has helped you, write to thank them. It is always better to write rather than simply using the phone. Everyone appreciates this type of attention - it shows that you remember and value them.

Thank as many people as you can think of. Even write to people you do not know. Incidentally, always write using a fountain pen, rather than a cheap ballpoint. A number of years ago I read a particularly interesting book on personal marketing called *Hype: The Essential Guide to Marketing Yourself* by Andrew Crofts. If you can find it, read it. Without requiring a reply, I simply wrote to his publisher congratulating him on such a good piece of work. They passedthe letter on to him. He telephoned to say that the letter had made his day. Why don't you make someone's day too? Most people don't get much positive feedback for what they do - if you are sincere when you praise someone, they will know and appreciate it.

Interestingly for me, Andrew Crofts contacted me a month or so later and interviewed me for a new book he was writing called *Using Television and Video in Business*. I was quoted a number of times in that book. I could never have predicted such a good outcome. But that was neither the point nor the intention.

Through networking it is possible to reach almost anybody you would want to, if you have developed a reputation for being unselfish and helpful. Become someone who cares about others and you will generate more contacts, business leads and added business and opportunities. Guaranteed.

The mark of someone's true character is how they treat those they don't know. Gaining access to important and influential people often requires knowing some of the "little people" in life. The best networkers find and look after such assistants.

So far we have only covered what you can do to help others. This is obviously only part of what Networking is about. Asking for help can produce remarkable results. Many of us find it difficult to do so. Asking for help is not a sign of weakness - it is proof of your intelligence.

So do not be afraid to ask for help - imagine how you would feel if someone asked you for help - you would probably be pleased to do whatever you could. Why should someone else be any different?

When asking for help do not say, *"Do you know anyone who could...?"* Ask the question in this way:*"Who do you know who could...?* This has the effect of getting the person you are talking to, to think about a solution to your problem. It cannot be answered using a yes or a no. When you ask for help, be open and honest about what you want or need. Don't try to manipulate or deceive anyone. Do not fall into the trap of believing the more well known you become, the easier it will be to network. If you have built a reputation for being selfish or self-focused, word about your selfishness will travel faster!

Each and every day offer help to someone before asking for it, and actively seek out opportunities to help the people that they know.

Think of any friend or colleague who you have known for many years. Has there ever been a situation where you have met some of his or her friends and thought, "Why didn't I know about this great person?" Why not spend an evening with a friend or two, going through each of your address books, talking about why your friends and colleagues are interesting or worth knowing? I challenge you not to unearth potentially valuable links between people in your networks. Some of them will be in a position to help you and even turn out to be future friends.

Just the job

A short-sighted employer may suspect that the next few pages will encourage all members of staff to leave. But high-performance employers know that they have a responsibility to keep high-performance people. Therefore they have to create an environment which nurtures those individuals and gives them ample reasons to stay. The information below is designed merely to demonstrate how self-marketing can be used.

As you will know by now, I am a devoted self-employed portfolio worker. But if you still need convincing that self-marketing can produce some astounding results, let me use the example of 'getting a job' - and not just any job: the best job you could ever dream of (why aim low?). You will see how effective personal marketing can make a difference to the outcome.

You have seen an advertisement for the job. It is genuinely perfect for you, calling for the qualifications, expertise and experience you already have. In return, the job has everything you could possibly want. The only thing missing from the actual advertisement is a headline mentioning you by name and pleading with you to take the job!

What happens? You write a letter, send off your application and wait for a response. You may then find that either you don't get an interview or, if you do, the job has been given to someone else; someone you feel certain is not the best person for the job. As you know, this can and does happen regularly. Employers often recruit the wrong people. They don't want to, but I'm sure you know of many occasions in which people seem to get promoted to their level of ineptitude.

When you don't get the 'perfect' job, it's easy to put it down to favouritism, nepotism, a personality clash, or plain bad luck. You probably feel initial disappointment and then try to rationalise the situation by telling yourself 'It wasn't to be'. The truth can be devastatingly simple and rather brutal. It is highly likely that you lacked the necessary control over the way you were perceived by the decision-maker. The presentation and content of your application letter and resume must have failed to convey how good you really are, or perhaps when you met the employer the signals you sent were not those received.

Obviously no one can ever be guaranteed success when applying for a job, but you can certainly shift the odds in your favour. In the sections which follow you will find detailed information on how to go about being offered a new and better job.

My views are not in line with accepted wisdom on the subject, but the information and the approach outlined below really work. There are many books on job hunting which advocate 'playing by the rules' - dictated by the terms of potential employers. Break whatever rules you can, to get the result YOU are looking for. Forget so called 'conventions' about job applications. Many of them are purely for the benefit of personnel managers. They encourage bland, impersonal applications. Conventional approaches will make you look like everyone else - dull. You must find a way to 'shine' and build a personal relationship on paper to persuade someone to meet you. You can't build rapport by producing an impersonal list of experiences.

Why is it that in business, an impersonal approach is often seen as being more 'professional? This attitude is a relic of the industrial age, where everyone was expected to perform clearly defined functions within a rigid hierarchy. This is precisely why this book is deliberately littered with personal anecdotes and stories. Most conventional book publishers insist on an impersonal style. Authors are often told to detach themselves from the subject. It just doesn't make sense. As discussed earlier, our networks and the relationships we create, often produce the best results for everyone concerned.

Business is changing dramatically and, increasingly, is looking for high calibre people who do not fit neatly within existing 'boxes'. Employers who insist on recruiting people in the old, outdated and conventional ways will lose out. Personnel and Human Resources (sometimes referred to as the 'human remains' department) are changing - some will be forced to change even more.

Through my training organisation, The Freelance Centre (http://www.freelancecentre.com) which offers seminars, audio tapes and other information products to the self-employed, we put a great deal of effort into persuading people to avoid writing or sending CVs and resumes to potential clients. A CV 'asks' for employment rather than demonstrating the benefits you can deliver to an individual or organisation. Worse still, an impersonal CV merely provides a listing of the 'tools' in your personal tool kit and leaves it up to the recipient to work out for themselves whether those tools can do what they need.

Most CVs are dull and lifeless. But the people who send them are usually not. There are many, more effective alternatives.

The CV

The good news is that when you apply for a superb job you are invariably competing with a lot of people who have submitted low-grade applications. The bad news is - yours could be one of them!

People who are unskilled at self-marketing often have totally unrealistic ideas about how to apply for a job. Being offered a worthwhile job is akin to running in a high-level athletics meeting. Without preparation, the right training and a winning approach to the task, you will get beaten at the tape. A docile approach rarely gets the desired result.

First, contrary to what most people think, a written job application rarely gets you a job - only an interview. Therefore it is essential that your letter and CV persuade the prospective employer to want to meet you. When large quantities of applications arrive they are usually sorted into three piles: 'A's

- definite interview material; 'B's - maybes; and 'C's - rejections. So your first persuasion task is to make sure you get into the 'A' pile - or at the very least the 'B' pile. If you go into the 'C's - it's instant death! I have seen countless applications handwritten on paper that has been ripped out of cheap notepads. Usually these are immediately put into pile D: the rubbish bin.

Employers advertising a job are telling you that they have a need - it is up to you to coax them into believing that only you can fulfil this need. Don't take what they state in the advertisement too literally. If you really want the job, set about manipulating them into seeing you as the best possible candidate and making you an offer. For instance, if they specify a particular age bracket and you don't satisfy this - still apply.

Most people who write job application letters merely ask to be considered for the job. Asking for something always puts you in a weak position. Offer something strong and relevant in your letter and you will begin to affect the decision-makers' perception of you in a positive way. Help them to solve their problem. Look at the situation from their point of view - not yours. Why are you worth seeing? What have you got to offer? How can you help them? If you cannot answer these questions, you certainly cannot expect a potential employer to do so.

If you are to reach the next stage, your overall presentation must be immaculate. Your accompanying CV or resume will be scanned for up to 20 or 30 seconds. If the reader does not find what he or she is looking for, it (and you) will be discarded. The style, layout, content and running order of most resumes are the same. They often also share one overriding feature - they're boring!

A resume that gets results is far more than just a list of your qualifications and achievements. It should persuade the reader to believe that you are worth meeting. It should hint at a lively, interesting personality - someone who would make a valuable contribution to the company in question. Your CV should be thought of as a personal advertisement - not merely a list of facts and dates. The secret is to include something that will intrigue the reader. Try to humanise yourself - you will appear more interesting. But don't try too hard. You are not trying to be 'Personality of the Month'!

Two personal examples come to mind. Sian Roberts has a naturally lively personality, but her CV did not reflect that - it was rather bland. No wonder she didn't get many job interviews. I spoke to her at length and it transpired that she had spent some time teaching English in Rio de Janeiro and, while there, went on a trip up the Amazon looking for crocodiles to photograph. She had also flown a light plane over the Andes in Peru (but only for about two minutes!) After some persuasion she agreed to include both items, although she was not that keen because, as she said, 'You don't put things like that in CVs.'

Her new CV got her a good job shortly afterwards, simply because it did what it was meant to do: it attracted attention and persuaded an employer to want to meet this remarkable-sounding woman. If you have done anything interesting or different - include it. So many interesting people send out dull resumes. Don't be one of them. Advertisers write copy that actively shows a product in its best light, you should do the same. If it includes showing a professional-looking photo of the product, they will. Do the same - if you look presentable. So many applicants insist on being too nice about the task in hand. Your aim is to get the result you want. Anything is fair game in writing job applications, so long as you don't lie.

George is an architect and friend - he is superb at both. He called to tell me he'd been made redundant. His firm didn't have enough work for him. He was understandably devastated. In his mind he was destined to yet another period of unemployment (he'd previously experienced over a year without a job). On the face of it, things did not look good. Together we set about creating a CV to give him an 'unfair' advantage. We broke all the rules.

Conventional wisdom dictates a CV should be no more than 1 or 2 pages. When we finished, his was 15 pages long! The experts will tell you that no one will bother to look at a CV that long. That's only true if you produce something boring. George sent out 40 copies to London firms he'd identified as ones he would want to work with. Not all of these firms were recruiting. He received 38 replies, attended 11 interviews and was offered 2 jobs.

What had we done? For an hour or so, I'd grilled George about what benefits he would bring to a company. How does he add value? How does he make the architects firm look good to its customers? How seriously does he take responsibility for solving problems and finding solutions? What were his most notable achievements? His answers were recorded onto cassette, transcribed, edited, polished and prioritised - the best 'strawberries' were put at the top. This became the first page of his CV.

The next three pages produced initial resistance from George. Just like Sian, he felt uneasy about breaking what seem to be the sacrosanct conventions of written applications. He wasn't sure he would be able to provide the information I demanded. But within two weeks he had compiled a series of high-quality, written testimonials from past employers and clients. (Everyone should build a file of written comments, testimonials and memos congratulating you for your achievements - one day they could be worth a fortune to you). These are fundamentally important to any job application. Why? When employers/clients appoint someone new, most recruiters are petrified of making a 'wrong hire'. It's a time-consuming and expensive process. We took the initiative by persuading the reader that George was worth employing. And it's far better to say so through other people's words!

Each of these testimonials carefully confirmed the qualities outlined on the first page. We made it clear; here was someone who was respected as a person and for his skill and conscientiousness. Incidentally, George was pleasantly shocked to find how willing people were to provide him with a written testimonial. Convention dictates you merely provide the names of references on applications. These are only followed up after you have been selected. **This is no use to you**. So don't conform! There are more details of how you can use testimonials in the 6 part audio tape series *The Secrets of Successful Freelancing*. See the back of this book for further details.

As for the remaining 11 pages of George's CV - all architects want to look at plans and drawings. So we incorporated pages and pages of selected drawings to illustrate his skill as a draughtsman. These were scanned into the computer and pasted into the word processed document. Each drawing was accompanied by a brief description of his role with that project and employer. No one had ever seen an architect's CV which looked like this. George stood out. So must you. His contact details were on the front page - not the last. The accompanying letter echoed the benefits he'd outlined on the first page of the CV, and suggested an informal meeting to discuss issues further.

How could you use such an approach?

If you have written articles, or had material written about your professional achievements - include them too. Computer technology is now so advanced it is relatively easy to produce highly professional documents with stunning graphics and photos in black and white or colour. Don't be limited by convention. Post them on your own internet site. See my personal website http://freespace.virgin.net/roy.sheppard for some ideas.

Ensure you include information about how your prospective employer would benefit from tapping into your wide and influential network if you have one. Self-starters are always in great demand. If you are new to the workplace, show initiative and demonstrate the fact that you understand the importance of adding value to the employer. How could you help to improve revenues and increase sales? You don't have to work in sales or marketing to do this.

Self-marketers earn a place in the lives of others. By focusing your attention on what's in it for others - you will benefit more.

By attracting attention to your application you will be far more likely to be invited for an interview. Assuming you are asked to attend one, you will have succeeded in stage one of the job-selection process: persuading the employer to take you seriously for the job or the promotion.

The Interview

Stage two involves more persuasion if you are to be successful. Traditionally, being interviewed is regarded as a bit like being the sacrificial lamb at the slaughter - but in reality an interview can be an opportunity to manipulate the interviewer(s) into wanting you to take the job. Somehow I can sense you don't believe me! Let's look at the situation logically. They have a need and you have been invited to satisfy that need. They are busy people who would not waste their time asking to see you if they thought you were not suitable for the post. All you have to do is show them that in choosing you, they will have made the right choice. To get the result you want, you must understand fully what they want and then tailor what you say, how you look and how you behave to match it completely. Interviews are little more than performances - for both interviewee and interviewer. No professional would perform without preparation and rehearsal. An amateur certainly cannot afford to go into such a situation without adequate preparation.

When you walk into the interview, the interviewer will genuinely want to feel that in meeting you, the right candidate has been found. Most interviewees want an easy life - so make it easy for them - gently take the lead. Once again, this does not mean rushing in as 'personality of the month' - aim for quiet self-confidence. Look in control. Tell yourself that they need you more than you need them. Even though you may feel nervous inside, it's highly unlikely that the interviewer will know this. Use the interviewer's name - if you did not catch it, ask again. You will appear more confident using his or her name, and he or she will like this. Maintain eye contact; don't look nervously at the floor. When asked to talk about yourself don't go on as if in the confessional - keep it brief, up-beat and relevant. Rehearse beforehand so you do not 'um' and 'er' too much.

In your preparation you should have found out as much as possible about the company. This can be done from newspaper cuttings, your local library and, most importantly, from the company itself. Feel free to telephone the company or if it's for a promotion, the new department. Speak to a few people about what they do. Large companies often have a PR department: tell them why you are calling. Ask for the names of employees they would recommend you talk to. Ask around within your network for information. By showing an interest you will learn a lot about what the company does, how it fits into its industry, and how well it is doing. To make a good impression, you should use this information throughout the interview. But do not make the common mistake of blurting it all out. Use the knowledge to formulate lots of intelligent questions about the company. Have them on a piece of paper if necessary. Let the interviewer do most of the talking. This way you will succeed in a number of ways; you will appear interested and, the more you let him or her talk, the more interesting you will seem! You will also be turning a one-sided interview into a two-way conversation. This is a technique you can and should use in all your relationships. Gently weave into the conversation some of the following questions:

- What are the key challenges the company is facing at the moment?
- Why is that do you think? What or who is to blame?
- Who are the biggest competitors and how are they doing? (If you've already done your research, as you should have, you'll know the answer to this one. How does what you are told compare with what you found out?)
- What is the company doing to cut its costs?
- What is being done to grow the business?
- What new technology is being implemented throughout the industry?
- How much of it is has been acquired by your company?
- How much more is going to be bought or leased in the next 12 to 18 months?
- How many layers of management are there? Why?
- How would they define the management style or culture of the company?
- If you could change anything about the company, what would it be?
- How many women are in senior management positions?

What you are trying to discover is how open, forward-thinking and realistic they are. Is the company thinking in the past or the future? By asking leading questions, you will also demonstrate how well informed you are about business. In some ways the answers you receive are unimportant. The blame question above is a particularly useful one to use. The answer you receive will tell you a great deal about attitudes within the company. If those you speak to are overly keen to point the finger of blame for poor performance elsewhere, be very wary of that company.

During the interview, concentrate on issues relating to your prospective employer's needs rather than just your own. Controlling the interview is important - controlling how it ends is crucial.

When you know that the interview is coming to an end, take control by gently asking if there is anything else the interviewer would like to know about you. If not, say thank you for the opportunity to meet with him or her and ask when you can expect to hear from the company. By gently taking charge of the meeting you will be asserting yourself and will ensure that you are not dismissed.

Using the example of getting a job has been deliberate, to show you that it is possible to exert a level of control in all situations that may at first seem totally uncontrollable.

"When an archer misses the mark, he turns and looks for the fault within himself. Failure to hit the bull's eye is never the fault of the target. To improve yourself-improve your aim." Gilbert Arland

Persuasion

The final stage in achieving maximum levels of control in your life is to know how to persuade others to help you achieve your goals and ambitions. I am not suggesting deviousness in your dealings with others, but once you have decided on your purpose in life and the goals you must meet to fulfil that purpose, it is often necessary to enlist the help of others. To take control effectively, without appearing pushy or arrogant, requires an ability to understand people. Like so many of the truly important things in life, we are not normally taught how to do this in our schools and colleges. Dealing with others is therefore left almost purely to chance. The ability to persuade others is probably the single most important quality we can ever possess.

If you can learn to be an effective persuader you will almost certainly achieve more in your life time. In his fascinating book *The Power of Persuasion*, Rupert Eales White cites four persuasion approaches:

* Logic: using structured facts or opinions.
* Incentives: dangling the most appropriate 'sticks or carrots' in front of the 'persuadee(s)'.
* Group: encouraging others to 'belong' when they need to share common concepts and visions.
* Empathy: concentrating attention on the needs of the persuadee to create a 'win-win' situation.

How you use these persuasion techniques, and in which combination, will determine how successful you will be as a persuader. In order to motivate others to do what you want, they must be inspired to want to do it for themselves. This is achieved by appealing directly to their needs. Try to put yourself in their place and work out what would make them want to take a particular course of action. Ask yourself what people do to make you feel good, then do those things for others.

Abraham Maslow's 'hierarchy of needs' defines our basic needs as: survival, shelter, food, love, security, acceptance, respect, knowledge, fulfilment, sex and self-esteem. You will be far more likely to succeed in persuading others if you can satisfy one or more of these needs for them. Choose your approach carefully and apply it appropriately - especially the second to last need! Tactless (and unsuccessful) persuaders might use threats to try to get someone to do what they want. They rely on fear, criticism, public ridicule and lecturing to 'motivate' others. A more effective persuader would offer 'persuadees' a genuine opportunity to lighten their workload, or help them to appear more effective to their superiors or colleagues. People you may be trying to persuade might be susceptible to an approach that allows them to join or stay within 'the safety' of a particular group. Others may want to be closer to those they admire - could you help them to achieve that? Can you offer them the chance to be seen to be the best? Can you appeal to their snobbishness? Will they be able to fulfil a goal or ambition if they help you? If you don't know what those around you want, don't just guess - ask. If at first you don't get a satisfactory answer, be persistent. Make them see that you are really interested in what they want and why they want it.

I know a successful computer salesperson who literally doubled his sales commission by incorporating the following question in his sales calls: *'What can I do to make you look good in your organization?'* The strong relationships he has forged this way have practically guaranteed him future business. To persuade effectively you must develop the ability to evoke genuine enthusiasm, not only for the tasks in hand, but for the people who can best perform them. The power of enthusiasm should never be underestimated. Enthusiasm alone is sometimes enough to galvanize support from others. If you also provide encouragement, honest and genuine praise, you will achieve even better results. A sincere 'thank you' will often make someone's day and motivate him or her to do even more for you next time. By showing a genuine interest in the well-being of those you work and live with, you will not only gain their respect, but their ongoing co-operation.

We often need to persuade anonymous officials and public servants to help us. Dealing with them can often be an uphill struggle. But try this approach: ask for their names (making sure that they don't suspect you of planning to use it against them) and then make a point of using it while you are talking to them. Our own names are the most important words we know, so making someone feel important (particularly someone who is rarely treated in this way) will often get the result you want. At all other times, try to get into the habit of asking for the names of everyone you come into contact with, then try to remember them for future use. It's a personal compliment when someone is made to feel that he or she is important enough for you to remember. Such behaviour will make you stand out. Being successful at persuading others requires practice and application. By giving 'persuadees' opportunities to contribute to the tasks you have set, you will succeed in getting them more involved and therefore more interested in the outcome.

A sustained self-marketing campaign over a long period will set you apart from those competing for work projects, jobs and new relationships. Initial discomfort about bringing attention to yourself will soon fade away, as those you live and work with begin to realise that you are someone who helps them to achieve their goals, and puts them in touch with others who can do the same.

After word

Predicting the future is impossible. Nobody has the answers. Who knows what cataclysmic events could occur tomorrow which would instantly change life for everyone on this planet forever? However, as we have explored within this book, we can each do more to minimise many of the threats that will shock or surprise millions of others in the decades to come. Understanding what threats exist represents the first step towards learning the key survival skills of self-reliance we will all need in the 21st century.

We are living in an exciting yet difficult and uncertain period of our history. The winds of global political and economic instability blow through all of our lives, wreaking havoc in some areas, while in others they have a bracing and refreshing effect. We all need to chart our own course through this turbulence or risk the consequences of being dashed against dangerous and sometimes submerged rocks. This is the time when we and those whom we entrust to govern need the necessary skills and knowledge for uncharted waters.

Tomorrow's societal and environmental problems will require rapid, international and decisive action that cuts through the vested interests of governments and corporations. Based on past experiences, to expect these old, crumbling institutions to 'do the right thing' is asking a great deal.

In Kenichi Ohmae's *The Borderless World*, he wrote *"... we are all in this together. The economies of individual nations, such as the United States and Japan, are not firmly on the ground. They are like two planes aloft with the hydraulics of each pilot's levers linked partially to the flaps of the other plane....Cooperation is essential, more so every day as the activities of global companies further spin the web of connectedness. This is the fact of life with which we all have to learn to make a productive peace. But this is not what we most talk or yell about."*

In the dependency decades of the 20th century millions became over-reliant on others. It is not that we are incapable of looking after ourselves, merely that the self-reliance skills our ancestors were forced into utilising seem to have gone to sleep for the last few hundred years. To become self-reliant again, we as individuals and as a nation are obliged to wake ourselves up and apply many new, and at times confusing types of literacy for the 21st century: new technologies, personal finance, a deeper understanding of how society and businesses function and our individual places within them. We are all self-employed, even those who work full time for large corporations. Who we are will change as we engage in new ways of working. Flexibility, uncertainty and change will become an integral part of our lives.

Possessing job skills will no longer be enough to thrive in the 21st century. Without developing our ability to market ourselves effectively such skills will have a limited value. We all need to accept this reality. For many of us, it will feel particularly uncomfortable to take charge of our own destiny in this way. Learning to cope will become a challenge for those who refuse or feel unable alter their behaviour in response to the new environment and global economy. We can no longer afford to function without self-awareness. We each need to re-appraise and audit our lives and the industries in which we derive our incomes. Anyone working in a dying industry must face up to such harsh realities and work towards providing their own solutions. Expecting others to assume what is our own responsibility will almost certainly lead to anger, disappointment and ultimately financial hardship.

We need to adopt new ways of thinking in order to resolve our new problems.

"You always get the behaviour you reward". Perhaps those in power need to look at all aspects of society to understand which anti-social behaviours are being rewarded. Until law makers, governments and community leaders can see why people behave in the ways they do, committing crimes will continue to be a viable option for a significant proportion of the population. When individuals are permitted to avoid the consequences of their behaviour, it always perpetuates that behaviour.

Predominantly male politicians, generals and executives strive to find ever more ingenious ways to cling on to their political, military and economic power. So far, individual countries and corporations that behave irresponsibly or against the interests of the majority rarely suffer the consequences of their behaviour. In the main, they continue to get away with whatever they can for as long as they can. But how long will this be permitted to continue? Global polluters from the old smokestack industries still wield their enormous industrial power; they grow fat as the rest of us are made to choke on their poisonous by-products. Even the mightiest governments are beginning to demonstrate their impotence against the demands of their political 'supporters', the mega tax-generating conglomerates. Buying the right to pollute is not an option. At the Climate Change Convention in Kyoto in December 1997, money, yet again shouted the loudest. But millions of citizens are becoming more demanding and less tolerant of those who destroy for profit, even though many of us are still happy to purchase their products.

"Since all of our decisions are made on the basis of what we think we need to be secure, if we change our idea of security, we will change the way we live, vote, and spend our money. If we could believe that global as well as national security was at stake here, we would quickly shift to seeing the world in a new way." John L Petersen, *The Road to 2015.*

Those whose preferred means of expression is through confrontation, rather than collaboration, will become increasingly marginalised in the future. How many businesses could survive and thrive in today's environment if they were required to function within the parameters of the past as laid down by parliamentary procedure and tradition, and from inside a building more suited as a museum? Few I suspect.

Collaboration is very difficult. In business, financial imperatives have forced many confrontational relationships to evolve into collaborative ones. Past competitors are now more likely to be partners, each working with one another to protect their individual survival in the marketplace. How long will it be before governments learn this lesson? Will politicians ever acquire the necessary confidence and earn the trust of their opponents to work together for the good of a nation?

Too many people believe that devoting a lot of time to something demonstrates its importance. Making fast decisions seems to imply a lack of respect for the issue or problem. But one of the key traits common amongst the most successful people and organisations is their ability and confidence to reach decisions quickly and then implement them. In the 21st century this will be a requirement. Response times will be short. If a decision turns out to be wrong for whatever reasons, an underlying confidence allows them to quickly re-appraise the situation just as quickly and pull the plug on a project if necessary. Decisiveness is the key. Ploughing additional effort or resource into a bad idea rarely turns it into a good one. So why prolong the agony and increase the costs? There is no time to take bad decisions personally (although if an individual or organisation is consistent in this respect - it does get personal!)

Focusing on solutions is often forgotten in the heat of the battle. It's worth remembering that confrontation kills, collaboration heals.

In Francis Kinsman's 1990 book *Millennium*, he explores the significance of research by the Taylor Nelson Group and Applied Fortunes Ltd which found that a growing number of people in Britain are becoming more 'inner-directed' and less concerned with conspicuous consumption and material possessions. This is in stark contrast to the prevailing attitudes in the US, Japan and Germany whose people are far more 'outer-directed' - committed, conspicuous consumers. In France and Italy in particular, society is still based on an agricultural or agrarian culture which is driven by a sense of survival and of 'belonging' to clearly defined groups. As we in Britain have progressed from being a wholly dependent population as determined by our feudal forebears, we have slowly become more independent since the beginning of the industrial revolution. During this time we have fought for our rights, our incomes and better working conditions. But we stand at the dawn of an era in which interdependence will take on a deeper significance in the lives of successful people.

By working together with our employers, clients, customers and families to achieve better results for everyone, more of our attention will shift fundamentally towards asking ourselves deeper questions about who we are and what we really want out of life. More people will learn to define what 'enough' means to them: enough money, fun, love, food or grown-up toys. For many, this will almost certainly mean choosing to save more, to consume less and eliminate the more unproductive, unsatisfying and unfulfilling activities which consume their time and energy. 'More of everything' is not the answer.

"The future belongs only to those who have adequately prepared for it."

So, what are the first things you are going to do to prepare yourself and your family for a more secure and fulfilling future?

Reading Resource

Accelerated Learning into the 21st Century by Colin Rose 1997 Dell Books

The Age of Unreason by Charles Handy 1990 Arrow Books Ltd.

Awaken The Giant Within by Anthony Robbins 1992 Simon & Schuster

Being Digital by Nicholas Negroponte 1995 Alfred A. Knopf Publishing

Betrayal of Trust by Dr. Vernon Coleman 1994. European Medical Journal

Better Change by The Price Waterhouse Change Integration Team 1995 Irwin Professional Publishing

Better Money Management; A Step by Step Guide to Making Your Money Go Further by Marie Jennings 1994. Piatkus Books

Beyond Humanity: CyberRevolution and Future Minds by Gregory S. Paul and Earl D. Cox. 1996. Charles River Media Inc.

Breaking into the Boardroom; What Every Woman Needs to Know When Talent and Hard Work Aren't Enough by Jinx Melia 1986 St Martin's Press

Cybertrends: Chaos, Power and Accountability in the Information Age by David Brown 1997. Viking Books

Digital Business: Surviving and Thriving in an On-Line World by Ray Hammond. 1996. Hodder & Stoughton.

Emotional Intelligence: Why it can matter more than IQ by Daniel Goleman 1995 Bloomsbury

The Empty Raincoat by Charles Handy 1994 Hutchinson

The End of Work:The Decline of the Global Labor Force and the Dawn of the Post-Market Era by Jeremy Rifkin. 1995. GP Putnam's Publishing

Excelerate: Growing in the New Economy by Nuala Beck 1996 HarperPerennial

The Fifth Discipline Fieldbook by Peter Senge with Richard Ross, Bryan Smith, Charlotte Roberts and Art Kleiner. *Nicholas Brealey Publishing 1994*

Fit For Life by Harvey & Marilyn Diamond 1985 Bantam Books

First Things First by Stephen R Covey, A. Roger Merrill and Rebecca R Merrill. 1994 Simon & Shuster Ltd.

Future In Sight: 100 of the Most Important Trends, Implications and Predictions for the New Millennium by Barry Howard Minkin 1995 Macmillan

Future Shock by Alvin Toffler 1970 Pan Books

Future Shop by Jim Snider and Terra Ziporyn 1992 St. Martin's Press

Going Digital: How New Technology is Changing Our Lives. 1996. The Economist.

Hardball For Women: Winning at the Game of Business by Pat Heim PhD 1993 Plume Books

Hype: The Essential Guide to Marketing Yourself by Andrew Crofts 1990 Hutchinson Business Books

Introducing NLP by Joseph O'Connor and John Seymour. Aquarian/Thorsons Books 1993

Jobshift by William Bridges 1995 Nicholas Brealey Publishing.

Learning to Learn by D. Trinidad Hunt 1991 Elan Enterprises

The Learning Revolution by Gordon Dryden and Dr. Jeanette Vos *1994 Accelerated Learning*

Living Health by Harvey & Marilyn Diamond *1987 Bantam Books*

Lick the Sugar Habit by Nancy Appleton PhD. *1988 Avery Publishing*

Megatrends 2000 by John Naisbett and Patricia Aburdene *1990 Avon Books*

Megatrends Asia by John Naisbett *1996 Simon & Shuster*

Millennium: Towards Tomorrow's Society by Francis Kinsman *1990 Penguin Books*

The Monster Under The Bed by Stan Davis & Jim Botkin *1994 Touchstone Books*

The Myth of Male Power by Warren Farrell Ph.D *1993 Simon & Schuster*

Navigating in Cyberspace by Frank Ogden. *1995. Macfarlane Walter & Ross Publishing.*

The Next Twenty Years of Your Life: A Personal Guide into the Year 2017 by Richard Worzel *1997 Stoddart Publishing*

NLP at Work by Sue Knight *1995 Nicholas Brealey Publishing*

Organise Yourself by Ronni Eisenberg with Kate Kelly *1986. Piatkus Books.*

Out of the Blue: Wild Cards and Other Future Surprises by John L Petersen, *1997 The Arlington Institute, 2101 Crystal Plaza Arcade, Suite 136, Arlington, VA 22202* www.arlinst.org

The Plug-In Drug by Marie Winn *1977. Penguin Books*

The Popcorn Report by Faith Popcorn *1992 Arrow Books*

Powershift by Alvin Toffler *1990 Bantam Books*

Preparing for the Twenty-First Century by Paul Kennedy *1993. HarperCollins Publishers*

Rethinking the Future Edited by Rowan Gibson *1996 Nicholas Brealey Publishing*

The Road Less Travelled by M. Scott Peck *1978 Arrow Books*

The Road to 2015: Profiles of the Future by John L Petersen *1994 The Arlington Institute, 2101 Crystal Plaza Arcade, Suite 136, Arlington, VA 22202* www.arlinst.org

The Richest Man in Babylon by George S. Clason *1926. Signet Books*

The Road Ahead by Bill Gates with Nathan Myhrvold and Peter Rinearson *1995 Viking Books*

The Secrets of Savvy Networking: How to Make the Best Connections - for Business and Personal Success by Susan RoAne. *1993 Warner Books*

The Seven Habits of Highly Effective People by Stephen R Covey *1989. Simon & Shuster Ltd.*

Shifting Gears: Thriving in the New Economy by Nuala Beck *1993 HarperPerennial*

Super-Learning 2000 by Shiela Ostrander & Lynn Schroeder with Nancy Ostrander *1994 Souvenir Press*

Technotrends: 24 Technologies That Will Revolutionize Our Lives by Daniel Burrus with Roger Gittines. *1993 HarperBusiness*

The Third Wave by Alvin Toffler *1980 Pan Books*

Thin Tastes Better by Dr. Stephen P. Gullo *1995 Dell Publishing*

What Colour Is Your Parachute by Richard Nelson Bolles *Published annually. Ten Speed Press.*

The World in 2020: Power, Culture and Prosperity, a Vision of the Future by Hamish McRae *1995 HarperCollins*

You and Your Money: Transforming Your Relationship with Money and Achieving Financial Independence by Joe Dominguez & Vicki Robin *1992. Penguin Books*

The Secrets of Successful Freelancing
How YOU can
Earn more, keep more and
work with better clients

Essential to every freelancer

- Avoid the 20 most common mistakes
- How to target and attract better clients with proven techniques
- How to overcome a client's fear of employing you for the first time
- What to include in a written agreement
- How to price yourself
- How to write business generating letters
- Ways to get paid more promptly

Packed with up to four hours of practical ideas, tips and secrets, this six part audio series will help you earn more as a freelancer. Based on the highly acclaimed seminar *The Secrets of Successful Freelancing.* Written and narrated by Roy Sheppard.

Hundreds of satisfied customers. See website for freelancer testimonials.

To order your cassettes send a cheque or money order for £49.95 inc. VAT (plus £3 p&p) to: Centre Publishing, Suite 2, 170 Kennington Park Road, London, SE11 4BT England.

Credit card orders accepted
Tel (+44) 171 820 8511
Fax: (+44) 171 793 7962

Orders can only be accepted when accompanied by full payment in pounds sterling. Please allow 28 days for delivery. Overseas orders should add £10 to cover additional postage costs.

Freelance Centre website http://www.freelancecentre.com

Who do you know
who would be delighted to receive
a copy of this book as a gift?

Quantity	ORDER FORM	Total
	Your Personal Survival Guide to the 21st Century book by Roy Sheppard @ £9.99 inc p&p. **Special Offer** 3 copies for the price of 2 (£19.98). See below for other volume discounts.	
	The Secrets of Successful Freelancing Audio Home Study Programme by Roy Sheppard @ £49.95 + £3 p&p	
	Yes You Can motivational audio cassette by Roy Sheppard @ £8.99 inc p&p	
	Sub total	
	Additional postage (if applicable)	
	Total enclosed	

**Simply fill in the order form above and send it to us
with your payment.**

Overseas orders please add £2 postage for **Your Personal Survival Guide to The 21st Century** book and **Yes You Can** tape. For **The Secrets of Successful Freelancing** please add £5. All orders must be in pounds sterling.

Volume discounts are available for larger orders of **Your Personal Survival Guide to the 21st Century:**

3 copies for the price of 2		£19.98 for 3 copies
4-9 copies	less 10%	£8.99 per copy
10-20 copies	less 20%	£7.99 per copy
20-99 copies	less 30%	£6.99 per copy
100+ copies	less 40%	£5.99 per copy

Substantial discounts available for specially produced corporate editions for employees or customer promotions; prices on application.

Cheques should be made payable to Centre Publishing.
Credit card orders can be faxed to 00 (+44) 171 793 7962. Include your credit card number and the card's expiry date, together with your signature.

Send your order to:
Centre Publishing, Suite 2, 170 Kennington Park Road, London SE11 4BT, England.

This order form may be photocopied

About the author

A corporate interviewer and international business speaker, Roy Sheppard gives talks and presentations on *Surviving the 21st Century* and a variety of business communication subjects such as *The Body Talk* (a one hour interactive talk on body language - how our bodies talk even when we are not speaking) and *Building Profitable Business Relationships through Networking.*

For further details of how Roy Sheppard could speak at your next conference, telephone 00 (+44) 171 820 8511 or fax 00 (+44) 171 793 7962

website http://freespace.virgin.net/roy.sheppard

If you have any ideas about how this book could be improved for later editions, please address them to Centre Publishing, Suite 2, 170 Kennington Park Road, London SE11 4BT, England.